" This artfully conceived collection is timely.
It combines perceptive commentary on issues of the day
with enduring insights on the nature of investing,
markets, and human affairs. A valuable resource
for investors seeking to understand the
forces at play in today's world. "

LYNN SHARP PAINE
John G. McLean Professor of Business Administration,
    Harvard Business School
Author, *Value Shift: Why Companies Must Merge Social and
    Financial Imperatives to Achieve Superior Performance*

Also available from
BLOOMBERG PRESS

Investing in REITs: Real Estate Investment Trusts
Revised and Updated Edition
by Ralph L. Block

Tom Dorsey's Trading Tips:
A Playbook for Stock Market Success
by Thomas J. Dorsey and the DWA Analysts

Wall Street Secrets for Tax-Efficient Investing:
From Tax Pain to Investment Gain
by Robert N. Gordon with Jan M. Rosen

Investing in Small-Cap Stocks
Revised Edition
by Christopher Graja and Elizabeth Ungar, Ph.D.

Investing in Hedge Funds:
Strategies for the New Marketplace
by Joseph G. Nicholas

The Money-Making Guide to Bonds:
Straightforward Strategies for Picking
the Right Bonds and Bond Funds
by Hildy Richelson and Stan Richelson

A complete list of our titles is available at
www.bloomberg.com/books

Investing Under Fire

Winning Strategies from the Masters
for Bulls, Bears, and the Bewildered

Edited by

A l a n   R .   A c k e r m a n

BLOOMBERG PRESS

PRINCETON

First edition published 2003
1 3 5 7 9 10 8 6 4 2

Library of Congress Cataloging-in-Publication Data

Investing under fire : winning strategies from the masters for bulls, bears, and the bewildered / edited by Alan R. Ackerman.-- 1st. ed.
        p. cm.
Includes index.
   ISBN 1-57660-137-4 (alk. paper)
   1. Investments.   I. Ackerman, Alan R.

   HG4521. I3858 2003
   332.6--dc21   2003006174

Book Design by LAURIE LOHNE / DESIGN IT COMMUNICATIONS

To my mother, Leona Ackerman, who during the Great Depression and World War II remained a cockeyed optimist. She continued to believe that a man's reach should exceed his grasp—or what's a heaven for?

And to GIs everywhere, who remain America's true heroes.

Contents

About the Contributors   xi

Preface   xxv

Aknowledgments   xxix

Introduction   xxxi

P a r t   O n e

Pitfalls and Hazards Facing Today's Investor

1   Today's Mutual Fund Industry: Back to the Future   3
John C. Bogle

2   Going Against the Grain   19
Ned Riley

3   The Importance of Being a Stock "Detective"   29
Foster Friess

4   The Search for Value   41
William C. Nygren

5   Technical and Sentiment Analysis—
   Timing, Discipline, and Contrary Thinking   51
Bernie Schaeffer

6   Inefficiencies in the Market   67
Louis G. Navellier

7   Ten Rules for Becoming Wealthy   77
Craig Brimhall

Part Two

Key Sectors Driving Market Opportunity

8 The Unquenchable Thirst for Oil   89
James T. Hackett

9 The Predictive Power of the Bond Market   99
Anthony Crescenzi

10 Gold and Monetary Disorder: Three Bullish
Gold Price Scenarios   109
John C. van Eck

11 Gold's Precious Secret: It's Money   127
James Turk

12 Small-Cap Stocks in an All-Weather Portfolio   137
James D. Awad

13 The Bright, the Brave, the Biotech   143
Mark Monane, M.D., M.S.

14 Foreign Direct Investment in Emerging Market
Countries: A Calculated Risk   155
Vladimir L. Kvint

15 The Changing Spectrum in Asia   169
Robert D. Hormats

Part Three

Tools of the Trade for Today's Investor

16 Equity Research and the Investor's Right to Know   183
Hendrik Kranenburg
Sam Stovall

17 The Promise and Peril of Fund Investing   191
Brian Portnoy

18 A Standard of Value   201
Jean Bernhard Buttner

19 A Sounding Board for Business   211
Randall Poe

20 Sarbanes-Oxley Act and Securities Fraud   219
Lewis D. Lowenfels
John D. Tortorella

P a r t   F o u r

Corporate Models of Excellence in Challenging Times

21 Toyota's Responsibility to People, Process,
and Environment   229
Toshiaki Taguchi

22 Middle-Market Mortgages ... Then More   237
Kerry Killinger

23 Transforming Whole Beans to "Coffee Experience"   245
Orin C. Smith

24 Immigration and Education: Two Great Resources   255
John T. Kernan

Part Five

Geopolitical Implications for Today's Investor

25 Investing in Our Physical and Fiscal Security   265
   Jules Kroll

26 Waging a Different Kind of War   275
   General Wesley Clark

27 Prospects for Containing Future Terrorism   287
   Graham Allison

28 Shifting Sands in the Middle East   299
   Ambassador Dennis Ross

29 Peace, Democracy, and Free Markets
   in the Twenty-First Century   307
   Michael Mandelbaum

Index   315

About the Contributors

Editor **Alan R. Ackerman**, global market strategist at Fahnestock & Co. Inc., has spent the past four decades in the investment banking business. He began his career at Merrill Lynch as an account executive and subsequently served as director of foreign research and investment for several other Wall Street firms. In addition to his Wall Street activities, Ackerman has served as a consultant to publicly owned companies, founded and was a major stockholder in several public companies, and has handled investments in Europe and Asia for major banks and international corporations. In the 1970s Ackerman served as Deputy Director of President Ford's Citizen Action Committee at the White House. Considered an expert in foreign affairs and international strategies, he has been quoted by Dow Jones, Reuters, the *Wall Street Journal, Investor's Business Daily,* and the *New York Times.* He also appears weekly on radio and television and has been a contributing editor to several financial publications. A resident New Yorker and graduate of the Horace Mann School and Brown University, Ackerman serves as a director of several charitable organizations.

Graham Allison is Douglas Dillon Professor of Government and Director of the Belfer Center for Science and International Affairs at Harvard's John F. Kennedy School of Government, where he also served as Dean of the School (1977–89). In the first term of the Clinton Administration, Dr. Allison served as Assistant Secretary of Defense for Policy and Plans where he coordinated Department of Defense strategy and policy towards Russia, Ukraine, and the other states of the former Soviet Union. Dr. Allison's publications include *Essence of Decision: Explaining the Cuban Missile Crisis* (1971), released in an updated and revised second edition (1999), which ranks among the best-sellers in political science with more than 400,000 copies in print; *Realizing Human Rights: Moving from Inspiration to Impact* (2000); and *Avoiding Nuclear Anarchy: Containing the Threat of Loose Russian Nuclear Weapons and Fissile Material* (1996). This chapter in *Investing Under Fire* builds on and extends the argument Allison previously presented in "Could Worse Be Yet to Come?" *The Economist* (November 1, 2001) and in "The New Containment: An Alliance Against Nuclear Terrorism," which he wrote with Andrei Kokoshin, in the Fall 2002 issue of *National Interest.* *(Chapter 27)*

James D. Awad is chairman of Awad Asset Management, an investment advisory firm which today manages approximately $800 million in assets for individuals and institutions. He has been in the securities industry for three decades as a portfolio manager and senior investment officer. A sought-after commentator to the investment community, he is a frequent guest speaker on CNBC, CNN, Fox Satellite, CNNfn, and Bloomberg TV. Active in community and philanthropic affairs, he also is a retired member of the Dean's Council at Harvard's John F. Kennedy School of Government. Awad received a B.S. from Washington & Lee University and an M.B.A. from Harvard University Graduate School of Business.   *(Chapter 12)*

John C. Bogle is founder and former chief executive of The Vanguard Group, Inc. and president of the Bogle Financial Markets Research Center. The organization he created in 1974 is now one of the two largest mutual fund organizations in the world, with current assets totaling some $550 billion. In 1975, Bogle also founded the first index mutual fund. In 1999, *Fortune* named him as one of the investment industry's four "Giants of the 20th Century." Earlier that year, Princeton University, his alma mater, awarded him its Woodrow Wilson Award for "distinguished achievement in the Nation's service." Bogle has been presented with the Award for Professional Excellence of the Association for Investment Management and Research, inducted into the Hall of Fame of the Fixed Income Analysts' Society, and in 2003 was given the Legends of Leadership Award by the Yale School of Management. A prolific writer and speaker, he is author most recently of *John Bogle on Investing: The First 50 Years* (2000) and *Character Counts: The Creation and Building of the Vanguard Group* (2002). Bogle served as a member of The Conference Board's Commission on Public Trust and Private Enterprise during 2002–2003 and as chairman of the Board of Governors of the Investment Company Institute in 1969–1970.   *(Chapter 1)*

Craig Brimhall is the vice president of wealth strategies at American Express Funds, headquartered in Minneapolis. He is a personal finance expert in the areas of retirement savings and distributions, with expertise in current tax law changes and how they affect retirement plans, and serves as national spokesperson for American Express Financial Advisors. Prior to assuming his current position, Brimhall served as region vice president of investments for the Virginia, District of Columbia, and Baltimore areas, providing support and training programs for advisers, sales consultants, and clients on topics including financial planning, investment strategies, stock market outlook, asset allocation, retirement, and estate planning. Brimhall is interviewed regularly by the news media on financial topics. He is licensed as a Certified Financial Planner, Certified Fund Specialist, and Chartered Retirement Planning Counselor and has also earned Series 7, 63, and 65 licenses.   *(Chapter 7)*

Jean Bernhard Buttner is the chairman, chief executive officer, and president of New York–based investment advisory and money management firm Value Line, Inc. She also is publisher and editor-in-chief of *The Value Line Investment Survey*, the nation's largest independent investment service. In addition, Buttner serves as chairman, chief executive officer, and president of Arnold Bernhard & Co. She is on the board of directors of the Associates of Harvard Business School and a member of the New York City Partnership Committee of 200 and the Harvard Business School Club of Greater New York. She was cited among *Working Woman*'s Top 500 Women-Owned Businesses, and named one of *Crain's New York Business*'s 100 Most Influential Women in Business. Buttner is a graduate of Vassar College.   *(Chapter 18)*

General Wesley K. Clark, U.S.A. (Ret.), who led the 1999 NATO campaign in Kosovo, served as NATO's Supreme Allied Commander, Europe, for the last four years of his military career. A four-star general, he is the recipient of numerous military honors and awards, among them the Presidential Medal of Freedom, the Nation's highest civilian honor. Clark, now a military analyst with Cable News Network, was formerly a managing director of merchant banking at Stephen's Group Inc., a venture capital firm. He is a senior adviser for the Center for Strategic and International Studies (CSIS), a director of the Atlantic Council, and a member of the board of the International Crisis Group. General Clark is a graduate of the United States Military Academy of West Point and holds a master's degree in philosophy, politics, and economics from Oxford University where he studied as a Rhodes Scholar. He is the author of *Waging Modern War: Bosnia, Kosovo, and the Future of Combat* (Public Affairs, 2002), from which General Clark's chapter in this book has been excerpted.   *(Chapter 26)*

Anthony Crescenzi is chief bond market strategist at Miller Tabak & Company and has been an active trader in government bonds and bond futures for institutional clients. He also is chief executive officer of BondTalk.com, a comprehensive website for bond investors, and has taught classes on the bond market at Baruch College's Executive M.B.A. program. The author of *The Strategic Bond Buyer*, Crescenzi has been quoted widely in the financial press, including the *Wall Street Journal,* the *New York Times, Barron's,* and *Investors Business Daily,* and appears frequently on CNBC, CNNfn, and Bloomberg TV. The Federal Reserve chose him to be a regular participant in the prestigious Livingston Survey of economic forecasters. Crescenzi holds an M.B.A. from St. John's University.   *(Chapter 9)*

John C. van Eck, chief gold strategist and chairman of Van Eck Associates and Van Eck Funds, is well known as a pioneer of international investing and as a leader in the gold sector, with over fifty years of investment experience. In 1955 he founded Van Eck Global, an investment firm specializing in global investments. He founded International Investors Incorporated mutual fund over forty-five years ago in order to provide a convenient investment vehicle with which Americans could invest in foreign growth stocks. Concluding that worldwide inflation would lead to gold mines offering better growth prospects than industrial and financial investments, van Eck moved the bulk of the portfolio into gold mining shares in 1968 in time to participate in the great gold bull market of the 1970s. Gold mining shares began to perform well again in 2002, and the Fund's performance that year put it in third place among all U.S.-based open-end mutual funds. Van Eck International Investors Gold Fund is the oldest U.S. mutual fund to concentrate in precious metals mining shares. In addition, van Eck has created ten other global and gold funds during his career. Van Eck received a B.A. from Williams College and his M.B.A. from Harvard Business School, and he is a Chartered Financial Analyst charter holder.   *(Chapter 10)*

Foster S. Friess is founder and chairman of Friess Associates, which manages approximately $5 billion in assets for clients including The John M. Templeton Foundation, the Brandywine Funds, Fortune 500 corporate pension plans, the mutual fund tracking firm Morningstar, and Friess's high school basketball coach. A $10,000 investment made with Friess when he launched his firm in 1974 would be worth, before taxes, nearly $1.2 million today. Friess Associates' flagship Brandywine Fund has appeared on *Money* magazine's list of the "World's Best Mutual Funds" every year since *Money* began compiling it. *BusinessWeek* called Friess "the longest-surviving successful growth stock picker," and Ron Insana of CNBC dubbed him "one of the last century's great investors." Brandywine's 20 percent annualized return throughout the 1990s won it a spot on *Mutual Funds* magazine's list of the "Best Funds of the Decade." Friess earned a degree in business administration from the University of

Wisconsin. A past president of the Council for National Policy, he was honored with its Rich M. DeVos Free Enterprise Award for Exceptional Leadership in 2000 and has received numerous awards over the years for his humanitarian and philanthropic activities.   *(Chapter 3)*

James T. Hackett is chairman of the board, president, and CEO of Ocean Energy, Inc., and becomes president and chief operating officer of Devon Energy Corporation in mid-2003 when the two companies merge to create the largest independent oil and gas exploration and production company in the United States. During his five-year tenure with Ocean, he doubled the size and scope of the company, positioning it as one of the leading independents in deepwater exploration and production, following a $3.6 billion merger with Seagull Energy Corporation in 1998. Earlier in his career, Hackett helped to lead a $7 billion merger between Duke Power and PanEnergy Corporation, where he was executive vice president. At Duke Energy his responsibilities included worldwide development of pipelines, processing facilities and power plants, nuclear and petroleum engineering services, and commodity marketing and trading. Prior to working for Duke Energy, he was president of the Natural Gas Liquids Processing division for Dynegy, Inc. Hackett joined Dynegy from Burlington Resources, where he was a vice president and served in production, drilling, and reservoir engineering functions. Active in energy industry public affairs, he chairs the Domestic Petroleum Council and is a member of the Policy Committee of the American Petroleum Institute and the Society of Petroleum Engineers. Hackett received a B.S. degree from the University of Illinois and his M.B.A. from Harvard Business School.   *(Chapter 8)*

Robert D. Hormats is vice chairman of Goldman Sachs International. He served as Assistant Secretary of State for Economic and Business Affairs in 1981–1982, Ambassador and Deputy U.S. Trade Representative in 1979–1981, and Senior Deputy Assistant Secretary for Economic and Business Affairs at the Department of State in 1977–1979. During his tenure in 1969–1977 as a senior staff member for international economic affairs on the National Security Council, he was Senior Economic Advisor to Dr. Henry Kissinger, General Brent Scowcroft, and Dr. Zbigniew Brzezinski. Hormats was a recipient of the French Legion of Honor in 1982. He was appointed by President Clinton in 1993 to the board of the U.S.-Russia Investment Fund. A board member of the Council on Foreign Relations, he is also a member of the Board of Visitors of the Fletcher School of Law and Diplomacy and the Dean's

Council of Harvard's John F. Kennedy School of Government. His pub-
lications include *American Albatross: The Foreign Debt Dilemma and
Reforming the International Monetary System* as well as articles in
Foreign Affairs, Foreign Policy, the *New York Times,* the *Washington
Post,* the *Wall Street Journal, American Banker,* and the *Financial Times.*
Hormats received his B.A. from Tufts University and an M.A. and a
Ph.D. from the Fletcher School of Law and Diplomacy.   *(Chapter 15)*

John T. Kernan is chairman and chief executive officer of Lightspan,
Inc., which creates interactive software and Internet products for elementary education, featuring entertainment-quality interactive curriculum programming. He was formerly chairman and chief executive officer
of Jostens Learning Corporation, the nation's largest educational software company and a leader in high-tech training for the military and
commercial aviation. Kernan has served as chairman and president of the
Software and Information Industry Association, the primary trade association of the computer software industry. He has been selected the
regional Entrepreneur of the Year by *Inc. Magazine,* Educator of the
Decade by *Electronic Learning Magazine,* and Portfolio Company
Executive of the Year by the National Association of Small Business
Investment Companies.   *(Chapter 24)*

Kerry Killinger serves as chairman, president, and chief executive officer
of Seattle-based Washington Mutual, Inc., a national financial services
retailer serving the needs of mass-market consumers as well as small and
medium-sized businesses. Under his leadership, WaMu has grown into the
nation's seventh largest financial services company, with over $261 billion
in assets, and an employee base of more than 50,000 people. In 2001,
American Banker magazine named Killinger its "Banker of the Year."
He is a member of the New York Stock Exchange Listed Companies
Advisory Committee and serves on the boards of the Financial Services
Roundtable, the Washington Roundtable, the Washington Financial
League, the Committee to Encourage Corporate Philanthropy, Achieve,
the Partnership for Learning, and the Greater Seattle Chamber of
Commerce. Killinger earned bachelor's and M.B.A. degrees from the
University of Iowa.   *(Chapter 22)*

Hendrik J. Kranenburg is executive vice president of Standard & Poor's,
a division of The McGraw-Hill Companies, Inc. He leads Standard &
Poor's Investment Services division, which provides financial commentary,
investment advice, and real-time market data to investment managers and

advisers. Kranenburg is a frequent commentator on world financial market developments. A graduate of the University of California at Berkeley, he holds a master's degree from the Woodrow Wilson School at Princeton University and is a Chartered Financial Analyst.   *(Chapter 16)*

Jules Kroll is executive chairman of the board of Kroll Inc., which provides a wide range of risk consulting services as well as investigations, intelligence, and security to a multinational client base of corporations, law firms, nonprofit institutions, government agencies, and individuals. Kroll is a leading authority on defensive tactics in contests for corporate control, industrial counter-espionage, and the prevention and detection of white-collar crime. Kroll Inc.'s reputation for high-quality investigative work was established on Wall Street in the 1980s and spread internationally in the 1990s as the firm successfully tracked down assets hidden by Jean-Claude "Baby Doc" Duvalier, Ferdinand and Imelda Marcos, and Saddam Hussein. A sought-after speaker at conferences and seminars worldwide, Kroll has been interviewed on *60 Minutes* and *CBS MarketWatch* and has been quoted in many publications including the *New York Times,* the *Wall Street Journal, Fortune, BusinessWeek,* the *Financial Times,* and the *Observer.* He is a graduate of Cornell University and Georgetown University Law Center.   *(Chapter 25)*

Vladimir L. Kvint has been a professor of management systems and international business at Fordham University's Graduate School of Business since 1990 and has served as adjunct professor at the Stern School of Business at New York University. In 1989–1990 he was a professor at the Vienna Economic University and in 1991 was the Distinguished Visiting Professor at Babson College. Between 1978 and 1989, he was the leading Research Fellow of the USSR Academy of Sciences. In 1992–1997, he was the director of emerging markets at Arthur Andersen. Since 1993 he has been a member of the Bretton Woods Committee. Kvint is a member of the Russian Academy of Natural Sciences and president of the International Academy of Emerging Markets. He is the author of more than 350 articles and eighteen books, including *The Global Emerging Market in Transition,* which was the subject of a special conference in UN headquarters in 1999. Kvint has served as adviser to governments and leaders of Balkan countries (Bulgaria, Albania, and Romania) and several other emerging market countries. He has a D.Sc. in economics and a Ph.D. in management economics, an M.S. in mining electrical engineering, and an honorary doctorate from the University of Bridgeport.   *(Chapter 14)*

Lewis D. Lowenfels, a partner in the New York law firm of Tolins & Lowenfels, has more than forty years of experience in practicing corporate and securities law representing public companies, investment banking firms, and many prominent Wall Street individuals in all facets of their businesses. *Forbes* magazine has called him "one of the best securities lawyers in the business." Lowenfels is coauthor with Professor Alan Bromberg of the six-volume *Securities Fraud and Commodities Fraud,* which is considered the definitive treatise in the field and has been cited hundreds of times over the years by the U.S. Supreme Court and circuit and district courts. A public governor of the American Stock Exchange from 1993 to 1996, he serves as an expert witness in litigation and arbitration, is quoted regularly in the print and electronic media, and serves as an adjunct professor of law at Seton Hall University Law School. Lowenfels graduated from Harvard College and received his juris doctor's degree from Harvard Law School. *(Chapter 20)*

Michael Mandelbaum is the Christian A. Herter Professor of American Foreign Policy at The Johns Hopkins University School of Advanced International Studies and Senior Fellow at The Council on Foreign Relations. Formerly director of the Project on East-West Relations for the Council on Foreign Relations, he has taught at Harvard University, Columbia University, and the U.S. Naval Academy. Mandelbaum is a regular foreign affairs columnist for *Newsday* and the author of several books on foreign policy, including *The Ideas That Conquered the World: Peace, Democracy and Free Markets in the Twenty-first Century* (PublicAffairs, 2002), from which his chapter in *Investing Under Fire* is adapted. He has a Ph.D. in political science from Harvard University. *(Chapter 29)*

Mark Monane, M.D., M.S. is principal of equity research at Needham and Company, an investment bank in New York City, where he serves as a senior analyst in biotechnology and biopharmaceuticals. His coverage universe focuses on small-cap and midcap companies in the cardiovascular and cancer areas. He was recently ranked number two in biotechnology in the 2002 Best on the Street Analysts Survey conducted by the *Wall Street Journal.* Dr. Monane formerly was a full-time faculty member and researcher at Harvard Medical School and also has worked at Merck-Medco Managed Care. His research has resulted in more than fifty articles and review publications in such journals as *Journal of the American Medical Association, Archives of Internal Medicine, Clinical Pharmacology* and *Therapeutics.* Dr. Monane holds an A.B. degree from Columbia University, an M.D. from New York University School of Medicine, an M.S. degree from Harvard School of Public Health, and an M.B.A. degree from Columbia Business School. He is an adjunct associate clinical professor at Rutgers College of Pharmacy in New Jersey.   *(Chapter 13)*

Louis G. Navellier, the president and chief investment officer of Navellier & Associates, Inc. and Navellier Management, Inc., is editor of *MPT Review* and *The Blue Chip Growth Stock* newsletters. Successful in translating what had been purely academic techniques into "real market" applications, he is committed to the principle that disciplined quantitative analysis can yield stock selections that will significantly outperform the overall market. Navellier employs a three-step, highly disciplined "bottom up" stock selection process, including quantitative analysis, fundamental analysis, and utilization of an allocation model, and publishes his research in his stock advisory newsletter *MPT Review.* He is active in the management of individual portfolios, pension funds, and institutional portfolios, with over $3 billion under management in the Navellier Funds. In addition to appearing on Fox News, CNBC, Bloomberg TV, *Nightly Business Report* and *Wall Street Week,* he has been featured in *Barron's, Forbes, Fortune, Investor's Business Daily, Money, Smart Money,* the *Wall Street Journal,* and *Worth.* Navellier is a graduate of California State University, Hayward, with an M.B.A. in finance.   *(Chapter 6)*

William C. Nygren is a partner and portfolio manager for Harris Associates L.P., a Chicago-based investment management firm that serves as the adviser to The Oakmark Family of Funds. Known in the investment marketplace for its strict adherence to a fundamental value approach, The Oakmark Family of Funds, whose first fund launched in 1991, is designed to follow the same long-term value investment approach practiced since 1976 by its investment adviser, Harris Associates L.P. The fund family has expanded to seven funds to take advantage of various investment opportunities. Nygren is portfolio manager for The Oakmark Fund and The Oakmark Select Fund. He joined Harris Associates as an analyst in 1983 and was director of research from 1990 through March 1998. Prior to joining Harris Associates, he was an analyst with Northwestern Mutual Life Insurance Company. Nygren received a B.S. in accounting from the University of Minnesota and an M.S. in finance from the University of Wisconsin–Madison, and he is a Chartered Financial Analyst charter holder.   *(Chapter 4)*

Randall Poe is executive director of communications at The Conference Board, the New York–based nonprofit business research group. His work on economic and social trends has appeared in the *New York Times, Washington Post,* the *Wall Street Journal, BusinessWeek, Newsday, Harper's, Esquire,* and other publications. Poe's critical column on the business media appears in *Across the Board,* The Conference Board's magazine of ideas and opinion, and on The Columnists.com. In his role with The Conference Board, he frequently is called upon to speak before a wide range of business and university audiences. Poe is a member of *Who's Who in the World* and the Overseas Press Club.   *(Chapter 19)*

Brian Portnoy is a senior mutual fund analyst for Morningstar, Inc., covering a broad range of growth and value funds. He also writes frequently on foreign investing and edits the "Foreign Fund Insight" feature on Morningstar.com. He speaks regularly on fund investing and is widely quoted in the media, including the *Wall Street Journal, Financial Times,* and CNBC. Portnoy holds a bachelor's degree from the University of Michigan and a master's degree and Ph.D. in international political economy from the University of Chicago.   *(Chapter 17)*

Ned Riley is a senior principal and chief investment strategist for State Street Global Advisors. He is responsible for developing fundamental investment policy for the firm's institutional and high-net-worth clients. Prior to joining the firm in 2000, Riley was BankBoston's chief investment officer, where he directed the development and implementation of investment policy for $32 billion in assets under management. In this role, he was responsible for the development of the Boston 1784 Funds and cofounder of Eagle Investment Associates. Riley is well known in the investment management field and makes frequent appearances on CNBC, CNN, Fox, NBC, WCVB-TV Channel 5, New England Cable News, and the BBC. He received a B.A. in economics from Providence College and is a member of the Association for Investment Management and Research.   *(Chapter 2)*

Ambassador Dennis Ross is director of the Washington Institute for Near East Policy. A highly skilled diplomat, he was this country's point man on the peace process in both the first Bush and the Clinton administrations. He was instrumental in assisting Israelis and Palestinians in reaching the 1995 Interim Agreement; he also successfully brokered the Hebron Accord in 1997, facilitated the Israeli-Jordan peace treaty, and intensively worked to bring Israel and Syria together. Prior to his service as Special Middle East Coordinator under President Clinton, he was director of the State Department's Policy Planning office in the first Bush administration. In that position, he played a prominent role in developing U.S. policy toward the former Soviet Union, the unification of Germany and its integration into NATO, arms control negotiations, and the development of the Gulf War coalition. He served as director of Near East and South Asian affairs on the National Security Council staff during the Reagan administration and as deputy director of the Pentagon's Office of Net Assessment. President Clinton awarded Ambassador Ross the Presidential Medal for Distinguished Federal Civilian Service, and Secretaries James Baker and Madeleine Albright presented him with the State Department's highest award. Ambassador Ross is a graduate of University of California at Los Angeles.   *(Chapter 28)*

Bernie Schaeffer, chairman and CEO of Schaeffer's Investment Research, Inc., began publishing *The Option Advisor* monthly newsletter in 1981. As senior editor, Schaeffer's aspiration was to show traders how they could use options to discover profit opportunities in both stable and volatile markets. Schaeffer has guided the monthly publication to growth and success as the nation's leading options newsletter. Along with developing the newsletter, several recommendation services, and the highly regarded SchaeffersResearch.com website, Schaeffer has authored *The Option Advisor: Wealth-Building Techniques Using Equity & Index Options.* Schaeffer's thriving approach to market timing has earned him the "Best of the Best" award in the field of sentiment analysis from the Market Technician's Association as well as top market timing rankings from *Timer Digest* for more than a decade. In 2002, he won *Business-Week*'s annual Market Forecast Survey for most accurately forecasting year-end levels for the DJIA, Nasdaq, and S&P. Widely recognized as an expert on options and investor sentiment, Schaeffer is often sought by the financial media for his views on the stock market and the economy. He appears regularly on CNBC, CNN, Fox News, and the *Nightly Business Report.*   *(Chapter 5)*

Orin C. Smith is president and chief executive officer of Starbucks Coffee Company. When he joined Starbucks in 1990 as vice president and chief financial officer, the company had only forty-five stores. Today, Starbucks is the leading retailer, roaster, and brand of specialty coffee in the world. Early in his career, Smith spent fourteen years with Deloitte and Touche in the management consulting division. Later, he worked in the transportation sector as the executive vice president and chief financial officer of two public companies. Active in public affairs,

Smith has served as an adviser to the last five governors of the state of Washington. He is a member of the board of directors for Conservation International, the University of Washington School of Business, and several other public and private institutions. Smith received a B.A. from the University of Washington and his M.B.A. from Harvard Business School. *(Chapter 23)*

Sam Stovall is chief investment strategist at Standard & Poor's, a division of the McGraw-Hill Companies, Inc. Stovall serves as analyst, publisher, and communicator of Standard & Poor's outlooks for the economy, market, sectors, and stocks. He is a member of the S&P Investment Policy Committee, where he focuses on market history and valuations as well as sector and industry recommendations. He is also the author of *The Standard & Poor's Guide to Sector Investing* and "Stovall's Sector Watch," a page on businessweek.com, which identifies sector top-outs and turnarounds. Stovall is a graduate of Muhlenberg College and received an M.B.A. from New York University. He is licensed as a Certified Financial Planner. *(Chapter 16)*

Toshiaki Taguchi is president and CEO of Toyota Motor North America, headquartered in New York City, and a member of the Board of Directors of Toyota Motor Corporation. He is responsible for enhancing the coordination, speed, and productivity of Toyota's North American business operations. He has also served as executive coordinator at Toyota Motor Sales based in California, overseas in general management positions in the Europe division, and in supervising Latin American operations and international public affairs, but his career has revolved primarily around North American operations. Active in both the Japanese and American communities in New York, Taguchi is a member of the Board of Directors of Japan Society, Japanese Chamber of Commerce and Industry of New York, and The Nippon Club. He is a trustee of Japan Educational Institute of New York and International House and is a member of the Carnegie Hall Corporate Leadership Committee and the Board of Advisors of the National Center for Family Literacy. He is a graduate of International Christian University in Tokyo. *(Chapter 21)*

John D. Tortorella is an associate with the law firm of Paul, Weiss, Rifkind, Wharton & Garrison LLC. His practice focuses on securities law and commercial litigation. Tortorella was formerly law clerk to Honorable Samuel A. Alito, Jr. of the United States Court of Appeals for the Third Circuit. He graduated from Georgetown University and received his juris doctor's degree from Seton Hall University Law School. The views expressed in Tortorella's chapter for this book are those of the author and not of the firm or its clients.   *(Chapter 20)*

James Turk is the founder of GoldMoney (www.goldmoney.com), a company that operates a digital gold currency payment system based on three U.S. patents awarded to him. He has specialized in international banking, finance, and investments since graduating from George Washington University with a B.A. degree in international economics. His business career began at The Chase Manhattan Bank (now J.P. Morgan Chase), which included assignments in Thailand, the Philippines, and Hong Kong. He later joined the investment and trading company of a prominent precious metals trader based in Greenwich, Connecticut. He moved to the United Arab Emirates in 1983 to be appointed Manager of the Commodity Department of the Abu Dhabi Investment Authority, a position he held until 1987. James Turk is the author of *The Illusions of Prosperity* (1985), *Social Security: Lies, Myths and Reality* (1992), and several monographs on money and banking. He writes *The Freemarket Gold & Money Report* (www.fgmr.com), an investment newsletter he began in 1987.   *(Chapter 11)*

Preface

My firm conviction is that only by studying the lessons of yesterday can investors avoid making damaging mistakes tomorrow. In no other area has history repeated itself as in the stock market.

— DANA THOMAS, historian, journalist, and author

I WAS BORN DURING the Depression, interestingly, just nine years before the New York World's Fair of 1939 and just ten years before France surrendered to Germany in World War II. Then, as an eleven-year-old, I witnessed the wrenching shock, on December 7, 1941, of Japan's attack on Pearl Harbor. The United States was taken by surprise; the U.S. fleet was wiped out by the attack. America lost both its innocence and isolation. The next day I was among the children called to the basement of Joan of Arc junior high school at 12:30 P.M. to listen to FDR's radio remarks to the nation vowing that the United States would "gain inevitable triumph" by defeating Japan and saving democracy. How quickly we stopped trying to memorize the baseball stats on our trading cards when learning to recognize silhouettes of enemy aircraft came to feel far more important.

From 1929 on, until Germany invaded Poland in 1939, many developed nations, America among them, traversed a dark valley inhabited by unemployment and hardship, strife and fear. The darkness deepened as the economic crisis condensed into one great political thundercloud. Not unlike today, this was a period when there were nations and individuals that stopped at nothing in developing new ways to poison and pollute man's quest for peace, prosperity, and truth. How did ordinary people learn the truth? "The historian," as Harvard's political scientist Carl Friedrich said, "is the prophet looking backward." The past is prologue.

My mother had been invited, as a guest of President Roosevelt, to attend the 1939 World's Fair opening ceremonies. That year's fair, nicknamed *World of Tomorrow,* was an optimistic view of the marvelous future that awaited humankind. With the showcasing of medical break-throughs, revolutionary inventions, and greater understanding between all peoples of the world, to a nine-year-old it all added up to unlimited possibilities. Mother tirelessly made sure that we visited most of the exhibits, including GE, GM, and IBM. We went to the Pavilion of Nations many times, and she, like many others, believed that the world was on its way to being better through peace, invention, and industry.

That uncanny symmetry of history was played out again when, on the morning of September 11, 2001, United Flight #175 crashed into the south tower of the World Trade Center—the north tower was already burning from an explosion caused by American Airlines Flight #11. I saw both towers collapse, and once again, America became a nation in crisis.

Not only were we to struggle with a challenge from a faceless, ter-rorist enemy, but within just a few short months we found ourselves at the very end of a stock market bubble that had both instanta-neously minted millionaires by the thousands and melted the dreams of millions of other investors. Several of the nation's biggest bank-ruptcies occurred at the same time, even after the corporations involved had just received a clean audit. The shocking events of the last months of 2001 underscored our inability to learn the political and economic lessons of history well.

The United States finds itself once again swimming in a sea of uncertainty, whipped by complex crosscurrents, some old, some new, but all challenging our daily routines and our daily decisions. Significant changes now in process compel each of us and the nation as a whole to undertake a new analysis of trials and opportunities, costs and benefits, while attempting to preserve our most important values. We are in a new learning cycle where a mosaic of history lessons, governmental policy, socioeconomic changes, business philosophy, technological innovations, and plain old survival techniques need to be established.

The collected wisdom in this book comes not only from carefully selected newsmakers but also from top moneymakers, market strate-gists, and geopolitical, academic, and business experts. There are new lessons, strategies, approaches, and a new resolve in the pages that follow. My contributors have successfully dealt with crisis and opportunity before, have maintained their standards and ethics, and have shown the ability to endure. Above all, they believe that our free enterprise system will fuel the triumph of democracy over totalitarianism.

As Gerald Loeb said in *The Battle for Stock Market Profits,* "...every investor should read stock market, monetary, and business history...you will secure great benefit from reading the life stories of successful men. I always see merit in reading about something that happened rather than theoretical tomes of what ought to happen but rarely does."

Our own twenty-first century "World of Tomorrow" may seem uncertain. But as each generation has shown, we have our moments of tremendous despair, yet we manage to persevere, prosper, and eventually thrive through great adversity.

The collection of ideas in *Investing Under Fire* is a reinforcement of my belief that America can never truly be defeated.

ALAN R. ACKERMAN

A c k n o w l e d g m e n t s

JOE PATERNO, America's winningest football coach, has provided the best example I know of teamwork that leads to a winning formula. He stresses togetherness—people doing things together and for one another. He has always stressed class, style, and humility, commodities quickly fading from our generations as key ingredients to success.

In keeping with Joe's philosophy, may I take this opportunity to individually thank the team of esteemed contributors to *Investing Under Fire*. With the completion of this book, they have shared with our readers their experience, wisdom, and advice during a time in history when so much in the world has quickly changed. They have successfully dealt with crisis before, maintained their standards, and shown the ability to endure successfully. Thank you one and all.

The list of those behind the scenes in a project of this magnitude is impressively reinforced by Bloomberg stalwarts Paul Ehrlich, Charlie Pellett, Catherine Cowdery, and John Tucker; by Bloomberg Press's immensely talented and dedicated production team; and by editors Heather Ogilvie, Tracy Tait, and senior acquisitions editor Kathleen Peterson, who moved mountains to complete this project on time amidst a host of challenges.

Many thanks to Melissa Kleiner, Bloomberg News reporter, whose incisive knowledge of international players added so much.

Special thanks to my lifelong friend, Alan Mirken.

And lastly, three stalwarts under pressure helped put "the ball in the end zone"; Elizabeth Valente, Suzanne Robinson, and Paul Schwartz.

Lou Dobbs, you continue to come up with great thoughts. On the night of September 10th, 2001, you said, "Bulls, Bears, and the Bewildered would make a great title for a book." Well, many thanks. Here it is.

Introduction

W HEN THE DEPARTMENT OF HOMELAND SECURITY can raise the
terrorist attack index in a moment's notice and send equity
markets into a spiral, it says much about the nervousness, anxiety, and
uncertainty 40 million investors live with every day—sometimes every
hour. And these conditions may not change any time soon. Political
instability throughout the globe, economic fits and starts in our own
country, corporate malfeasance, and the resulting crisis of confidence
it has engendered seem intractable problems that continue to
confound policymakers and market players alike.

At no time in the nation's recent history have there been such
domestic and international cycles of uncertainty and real political
threat from countries aiming to advance their causes with nuclear and
other weapons of mass destruction. All Americans need to note that
since September 11 we are more aware, but we are not more secure.
Our country has been attacked by a faceless enemy at great cost, at a
time when a decade-long investment bubble decimated personal
holdings at a rate not seen since the Great Depression. We are
currently dealing with a crisis of confidence as a nation—and as individuals, we are all characters in crisis. The question for the average
investor is what to do next in terms of protecting one's portfolio and
planning for the future.

In *Investing Under Fire: Winning Strategies from the Masters for
Bulls, Bears, and the Bewildered,* I have aimed to provide insights
into the issues market players must wrestle with now and going
forward. In doing so, I've assembled the perspectives of pillars of
wisdom, financial industry experts, academics, corporate leaders,
newsmakers, and moneymakers on how the investor should interpret
and react in these tumultuous times. The book is organized into five
parts, each dealing with a separate aspect of the uncertainty facing the
investor in today's volatile, geopolitically jittery market environment.

Part One highlights the diverse perspectives and strategies of seven superstars in the investing arena, offering their points of view on how to win in the market under difficult circumstances. Legendary Vanguard founder John C. Bogle starts the section with a revealing analysis of the mutual fund industry's dramatic evolution and what this portends for investors. State Street Global Advisors' chief investment strategist Ned Riley, one of Wall Street's foremost spokespersons on investments, traces a fascinating history of stock market bubbles and bursts and how investors can seek out telling countercurrents for safe, intelligent investment decisions. Next, Brandywine Fund's distinguished founder Foster Friess offers nine seemingly counterintuitive guidelines that underscore the importance of assiduous "tire kicking" in stock research. Bill Nygren of the Oakmark Funds, a superstar of value investing, then describes the essential criteria investors must identify in the search for value. Acclaimed market maven Bernie Schaeffer reveals how his advanced technical analysis combined with timely sentiment analysis creates a powerful and unique set of arrows in an investor's quiver. Growth stock expert and investment all star Louis Navellier, with over $3 billion under management, argues in his chapter that the stock market is indeed inefficient as demonstrated in his robust reward/risk ratio and multifactor analysis stock-picking models. The section concludes with head of American Express Funds' wealth strategies division Craig Brimhall, who offers ten time-tested investing rules for weathering even the stormiest of market conditions.

Part Two showcases the views of eight leading-edge market experts on key investment sectors that are especially worthy of serious consideration in these uncertain times. The section begins with a penetrating chapter by global energy expert Jim Hackett, president, chairman, and CEO of Ocean Energy Inc., on the world's unquenchable thirst for oil and the critical challenges and prospects associated with this significant commodity. Next, Wall Street economist Tony Crescenzi describes in fascinating detail the predictive power of the bond market and the competitive advantage investors can gain in paying attention to its ripple effect on the broader trading world. Pioneering gold strategist and international fund manager John C. van Eck then traces gold's historical saga as a safe-haven investment, concluding with three bullish gold price scenarios that wary investors will find compelling. Van Eck's incisive analysis, which has withstood the vicissitudes of the markets, is followed by GoldMoney founder James Turk's provocative chapter that delves further into gold's shifting role over the decades and offers prospects for a new role for gold in today's global, wired economy. Next, Awad Asset Management's esteemed chairman and CNBC's stock-picking contest winner Jim Awad offers insights on the unique characteristics and special investment advantages of keeping small-cap stocks—"diamonds in the rough"—in an all-weather portfolio. Jim's chapter is followed by the clear insights of Needham & Co.'s star biotechnology and biopharmaceutical analyst Mark Monane on prospects and stock-selection principles for the biotech sector. This section's penultimate chapter, by world-renowned emerging markets expert and *Forbes'* spokesperson Vladimir Kvint, presents trends in the global emerging market, together with opportunities and risks associated with such investment. Vladimir's chapter is followed by that of another geopolitical affairs giant and revered market strategist, Goldman Sachs International's Bob Hormats, on the investor outlook in Asia and the pervasive, dynamic influence of China on Asian growth.

In Part Three, "Tools of the Trade for Today's Investor," contributors present a series of time-tested, independent resources investors can turn to for knowledge, reliability, and objectivity in research. The first chapter, by Standard & Poor's Hendrik Kranenburg and Sam Stovall, addresses S&P's approach to equity research and the broad suite of tools they offer. Next, Morningstar's Brian Portnoy describes how Morningstar's methodology supports the investor with unbiased, objective evaluations and analytical tools. Jean Bernhard Buttner, chairman and CEO of Value Line and the daughter of its legendary founder, then relates the history and rationale behind the company and its products. The fourth chapter in this part, by Randall Poe of The Conference Board, outlines the service profile of that organization as well as its economic analyses and management reports that have become trusted guides on the economy and a sounding board for business. The last chapter in this part, by one of the best securities lawyers in the business, Lewis Lowenfels, and his colleague John Tortorella, describes the substantially greater legal recourse afforded the investor to resolve cases of securities fraud with recent passage of the Sarbanes-Oxley Act.

Part Four offers the reader four case studies of companies that have faced vast business and social environmental change, pioneered a vision of how to prosper, and been significantly successful. Innovative companies of this genre are ones that investors may seek out and invest in for long-term gain. The first chapter, by Toyota North America president and CEO Toshiaki Taguchi, addresses major influences increasingly affecting his industry, with particular attention to "greener" cars and clean manufacturing. The next chapter, by Washington Mutual CEO Kerry Killinger, is the story of how a middle market bank from the Northwest ignored market trends toward depersonalization of service and remained true to its focus— treating every customer not as an account but as a "person," helping it grow into today's $260 billion business from $44 billion in 1996. In a similar story of market opportunity, Starbucks Coffee Company CEO Orin Smith traces the factors that have led to its phenomenal growth, among them social responsibility and sustainability-focused practices it continues to foster among its coffee growers. The last chapter in the section, by Lightspan Inc. president and CEO John Kernan, is about education, immigration, and the hugely significant challenge to develop educational strategies that effectively integrate immigrants into the growing workforce.

Part Five, exploring geopolitical implications for today's investor, assembles some of today's most respected thinkers and advisers from the worlds of public affairs, the military, and academia, including global risk consulting firm founder Jules Kroll, General Wesley Clark, Harvard's Graham Allison, Ambassador Dennis Ross, and Johns Hopkins University's Michael Mandelbaum. These experts address the complex geopolitical situations in many parts of the world with depth and perception rarely available to the average investor. In this section, and as a result of the 9/11 terror attacks, which claimed victims from thirty-six countries around the world, special emphasis is placed on the new politics of terrorism and warfare and how the investor should understand their implications.

The five parts of *Investing Under Fire* together are intended to provide an enlightening, broad-scope panorama of the most important issues and options challenging investors in today's markets. As such, I hope you will turn to these pages again and again for insight, strategies, and lessons to guide you.

Investing
Under Fire

Part One

Pitfalls and Hazards Facing Today's Investor

C h a p t e r   One

Today's Mutual Fund Industry: Back to the Future

JOHN C. BOGLE

Founder and former Chairman, The Vanguard Group

S OME FIFTY-THREE years ago, when I was trying to come up with a topic for my Princeton thesis, I stumbled upon an article describing the mutual fund industry in the December 1949 issue of *Fortune* magazine. The article, "Big Money in Boston," featured the nation's oldest and largest mutual fund, Massachusetts Investors Trust (M.I.T.). The story described it as "the leader of a rapidly expanding and somewhat contentious industry of great potential significance to U.S. business." I immediately realized that I had found my topic.

The extensive study of the industry that followed led me to four conclusions: One, that mutual funds should be managed "in the most efficient, honest, and economical way possible," and that fund sales charges and management fees should be reduced. Two, that mutual funds should not lead the public to the expectation of miracles from management, since funds could "make no claim to superiority over the (unmanaged) market averages." Three, that "the principal function [of funds] is the management of their investment portfolios"— the trusteeship of investor assets—focusing "on the performance of the corporation ... [not on] the short-term public appraisal of the value of a share of stock." And four, that "the prime responsibility" of funds "must be to their shareholders," to *serve* the individual investor and the institutional investor alike.

In retrospect, the seminal *Fortune* article that inspired my thesis described an industry that is barely recognizable today. Not just in size, for, as I predicted, an era of growth lay ahead for this industry. If "Big Money" described a *tiny* industry, I'm not sure what adjective would be adequate to describe today's giant. And while more than one-half of fund assets were managed "in Boston" then, that share is now down to one-sixth. The mutual fund industry today is international in scope.

The vast changes in the size of this industry and in the types of funds we offer today—the difference between funds *past* and funds *present*—are but one reflection of the radical change in the very character of this industry. What *Fortune* described a half-century ago was an industry in which the idea was to sell what we made: *funds that offer the small investor peace of mind,* an industry that focused primarily on stewardship. By contrast, the industry we see today is one focused primarily on salesmanship, an industry in which marketing calls the tune in which we make what will sell, and in which short-term performance is the name of the game.

This change in character is not an illusion. Since that *Fortune* article was published slightly over a half-century ago, there are specific, quantifiable ways in which this industry has changed. I'll describe nine of them, and then conclude with an appraisal of whether these changes have been good for investors. I'll use industry averages to measure these changes. Of course some fund firms—but not nearly enough, in my view—have strived to retain their original character. But overall, the mutual fund industry has changed radically. Let me count the ways:

Funds Are Far Bigger, More Varied, and More Numerous

THE MUTUAL FUND INDUSTRY has become a giant. From its 1949 base of $2 *billion,* fund assets soared to $6.5 *trillion* at the outset of 2003, a compound growth rate of 16 percent. If it had grown at the 7 percent nominal growth rate of our economy, assets would be just $72 *billion* today. (Such is the magic of compounding.) Then, 90 percent of industry assets were represented by stock funds and stock-oriented balanced funds. Today such funds compose only about half of industry assets. Bond funds now represent one-sixth of assets, and money market funds—dating back only to 1970—constitute the remaining one-third. Once an equity fund industry, we now span the universe of major financial instruments—stocks, bonds, and savings reserves— a change that has been a boon not only to fund managers, but to fund investors as well.

So, too, has the number of funds exploded. Those 137 mutual funds of yesteryear have soared to today's total of 8,300. More relevantly, the total number of common stock funds has risen from just seventy-five to 4,800, although it is not at all clear that the nature of this increase has created investor benefits, for, in retrospect, choice has done investors more harm than good.

Stock Funds: From the Middle of the Road to the Four Corners of the Earth

AS THE NUMBER of stock funds soared, so did the variety of objectives and policies they follow. In 1950, the stock fund sector was dominated by funds that invested largely in highly diversified portfolios of U.S. corporations with large market capitalizations, with volatility roughly commensurate with that of the Standard & Poor's 500 Stock Index. Today such middle-of-the-road funds represent a distinct minority of the total, and most other categories entail higher risks. Only 560 of the 3,650 stock funds measured by Morningstar now closely resemble their blue-chip ancestors. The accepted terminology in equity funds reflects this change. We have come to accept a nine-box matrix of funds arranged by market capitalization (large, medium, or small) on one axis, and by investment style (growth, value, or a blend of the two) on the other. Yesteryear's middle-of-the-road funds would today find themselves in the "large-cap blend" box, constituting just 23 percent of the funds in the diversified U.S. fund category, and 15 percent of the Morningstar all-equity fund total.

What's more, we now have 450 specialized funds focused on narrow industry segments, from technology to telecommunications (particular favorites during the late bubble), and 750 international funds, running the gamut from diversified funds owning shares of companies all over the globe to highly specialized funds focusing on particular nations, from China to Russia to Israel. Among our 4,800 stock funds, there must now be one for every purpose under heaven.

A half-century ago, investors could have thrown a dart at a list of stock funds and had nine chances out of ten to pick a fund whose return was apt to parallel that of the market averages. Today, they have just one chance out of eight! When that old *Fortune* article noted that most funds did no more than give investors "a piece of the Dow Jones Average," it presciently added, "the average is not a bad thing to own." But today, for better or worse—probably worse— selecting mutual funds has become an art form.

From Investment Committee to Broadway Stardom

THESE VAST CHANGES in fund objectives have led to equally vast changes in how mutual funds are managed. In 1950, the major funds were managed almost entirely by investment committees. But the demonstrated wisdom of the collective was soon overwhelmed by the perceived brilliance of the individual. First, the "Go-Go" era of the mid-1960s and then the recent bubble brought us hundreds of more aggressive "performance funds," and the new game seemed to call for freewheeling individual talent. The term "investment committee" vanished, and "portfolio manager" gradually became the industry standard, now the model for some 3,200 of the 3,650 stock funds listed in Morningstar. ("Management teams" run the other 450 funds.)

The coming of the age of portfolio managers whose tenures lasted only as long as they produced performance moved fund management from the stodgy old consensus-oriented investment committee to a more entrepreneurial, free form, and far less risk-averse approach. Before long, moreover, the managers with the hottest short-term records had been transformed by their employers' vigorous public relations efforts and the enthusiastic cooperation of the media, into "stars," and a full-fledged star-system gradually came to pass. A few portfolio managers actually *were* stars—Fidelity's Peter Lynch, Vanguard's John Neff, Legg Mason's Bill Miller, for example—but most proved to be comets, illuminating the fund firmament for a moment in time before they flamed out. Even after the devastation of the recent bear market, and the stunning fact that the average portfolio manager's tenure is just five years, the system remains largely intact.

Turnover Goes Through the Roof

TOGETHER, THE COMING OF more aggressive funds, the burgeoning emphasis on short-term performance, and the move from investment committees to portfolio managers had a profound impact on mutual fund investment strategies—most obviously in soaring portfolio turnover. M.I.T. and the other funds described in that *Fortune* article didn't even *talk* about long-term investing. They just *did* it, simply because that's what trusteeship is all about. But over the next half-century that basic tenet was turned on its head, and short-term speculation became the order of the day.

Not that the long-term focus didn't resist change. Indeed, between 1950 and 1965, it was a rare year when fund portfolio turnover much exceeded 16 percent, meaning that the average fund held its average stock for an average of about six years. (See Figure 1-1.) But turnover then rose steadily, and fund managers now turn their portfolios over at an astonishing average annual rate of 110 percent. Result: Compared to that earlier six-year standard that prevailed for so long, the average stock is now held for just eleven months.

The contrast is stunning. At 16 percent turnover, a $1 billion fund sells $160 million of stocks in a given year and then reinvests the $160 million in other stocks, $320 million in all. At 110 percent, a $1 billion fund sells and then buys a total of $2.2 billion of stocks each year—nearly seven *times* as much. Even with lower *unit* transaction costs, it's hard to imagine that such turnover levels aren't a major drain on shareholder assets.

Let me be clear: If a six-year holding period can be characterized as long-term investment and if an eleven-month holding period can be characterized as short-term speculation, mutual fund managers today are not investors. We are speculators. When I say that this industry has moved from investment to speculation, I do not use the word "speculation" lightly. Indeed, in my thesis I used Lord Keynes' terminology, contrasting "speculation" ("forecasting the psychology of the market") with "enterprise" ("forecasting the prospective yield of an asset"). I concluded that as funds grew they would move away from speculation and toward enterprise (which I called "investment"), focusing not on the price of the share, but on the value of the corporation. As a result, I concluded, fund managers would supply

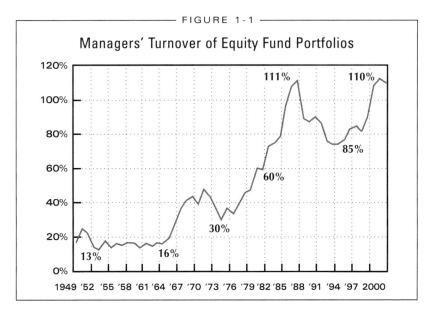

FIGURE 1-1

Managers' Turnover of Equity Fund Portfolios

the stock market "with a demand for securities that is *steady, sophisticated, enlightened,* and *analytic.*" I was dead wrong. We are no longer stock *owners.* We are stock *traders,* as far away as we can possibly be from investing for investment icon Warren Buffett's favorite holding period: Forever.

High Stock Turnover Leads
to Low Corporate Responsibility

WHATEVER THE CONSEQUENCES of this high portfolio turnover are for the shareholders of the funds, it has had dire consequences for the governance of our nation's corporations. In 1949, *Fortune* wrote, "one of the pet ideas (of M.I.T.'s Griswold) is that the mutual fund is the ideal champion of … the small stockholder in conversations with corporate management, needling corporations on dividend policies, blocking mergers, and pitching in on proxy fights." And in my ancient thesis that examined the economic role of mutual funds, I devoted a full chapter to their role "as an influence on corporate management." Mr. Griswold was not alone in his activism, and I noted with approval the SEC's 1940 call on mutual funds to serve as "the useful role of representatives of the great number of inarticulate and ineffective individual investors in corporations in which funds are interested."

It was not to be. Just as the early hope I expressed that funds would continue to invest for the long term died aborning, so did my hope that funds would observe their responsibilities of corporate citizenship. Of course the two are hardly unrelated: A fund that acts as a trader, focusing on the price of a share and holding a stock for but eleven months, may not even own the shares when the time comes to vote them at the corporation's next annual meeting. By contrast, a fund that acts as an owner, focusing on the long-term value of the enterprise, has little choice but to regard the governance of the corporation as of surpassing importance.

Although funds owned but 2 percent of the shares of all U.S. corporations a half-century ago, today they own 23 percent. They could wield a potent "big stick," but, with few exceptions, they have failed to do so. As a result of their long passivity and lassitude on corporate governance issues, we fund managers bear no small share of the responsibility for the ethical failures in corporate governance and accounting oversight that were among the major forces creating the recent stock market bubble and the bear market that followed. It is hard to see anything but good arising when this industry at last returns to its roots and assumes its responsibilities of corporate citizenship.

The Fund Shareholder Gets the (Wrong) Idea

THE CHANGE in this industry's character has radically affected the behavior of the mutual fund shareholder. In the industry described in the *Fortune* article as having "tastes in common stocks that run to the seasoned issues of blue-chip corporations," shareholders bought fund shares and held them. In the 1950s, and for a dozen years thereafter, fund redemptions (liquidations of fund shares) averaged 6 percent of assets annually, suggesting that the average fund investor held his or her shares for sixteen years. Like the managers of the funds they held, fund owners were investing for the long pull.

But as the industry brought out funds that were more and more performance oriented, often speculative, specialized, and concentrated —funds that behaved increasingly like individual stocks—it attracted more and more investors for whom the long term didn't seem to be relevant. Up, up, up went the redemption rate. In 2002 it reached

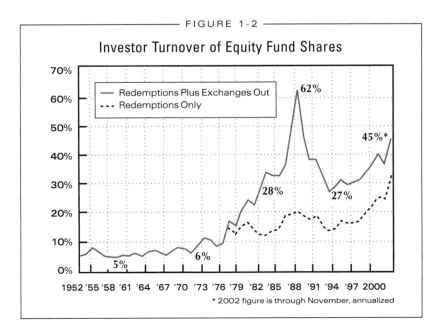

FIGURE 1-2

Investor Turnover of Equity Fund Shares

45 percent of assets, an average holding period of slightly more than two years. (See Figure 1-2.) The time horizon for the typical fund investor had tumbled by fully 90 percent.

As "buy and hold" turned to "pick and choose," the average fund owner who once held a single equity fund came to hold four. "Freedom of choice" became the industry watchword, and fund supermarkets, with their "open architecture," made it easy to quickly move money around in no-load funds. Trading costs are hidden in the form of access fees for the shelf space offered by these supermarkets, paid for by the funds themselves, so that swapping funds seemed to be free, tacitly encouraging fund shareholders to trade from one to another. But while picking tomorrow's winners based on yesterday's performance is theoretically attractive, in practice it is a strategy that is doomed to failure.

The Modern Mutual Fund: Made to Be Sold

IT IS EASY to lay the responsibility for this astonishing telescoping of holding periods on gullible, flighty, and emotional fund investors, or on the change in the character of our financial markets, especially in the boom and bust in the stock market bubble that happened between 1997 and 2002. It was clearly a mania driven by the madness of crowds. But by departing from our time-honored tenet, "we sell what we make," and jumping on the "we make what will sell" band-wagon, creating new funds to match the market mania of the moment, this industry was a major contributor to that bubble. As technology and telecom stocks led the way, we formed 494 new tech-nology, telecom, and Internet funds, and aggressive growth funds favoring these sectors. In all, the number of stock funds, which grew by 80 percent in the 1950s and 48 percent in the 1970s, burgeoned almost 600 percent in the 1990s.

Not only did we form these funds, we marketed them with vigor and enthusiasm, through stockbrokers and through advertising. Case in point: Right at the market peak, 44 mutual funds advertised their performance in the March 2000 issue of *Money*. *Their average return over the previous twelve exuberant months came to more than 85.6 percent!* Small wonder that this industry took in $555 billion of new money—more than a *half-trillion dollars*—during 1998–2000, over-whelmingly invested in the new breed of speculative high-perform-ance funds. Most of the money, of course, poured into those winners of yesteryear *after* they led the market upward. So their assets were huge when they led the market on the way down, the investors' money gone up in smoke. First the cash flow stopped, and then it turned negative—an $18 billion outflow in the year just ended. Today, it is not *irrational exuberance* but *rational disenchantment* that per-meates the community of fund owners, many of whom, unaware that the great party was almost over and that a sobering hangover lay ahead, imbibed far too heavily at the punch bowl.

It was not long until this flagrant formation of opportunistic new funds soon began to unwind. Fund deaths began to match, and will surely soon exceed, fund births. But it is not the old middle-of-the-road funds that are dying; it is largely the new breed of funds—those that sought out the exciting stocks of the new economy and hyped their records. While those conservative early funds were, as the say-ing goes, "built to last," their aggressive new cousins seemed "born to die." The fund failure rate soared. Whereas only 10 percent of the funds in the 1950s were no longer in business at the end of that decade, more than half of the funds that existed during the past decade are in not business today. And this trend shows no signs of slowing, with nearly 900 funds giving up the ghost in the 2000–2002 period alone, a rate that, if it continues, will produce another decade in which more than half of all equity funds cease to exist.

The Costs of Fund Ownership Have Soared

WHEN "BIG MONEY IN BOSTON" featured Massachusetts Investors Trust, it was not only the oldest and largest mutual fund, but also the least costly. The *Fortune* article reported that its annual management and operating expenses, paid at the rate of just 3.20 percent of its investment income, amounted to just $827,000. In 1951 its expenses came to just 0.29 percent of its assets. The average expense ratio for the twenty-five largest funds, with aggregate assets of but $2.2 billion, was only 0.64 percent.

What a difference five decades makes! In 2001 M.I.T.'s expense ratio had risen to 1.20 percent—a 300 percent increase—and its $141 million of expenses consumed 87 percent of its investment income. The expense ratio for the average equity fund has risen by 100 percent, to 1.54 percent, despite the fact that equity fund assets have soared 1,500-fold to $2.7 trillion. (See Figure 1-3.) The dollar amount of direct fund expenses borne by shareholders of all equity funds has risen from an estimated $15 million in 1950 to something like $35 *billion* in 2002. Despite the truly staggering economies of scale in mutual fund management, fund investors have not only *not* shared in these economies, they have been victims of far higher costs.

The fund industry reports that the costs of fund ownership have steadily declined, but it is difficult to take that allegation seriously. The decline, if such it be, arises from investors increasingly choosing no-load funds and low-cost funds, *not* from substantial management fee reductions. But even accepting the industry data at face value, the cost of mutual fund ownership is vastly understated. Why? *Because management fees, operating expenses, and sales charges constitute only a fraction of fund costs.* Portfolio transaction costs—an inseparable part of owning most funds—are ignored. Out-of-pocket costs paid by fund investors are ignored. Fees paid to financial advisers to select funds (partly replacing those front-end loads) are ignored. Put them all together, and it's fair to estimate that the all-in annual costs of mutual fund ownership now runs in the range of 2 to 3 percent of assets.

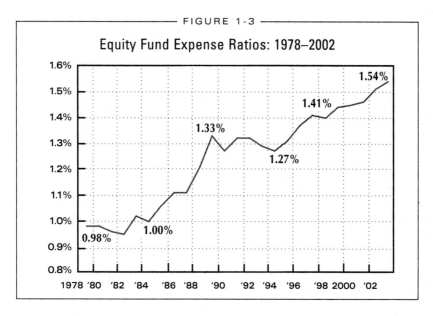

FIGURE 1-3

Equity Fund Expense Ratios: 1978–2002

What does that mean? While 2 percent may look like small potatoes compared to the value of a typical fund investment, such a cost could cut deeply into the so-called "equity premium" by which investors expect stock returns to exceed bond returns, giving the average equity fund investor a return little more than that of a bondholder, despite the extra risk. Looked at another way, 2 percent would consume 25 percent of an annual stock market return of 10 percent. Over the long term, $1 compounded in a 10 percent stock market would grow to $17.50 over thirty years; compounded at 7 percent—a typical fund's return *after* such costs—would reduce that value by exactly one-half, to $8.75. *Costs matter!* Yet costs rise and sharply, one more indication that the fund industry has veered from its roots as an investment *profession,* moving ever closer to being just another consumer products *business*.

The March of the Entrepreneur

THE INDUSTRY that *Fortune* described all those years ago clearly placed the emphasis on fund management as a profession— the trusteeship of other people's money. The article is peppered with the words "trust" and "trustee," and frequently refers to the "investment-trust industry." Today, it seems clear that salesmanship has super-seded trusteeship as our industry's prime focus.

What was it that caused this sea change? Perhaps it's that trustee-ship was essential for an industry whose birth in 1924 was quickly followed by tough times—the Great Depression, and then World War II. Perhaps it's that salesmanship became the winning strategy in the easy times thereafter, an era of almost unremitting economic prosperity. But I believe that the most powerful force behind the change was that mutual fund management emerged as one of the most profitable businesses in our nation. *Entrepreneurs could make big money managing mutual funds.*

The fact is that, only a few years after "Big Money in Boston" appeared, the whole dynamic of entrepreneurship in the fund indus-try changed. Up until 1958, a trustee could make a tidy profit by man-aging money, but could not *capitalize* that profit by selling shares of the management company to outside investors. The Securities and Exchange Commission (SEC) held that the sale of a management company represented the payment for the sale of a fiduciary office, an illegal appropriation of fund assets. If such sales were allowed, the SEC feared, it would lend to "trafficking" in advisory contracts, lead-ing to a gross abuse of the trust of fund shareholders.

But a California management company challenged the SEC's posi-tion. The SEC went to court, and lost. As 1958 ended, the gates that had prevented public ownership since the industry began thirty-four years earlier came tumbling down. A rush of initial public offerings (IPOs) began with the shares of a dozen management companies quickly brought to market. Investors bought management company shares for the same reasons that they bought Microsoft and IBM and, for that matter, Enron: because they thought their earnings would grow and their stock prices would rise accordingly.

But the IPOs were just the beginning. Even privately held man-agement companies were acquired by giant banks and insurance com-panies, taking the newly found opportunity to buy into the burgeon-ing fund business at a healthy premium—averaging 10 times book value or more. "Trafficking" wasn't far off the mark; there have been at least forty such acquisitions during the past decade, and the owner-ship of some firms has been transferred several times. In 2003, among the fifty largest fund managers, only six were privately held, plus mutually owned Vanguard. Twenty-three managers were owned by giant U.S. financial conglomerates, six were owned by major brokerage firms, and seven by giant foreign financial firms. (In 1982, even the executives of M.I.T. and its associated funds sold their management company to Sun Life of Canada.) The seven remaining firms were publicly held.

It must be clear that when a corporation buys a business—whether a fund manager or not—it expects to earn a hurdle rate of, say, 12 percent on its capital. So if the acquisition cost were $1 billion, the acquirer would likely defy hell and high water in order to earn at least $120 million per year. In a bull market, that may be an easy goal. But when the bear comes, we can expect some combination of (1) slashing management costs; (2) adding new types of fees (distribution fees, for example); (3) maintaining, or even increasing, management fee rates; or even (4) getting its capital back by selling the management company to another owner. (The SEC's "trafficking" in advisory contracts writ large!)

It's not possible to assess with precision the impact of this shift in control of the mutual fund industry from private to public hands, largely those of giant financial conglomerates, but it surely accelerated the industry to change from profession to business. Such a staggering aggregation of managed assets—often hundreds of billions of dollars—under a single roof, as much as it may serve to enhance, to whatever avail, the marketing of a fund complex's "brand name" in the consumer goods market, seems unlikely to make the money management process more effective, nor to drive investor costs down, nor to enhance this industry's original notion of stewardship and service.

Summing Up the Half-Century: For Better or Worse?

IN SHORT, THIS industry is a long, long way from the industry described in "Big Money in Boston" all those years ago. While my characterization of the changes that have taken place may be subjective, the factual situation I've described is beyond challenge. This *is* an infinitely larger industry. The variety of funds *has* raised the industry's risk profile. The management mode *was* largely by committee but *is* overwhelmingly by portfolio manager. Fund turnover *has* taken a great upward leap. Fund investors *do* hold their shares for far shorter periods. Marketing *is* a much more important portion of fund activities. Fund costs, by any measure, *have* increased, and sharply. And those closely held private companies that *were* once the industry's sole modus operandi *are* an endangered species.

All this change has clearly been great for fund managers. The aggregate market capitalization of all fund managers fifty years ago could be fairly estimated at $40 *million*. Today, $240 *billion* would be more like it. Way back in 1967, Nobel Laureate Paul Samuelson was smarter than he imagined when he said, "There was only one place to make money in the mutual fund business—as there is only one place for a temperate man to be in a saloon, behind the bar and not in front of it ... so I invested in a management company."

But returning to the question posed at the start of this text: Have these nine changes served the interest of the mutual fund investor? The answer is a resounding no. It's a simple statistical matter to determine how well those on the other side of the bar in that saloon, using Dr. Samuelson's formulation, have been served, first by the old industry, then by the new.

➤ In the first two decades of the mutual fund era (1950–70), the annual rate of return of the average equity fund was 10.5 percent, compared to 12.1 percent for the Standard & Poor's 500 Stock Index, a shortfall of 1.6 percentage points, doubtless largely accounted for by the then-moderate costs of fund owner-ship. The average fund delivered 87 percent of the market's annual return.

➤ During the past twenty years (1982–2002), the annual rate of return of the average equity fund was 10.0 percent, compared to 13.1 percent for the S&P 500 Index, a shortfall of 3.1 percentage points, largely accounted for by the now-far-higher levels of fund operating and transaction costs. The average fund delivered just 76 percent of the market's annual return.

It is the increase in *costs,* largely alone, that has led to that sub-stantial reduction in the share of the stock market's return that the average fund has earned. But it is the change in the industry's *char-acter* that has caused the average fund *shareholder* to earn far less than the average *fund.* Why? First, because shareholders have paid a heavy *timing* penalty, investing too *little* of their savings in equity funds when stocks represented good values during the 1980s and early 1990s. Then, enticed by the great bull market and the wiles of mutual fund marketers as the bull market neared its peak, they invested too *much* of their savings. Second, because they have paid a *selection* penalty, pouring money into "new economy" stocks and withdrawing it from "old economy" stocks during the bubble, at what proved to be precisely the wrong moment.

The result of these two penalties: While the stock market provided an annual return of 13 percent during the past 20 years, and the average equity *fund* earned an annual return of 10 percent, the average fund *investor,* according to recent estimates, earned just 2 percent per year (see Figure 1-4). It may not surprise you to know that, compounded over two decades, the 3 percent penalty of costs is huge. But the penalty of character is even larger—another 8 percentage points. *One dollar compounded at 13 percent grows to $11.50; at 10 percent, to $6.70; and at 2 percent, to just $1.50.* A profit of just fifty cents!

The point of this exercise is not precision, but direction. It is impossible to argue that the totality of human beings who have entrusted their hard-earned dollars to the care of mutual fund managers has been well served by the myriad changes that have taken place from mutual funds past to mutual funds present. What about mutual funds yet to come? My answer will not surprise you. It is time for the industry to go back to its roots, to put mutual fund sharehold-

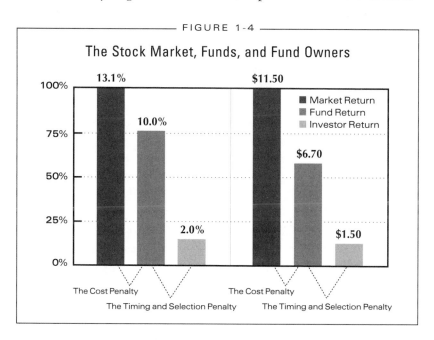

FIGURE 1-4

The Stock Market, Funds, and Fund Owners

ers back in the driver's seat, to put the interests of shareholders ahead of the interests of managers and distributions, just as the 1940 Investment Company Act demands.

This industry must return to its focus on broadly diversified funds with sound policies, sensible strategies, long-term horizons, and minimal costs. Some of the steps we must take are relatively painless—reducing turnover costs, by bringing turnover rates down to reasonable levels, for example—and some would be very painful—reducing management fees and sales commissions, and cutting our operating costs. But such cost reductions are necessary if we are to increase the portion of the stock market's return earned by *funds*.

To enhance the share of fund returns earned by *shareholders*, on the other hand, the industry needs to reorder it's "product line" strategies by taking a foot off the marketing pedal, and pressing down firmly on the stewardship pedal, giving the investor better information about asset allocation, fund selection, risks, potential returns, and costs, all with complete candor. After the market devastation of the past three years, I have no doubt that is what shareholders will come to demand. After all, as an article in an early 2003 issue of *Fortune* notes, "People won't act contrary to their own economic interests forever."

Fifty-plus years ago, the headline in that original *Fortune* article read: "The Future: Wide Open." So it was then. Now, the same headline applies, but it remains wide open only if the mutual fund industry goes back to the future—only if we return funds present to funds past—to our original character of stewardship and prudence. If funds come yet again to focus above all on serving shareholders—serving them "in the most efficient, honest, and economical way possible"—the future for this industry will be not just bright, but brilliant.

Chapter Two

Going Against the Grain

NED RILEY

Senior Principal and Chief Investment Strategist,
State Street Global Advisors

S TORIES OF LEMMINGS enthusiastically following one another off cliffs are scientifically untrue. Evidently, this fallacy came into vogue thanks to the fertile minds at Disney, who decided that it would be a heartrending plot twist if thousands of these cute creatures plunged to their deaths in a film—an animated film, of course.

Fortunately for those in Punditland, however, this oft-applied investor metaphor appears to hold true. Lemmings do, in fact, migrate in thundering (or at least tittering) herds when food becomes scarce. But instead of plunging off cliffs en masse, they will follow one another into any body of water in their way, swimming into eternity, if that's what it takes, in search of nourishment.

Just like investors in the grip of upside fever or downside fear.

Lemmings have an excuse, though: They are biologically programmed to follow one another around in search of food, so their behavior is unavoidable. Investors, on the other hand, operate on a higher level of consciousness and are capable of rational decisions. Theoretically, anyway. The reason investors keep swimming, even when they are in way over their heads and they know it, is herd psychology.

Much has been written about investor psychology and emotion in the markets, and just as much has been ignored. No matter how many times it happens, investors—on Wall Street as well as Main Street—get caught up in the emotion of the market: the thrill of the chase when times are good—despondency and sloth when times are bad. They come to believe that the good times or the bad times will last forever. No matter how many times this hypothesis is proved wrong, a large percentage of investors will inevitably behave, to their peril and eventual sorrow, as if it were one of the truths of the universe. And worse, this belief can become a self-fulfilling prophecy that actually expands a bubble beyond all proportion or elongates a bear market.

Why do investors behave this way? Emotion, pure and simple, fueled by those old standbys, fear and greed.

Compared to managing one's emotions in the face of a charging bull or a clawing bear, managing investments is a piece of cake. But then, successful investment management and emotional management are often the same thing. Unfortunately, this lesson can take a lifetime to learn, and it is virtually impossible to teach it to someone who has not made stupid mistakes, expensive missteps, and embarrassing pronouncements.

Of the above, I have certainly made my share, but I am willing to share my tales of bumps and bruises to help you avoid following the same misguided trail.

Learning from Experience

YOUNGER INVESTORS HAVE only the bull-to-bear market transition of 2001 as proof of the detrimental power of emotions. Indeed, this was a brutal but essential lesson in life for these newcomers, whose experience was that markets simply went up about 20 percent year after year. But those investors who have been around longer can point to lessons painfully learned in other market cycles.

Consider the end of the bull market of the 1960s, when I began my career working in a bank trust department. Those were the days of the Nifty 50—a bunch of technology, consumer, photography, and other companies destined for business nirvana. Today, a surprising number of those companies no longer exist—an important Darwinian lesson in itself. Back then, accepted wisdom in trust departments, which managed the lion's share of money for pension funds and individuals, and certainly the accepted wisdom for this then-young investment analyst, was that these stocks would go up and up forever and that earnings could increase 15 percent per year indefinitely. The result: Everybody had to own them—and did, to the virtual exclusion of everything else.

It turned out that those 15 percent projections were often merely justifications for unreasonably high valuations. In the course of the economic cycle, more and more of these companies began to miss this target, and their stocks suffered accordingly. Market leadership shifted away from the Nifty 50 and toward smaller-capitalization and nitty-gritty, commodity-driven stocks like mining, oil, and oil exploration companies. The price of gold, which had been fixed at $35 an ounce, was "unpegged" and went beyond $800 by the end of the decade. Oil soared to $40 a barrel, with many pundits projecting $100 a barrel in the foreseeable future. Companies linked to these and other commodities soared as the Nifty 50 tanked. At about the same time, some very smart investors broke from the crowd and began touting investment boutiques with diversified mutual funds focusing on a variety of market sectors. Soon these upstarts replaced banks as the preeminent money managers.

This writer was blindsided by the Nifty 50 mania, just like everyone else in my limited investment sphere—blindsided but not yet suspicious. After all, the old pros around me circled the wagons and said it was all temporary, an anomaly. The psychology of self-justification reigned supreme, as it so often does in this business. Unfortunately, I had to take another beating or two to realize that there are limits to valuations, that no stock or industry is immune to economic cycles, and that what goes up, comes down—often hard and often quickly.

I began to sense the truth, as scarcity became the watchword, OPEC the acronym of the day, and embargoes the bane of America's existence. In the midst of a mild recession, the growing belief that oil prices would rise forever and submerge our economy in the process sank the stock market. At about this time, I began to notice that stocks were moving quite differently from what I expected based on what I was hearing in the business and reading in the headlines. For example, in its "Investment Outlook" issue in January 1973, *BusinessWeek* reassured the world that in "1973: Bulls Will Control the Market." And one of *Barron's* famous panels was introduced with the headline, "Not a Bear Among Them." At about the same time, as if to confound the headline writers (not to mention the pros), the market started an almost unprecedented two-year slide—the worst since the Depression—that didn't end until *Newsweek* seemed to prompt a turnaround with its cover story, "How Bad a Slump?"

"Pessimism Dampens the Stock Market Outlook"

(*BusinessWeek*, January 1976)

THAT'S HOW *BusinessWeek* attempted to prepare investors for a sour 1976. Attentive readers will by now have realized that from pessimism sprang a bullish rally, one that seemed to end on cue when *Barron's* panelists were heralded as "Seven Bulls, One Bear" in January 1977.

It had taken only a decade, but this thick-headed writer was really beginning to get it—namely that when everyone seems to agree on the direction of something, there's bound to be a turning point out there waiting to jab them in the backside. Of course, other investors (although surprisingly few, it seems) had realized this truth before I did, and had probably made mountains of money by thinking for themselves rather than letting the crowd do it for them. If the price of a commodity like oil or Nelson Bunker Hunt's silver (or twenty years later, semiconductor chips or PCs) had been bid up beyond any rational measure, supply would eventually catch up with demand, product prices would drop, and along with them, the value of the stocks linked to those products.

At the same time, it was also becoming abundantly clear how difficult it can be to think for oneself when everyone else is saying the opposite or, as is more often the case, making so much noise that individuals are too confused to think. Thinking is one thing; however, acting is quite another.

The 1980s dawned with the stock market stumbling a bit and then appearing to recover. The question was, bull or bubble? After all, inflation had sunk its teeth into the economy fairly deeply by the end of the 1970s. The consumer price index (CPI) was increasing at a double-digit rate, the prime rate was nudging 20 percent, and home buyers thought themselves fortunate if they could get a mortgage at 17 percent. The Fed was not happy, and Chairman Volcker chomped down on the economy as if it were one of his cigars, pushing interest rates up even more and catapulting the economy into recession. The bubble burst.

I had been attempting to position my portfolios for the pop, but I learned quickly that when you work for a big organization, it can be hard to apply the principles of common sense and objectivity. The pressures to play the game, or to follow the herd, can be almost overwhelming. Sooner or later, your colleagues will cajole you into line, or the market itself will get you by moving up too fast or recovering too slowly—by which point your clients will already be complaining that you missed the rally or getting nervous that you are being too aggressive.

But bear markets don't last forever. At about the same time that headlines like "The Depression Syndrome" were appearing in the nation's papers and a *Newsweek* cover asked "How Safe Are Your Savings?" the market turned around. And in general, the bull didn't look back for quite a spell—except, for instance, when *BusinessWeek* declared "The Rebirth of Equities" (it had laid them to rest a few years earlier), which predictably coincided with a 10 percent retrenchment.

"Why Greenspan Is Bullish" (*Fortune,* summer 1987)

IF YOU LIKE EXTREME carnival rides that last for months, the real fun started in 1987. The Dow opened at about 2000 and by the end of August had risen to around 2700. But, ominously ignored, the inflation rate had doubled in twelve months, the Fed was tightening consistently, and signs of a weak market were becoming increasingly plentiful.

Fortune's late-summer headline about Dr. Greenspan should have been a dead giveaway. Some of us were nervous already. It didn't make sense that the market could keep up this pace in the face of rising interest rates; all the signs of potential weakness were there. At the same time, however, groupthink held that "This time it's different. This market can outrun the economy." And on and on. Black Monday came with a teeth-rattling 20 percent crash, with the sharpness of the descent nicely mirroring the steepness of the market's ascent over the previous year.

Again, the headlines did a fairly good job of indicating professional investor sentiment. "How Bad?" asked *BusinessWeek* immediately after the crash. *Newsweek* weighed in with "Heading Off Hard Times," while *US News and World Report* offered advice on "How to Ride Out the Bear Market." There were widespread doubts in the money management community, and who is the press going to call for quotes if not the big names on Wall Street? The Fed pumped enormous liquidity into the market to avoid a crisis of confidence and began a short-lived easing of interest rates. The market recovered even faster than the Fed's priming would justify and began a fairly steady climb for the next few years, leaving many of the professional victims of groupthink standing in the dust.

The Fed began to push interest rates up in 1988 and 1989 to fight the specter of inflation and hiked the federal funds rate to nearly 10 percent in 1989 before starting to ease. Some would say that's why the nineties began with a market decline wrapped in a recession against the backdrop of a real estate and banking crisis. To make matters worse, the news was filled with portents of war with Iraq. The easing was not enough, and the combination of looming war and downbeat economic news was too much for the market, which bottomed in September 1990.

The consensus held that war would be neither good for the economy nor the stock market, and that it was likely to result in oil prices that would suffocate growth. Once again, the consensus was wrong. That first quick victory over Saddam was a tremendous confidence builder, and coupled with the Fed's easing, jolted the markets back to life. The economy was another story. Recovery was slow and job creation was minimal. But by January 1991, the market was on a roll, while the Fed kept cutting rates, eventually leaving a 3 percent federal funds rate untouched for eighteen months, starting in 1992 and into 1994. Those low rates provided the launching pad for the greatest bull market in history.

The bandwagon effect was powerful, and virtually everyone had jumped on by the end of the nineties. Naturally, the market indexes did not move vertically, and there were bumps along the way. The ghost of inflation past was always present, and the Fed played wet blanket several times, such as when it took interest rates from 4 percent to 6 percent in just twelve months in 1994–1995. But the Fed eased at the end of 1995, and the market took off like a rocket, prompting Dr. Greenspan's famous and ultimately premature "irrational exuberance" remark in 1996, when the Dow stood at about 6000. Most people did not agree with him. Foreign investors showered money on U.S. stocks. Employees plowed their 401(k) money into stocks. Seed money for technology companies poured in by the bucketful, to the point where many infant, untested companies had a cost of capital that was essentially zero.

"How Worried Should You Be?" (*BusinessWeek,* 1998)

BY THE LATE 1990s, some investors (myself among them) who had earned or lost their share of grey hair during other bubbles and busts began to get nervous. The headline above simply heralded a dip in the Dow, but with valuations stretched to the limit and the world caught in an IPO frenzy, the market showed all the warning signs of a speculative trap.

It was at this point that all the lessons learned about emotion and groupthink in the markets became both vivid and valuable to me. It didn't take a genius to realize that dot-com companies selling for 200 times *sales* (who cared about earnings?) might not be a bargain or that something could be amiss when investors bid up the price of an IPO threefold in the first few hours of trading. Certain phrases resonated with ones I had heard in bygone days: "This time it's different ... , Old valuation models don't make sense in today's economy, ... , This economy is recession-proof," and worst of all, "Market corrections just don't happen anymore."

Oh yeah? Where were the Nifty 50 now? And weren't they supposedly recession-proof, too? And hadn't overvalued oil stocks climbed to 31 percent of the S&P 500 twenty years ago, just as technology stocks were in 1999? Didn't the stratospheric rise in U.S. stock indexes have a spooky resemblance to what had happened in Japan a decade earlier? But the laws of logic seemed to have been repealed. Investment fundamentals were old hat, obsolete. Common sense had become nonsense. Emotion was the currency that propelled the market, and there seemed to be no limit to how much emotion was available.

There also seemed no limit to the resistance that the press, investment professionals, or individual investors had to the naysayers. But with huge sums of money flowing into equity mutual funds (and mostly into growth and aggressive growth funds at that), the market and ecstatic managers were awash in liquidity that had to go somewhere. Retail investors were happy because their 401(k) plans looked like solid gold and shone brighter every day. And with publications like *BusinessWeek* saying, in January 2000, "This spectacular boom was not built on smoke and mirrors," what could go wrong?

Hindsight may be 20/20, but some find it hard to believe what they see in the present. Commentators have offered many rational explanations for what happened in 2001, but "rational" was not the operative word then. Nor is it now. The market is as mired in negativity as it was hopped up on adrenaline less than three years before. Where were the folks who, back then, were touting another year of 25 percent returns? They claimed to be looking at horrible numbers and studying a wretched economy. But might they not also have been listening to a Greek chorus of dirge-singing groupthinkers? They might have been better off studying their own psyches.

The most common investment tool today is not the computer, but the same tool it was thirty-five years ago: the rear-view mirror. Investors all too often look back at where they have just been and mistake it for where they are going. Stocks went up (or lost) 25 percent last year, so they will this year, too. XYZ Fund earned a five-star (or two-star) Morningstar rating last year, so it will this year, too. Bonds were a great strategic alternative three years ago, so they must be now, even though interest rates have already been sliced in half. Evidence to the contrary—not to mention common sense—is mistrusted, and confirming evidence is accepted uncritically. In the up-and-down world of the financial markets, it becomes an insidious and expensive cycle of buy high and sell low that is likely to be played out in future generations as well.

To make matters worse, going against the grain is not only tough, but fraught with its own potential costs and errors. For instance, I became skeptical of the most recent boom about eighteen months before the bubble burst. And I most assuredly took a favorable view of the market months before the eventual bottom. Both confirmed another lesson: The earlier you speak up about an out-of-whack market, the longer the market has to make you look foolish and trash your credibility before it eventually cooperates.

Even so, among the most valuable lessons of the past few years is this one: It is better to pass up the last 25 percent of a bubble market than to lose 80 percent when it bursts. The same is true of recoveries: More money will always be made by buying low—even if stocks still have not bottomed out—and selling high than the other way around.

Ned Riley's Top 10 Warning Signs
That You Are Losing Your Perspective

10 You listen closely to cab drivers, your brother-in-law, or famous athletes when they talk about the market.

9 You claim to be a long-term investor, but you have your cell phone programmed to alert you when one of your stocks moves up or down 3 percent.

8 You think about mortgaging your house to buy more stock because the Dow is so high, or ...

7 ... You refuse to buy more stock because the Dow is just too low.

6 You start throwing around terms like "yield curve" and "valuation" in everyday conversation.

5 You think about ordering a Bloomberg terminal for your home.

4 You start turning on the TV at 3 A.M. to see in real time where Hong Kong is closing.

3 You start turning off the evening news so you won't have to see the Dow.

2 You catch yourself saying "This time it's different..."

AND the #1 sign that you are in real trouble:

1 You start to think that you're an infallible investor.

It sounds so simple: Buy low and sell high. It has always been the cardinal rule of investing.

But it is the hardest one to follow when trapped in a herd of charging lemmings.

C h a p t e r 3 *T h r e e*

The Importance of Being a Stock "Detective"

FOSTER FRIESS
Founder and Chairman, Friess Associates

O NE OF THE MOST ENDURING investment strategies, based on intensive and critical research into the fundamentals of the companies, is to invest in companies that are growing earnings per share rapidly and have a reasonable ratio of the stock's price to its expected earnings for the upcoming twelve months. A desirable growth rate would be at least 15 percent year over year, and a reasonable price-to-earnings ratio (P/E) would typically be less than 25 to 30 times projected earnings.

To maximize the effectiveness of such a strategy requires facts, data, and perception of trends to be accurate. The *detective* work required to gather pertinent information, learn about potential surprises, and gauge market reaction ahead of "the Street," is more vital than the *analysis* of data.

To maximize returns while reducing risk, it is wise to concentrate on companies that have transcended the small, embryonic start-up stage but have not yet prospered and grown into huge, over-researched behemoths that have greater difficulty achieving a dynamic growth rate. Companies earning at least $3 million in after-tax income with at least three years of profitability create a reasonable "first look" threshold.

Most of America's largest 200 companies are either too large to sustain a 15 percent growth rate or too popularized to provide much opportunity for price-to-earnings ratio expansion. That doesn't mean good investments cannot be found among them, but it is less likely. Imagine the size and impact of a product required to grow a $10 billion company by 15 percent! It's better to isolate companies moving from #7 to #3 in their industries rather than high-profile market leaders that are in the precarious position of having to justify their high P/E ratios.

Severe bear markets, like the ones in 1974, 1987, 1990, 1994 and most recently in 2001–2002, are a not-so-subtle reminder that investors need a strategy "to invest under fire" when the bad markets come, as they inevitably will. Founded in the face of one of the worst bear markets on record in 1974, Friess Associates, managers of the Brandywine mutual funds, is no stranger to weathering some of the most turbulent storms in recent memory.

The firm has developed a time-tested strategy for investing soundly whether "under fire"—or in whatever type of market one faces. To gain insights into the success of the Friess Associates strategy, you must examine several conventional approaches this firm *does not* embrace and question some of these long-held axioms on Wall Street.

QUESTIONABLE AXIOM #1:
It's Essential to Be Diversified

THIRTY YEARS AGO being diversified meant owning the best steel company, the best oil company, the best bank, as well as the best chemical, paper, airline, and insurance companies. This diversification offers the investor equal opportunity to participate in all the sick or tired areas of the economy.

A new definition of diversification arose with the advent of "asset classes" based largely on the market capitalization of companies—midcap growth, small-cap value, large-cap core, and so on. Diversification among these "asset classes" failed to recognize that when Intel and Texas Instruments encountered headwinds, so did their midcap and small-cap counterparts in the semiconductor industry. For the most part, the semiconductor industry experienced declines across the board, regardless of market capitalization. In other words, earnings trends and stock-price movements correlate more closely to industry groups than to "style boxes."

This definition of diversification kept investors stuck in "large-cap growth" stocks at a time when the Friess approach condemned them to the "outrageous" price-to-earnings category. Why own companies selling at 70, 80, or even 100 times projected earnings, even though their fundamental outlooks are positive, just because they have achieved a certain market-cap size?

It is more effective to redefine diversification in the context of societal changes, spreading one's risks among the hundreds of companies participating in these changes if they meet growth and P/E criteria and possess clean accounting and solid balance sheets. All investors have the ability to ask themselves, "How is society changing, and which companies are not only benefiting from that change but even orchestrating it?" If that means you don't own any steel, paper, or aluminum companies, that's OK.

What are some of these societal changes? Here are a few examples:

➤ Major technology companies are selling their manufacturing facilities to contract manufacturers.

➤ Hobby and craft companies and video rental companies are flourishing as people stay closer to home.

➤ Financial companies are refinancing home mortgages as interest rates fall.

➤ Rising unemployment has forced workers to seek retraining in new fields. (Corinthian Colleges, which educates health care workers, trains chefs, and qualifies others for new jobs, is prospering from this trend.)

➤ Advances in medical technology, such as intensity modulated radiation therapy (IMRT), have spawned hospital equipment purchases.

➤ Congestion in major airports has encouraged new business models in the airline industry. (Southwest Airlines and Jet Blue are thriving in smaller markets.)

Especially in an environment where broad economic growth has slowed or even retraced, it is important to uncover these trends and societal shifts in order to isolate the companies that have the best prospects for future growth.

Active Management Won't Succeed—So, Index

INDEXING WAS PARTLY responsible for the stock market bubble. Investors poured money into companies simply because they were a component of an index created by a committee at Standard & Poor's or Frank Russell. Companies were selected on the basis of their past track records. Indexing affords investors the opportunity to invest in sick and over-priced companies. The lethargy with which a company is removed from an index suggests little attention is paid to the day-to-day developments that can cause prospects to deteriorate.

To steer clear of this pitfall, be sure never to invest in the "stock market;" invest in individual companies. Harness your own research techniques or those of your investment manager or advisor to isolate *individual companies* that fit your investment criteria, regardless into which index category others may assign it.

Buy Good Managements; Stick with Good People

THE MANAGEMENT FACTOR alone won't guarantee success. We know a myriad of companies that lost their luster through no fault of the competent people running them. It is important to have a business that is so well positioned that it doesn't take a genius to run it. As an investor in such businesses, it is crucial to have a mechanism to continually monitor the changing conditions that businesses encounter.

The more than thirty "detectives" of the Friess research team conduct over 1,000 interviews a week not only with company managements, but also, more important, with their competitors, suppliers, and customers. Even so, it is easy to fail to give adequate weight to what might seem to be a trivial departure from the company's success trail. This is not an easy endeavor.

Stick to the Strategy You Have Selected

RELIGIOUSLY ADHERING to a strategy isn't sound *unless the strategy itself is sound*. The Friess strategy of investing and closely monitoring proven companies that are growing rapidly, selling at reasonable price-to-earnings ratios, and have honest management and clean accounting is a sound strategy. Nevertheless, there will be times when other approaches are going to outperform. Investors must be patient and savvy enough to accept these periods and stay put to weather the "storms."

Often a fund can best be evaluated as a superior investment vehicle during years of *underperformance* rather than during years when it outperforms certain benchmarks. *Mutual Funds* magazine's January 2000 issue, when highlighting Brandywine Fund as one of the "Best Funds of the Decade" said: "Any team can win the World Series or the Super Bowl in any given year, but bringing home the trophy year after year requires something special." What is "special" is not only the sound strategy, but also more important, the people who implement it.

In 1998, when Friess Associates stuck with its discipline of owning companies with solid earnings growth and reasonable multiples, investors preferred to own the Wall Street darlings like Cisco, Dell, and Microsoft. Commitment to this approach caused several quarters of Friess underperformance as the high multiple stocks began their ascent. This signaled investors' shift toward the "new paradigm" in which earnings no longer mattered, only revenue growth. But Brandywine funds' short-term underperformance paved the way for superior performance during the subsequent bear market.

QUESTIONABLE AXIOM #5:
Buy Rapidly Growing Revenues; Think about Earnings Later

FOCUSING ON REVENUE growth rather than on earnings growth we've come to call the *I Love Lucy* method of investing. In one episode, Desi and Fred confronted Lucy and Ethel with the fact that they were losing ten cents on each jar from their kitchen-based jam-making venture. "We'll make it up in volume," Lucy retorted. The criteria of three years of earnings history and $3 million of after-tax income before a company crosses the Friess radar screen shielded Friess Associates clients from the bursting of the dot-com bubble. Three things determine a stock's future value: (1) earnings, (2) earnings, (3) earnings.

QUESTIONABLE AXIOM #6:
As Long as a Company Is Growing, Price-to-Earnings Ratios Don't Matter

FROM MARCH 2000 highs, indexes whose companies had the highest P/E ratios suffered the biggest losses: The Nasdaq Composite and the Nasdaq 100 plummeted 72 and 77 percent respectively, while the Goldman Sachs Internet Index plummeted 89 percent. Obviously, some of this decline resulted from the realization that fundamentals weren't as rosy as analysts thought. However, an even greater part of this drop came from lower price-to-earnings ratios that people accorded to declining fundamental outlooks. In some cases, price-to-revenue ratios were used for those companies that had no earnings, as was the case with many of the Internet stocks.

Some of the greatest companies in the world become terrible investments because their price-to-earnings ratios simply get too high. There gets to be no room for expansion, only potential disappointment and P/E ratio shrinkage. The December quarters of both 2001 and 2002 were characterized by sharp upward price movements of companies that could have been characterized as "broken stocks." Movements were triggered by a "macro" feeling that things were getting better in the economy and price-to-earnings ratios soared, sometimes 50, 60, or 80 percent, with no sign of any internal improvement in the companies whatsoever. These "rubbish rallies" subsequently fell back into ashes as true earnings outlooks came into focus and the multiples people were willing to attach to those less-than-enthusiastic earnings became better understood.

At their peaks, both Dell Computer and Microsoft sold for about $60 per share yet were earning well under $1. Cisco's P/E ratio reached over 140 times earnings. There is a corollary Wall Street axiom that says, "You can never pay too much for a great company." Yes you can. The statistics above prove what damage can be done to stock market values when sensitivity to price-to-earnings ratios is disregarded.

If one looks at the excessive price-to-earnings ratios accorded back in the early 1970s, it's not hard to find many Wall Street darlings that took eight or nine years to recover to those levels after they plummeted. Price-to-earnings ratios *do* matter.

QUESTIONABLE AXIOM #7:
Always Stay 100 Percent Invested

MANY INVESTORS FOUND Friess cash levels in early 1998 antithetical to their asset allocation strategy. By sticking to the belief that earnings matter and how much you pay for those earnings also matters, for the Friess team it became obvious during that period that many holdings, particularly those in the oil-service and semiconductor industries, were about to experience some rough sledding. Cash levels should not be driven by a dogmatic adherence to a flawed strategy. Cash levels should be derived solely from the number of great investments one uncovers. Holding a company with less-than-great prospects in order to stay "fully invested" is a recipe for losing money.

Friess researchers sold aggressively at the end of 1997. New investment ideas they investigated suffered from some of the same problems as the companies they sold. Therefore, they slowed their normal buying rate, and cash balances drifted as high as 78 percent for several weeks. Former "long-term investors" fled a proven, sound strategy due to these several weeks of elevated cash. By October, half of those stocks sold had declined between 50 and 90 percent.

Investors compared Brandywine's 0.7 percent decline in 1998 to indexes that favored the large-cap, high-profile stocks the Friess strategy rarely embraces. The Russell 3000, for example, was up 24 percent that year but those *same* 3,000 stocks, if evaluated on an equally weighted basis (to eliminate the exaggerated impact of the small number of large companies), grew only 1.4 percent that year.

Investors who stuck with the Friess strategy were soon rewarded. The Brandywine Fund soared 168 percent in the next eighteen months following the October 8, 1998 market low. It also weathered the subsequent market meltdown relatively well, booking a 55.3 percent gain from that low through December 31, 2002, in contrast with declines of 3.1 and 5.9 percent in the S&P 500 and Nasdaq Composite, respectively.

Brandywine is among only a minority of funds still up since 1998. It garnered kudos from the *Wall Street Journal* as one of only eight funds with over $1 billion in assets to outpace the Wilshire 5000 Index by at least 15 percentage points in 1999 and 2000 (+53.5 and +7.1 percent). The latter is particularly relevant in pointing out the strategy's focus on reasonable price-to-earnings ratios, as the Nasdaq Composite, full of high-multiple Wall Street darlings, plunged close to 40 percent.

Barron's later called Brandywine's subsequent performance "vindication of the fund's discipline in the 1998 tumble and aftermath." TheStreet.com reported: "They didn't get crushed by the dot-com and they didn't get lured into buying the wrong tech, the stuff that has crashed to earth so infamously." *Money* wrote: "Today, after the collapse of many high-priced stocks, Friess' caution looks a lot like prescience."

Investors should not be bullied into being fully invested if portfolio companies start to sour and good replacements can't be found. Sell bad investments, buy good ones, and let the cash levels settle where they may.

QUESTIONABLE AXIOM #8:
Buy and Hold

TRY TO FIND executives who are willing and able to predict what their company earnings will be six quarters out. Not only are they scarce, but also when you find them, they are probably going to be wrong. Our world simply changes too fast. A superior axiom would be "Buy and Prepare to Replace."

Therefore, it is important to constantly revisit current holdings and assess whether the investment is not only prudent, but effective as well. Selling good companies to make room in the portfolio for better companies is referred to as the "Pigs at the Trough" selling discipline. When ten pigs are feeding at the trough and the eleventh and hungriest pig comes along, it bumps out the pig that has been feeding the longest. In the same way, when research uncovers a great investment idea, another stock must be sold to make room. By adhering to this "forced displacement" sell strategy, or selling when holdings reach individual price targets or when fundamentals deteriorate, it will ensure that a portfolio always represents a collection of the strongest ideas.

As noted above, every week Friess researchers conduct 1,000-plus interviews, each of which is logged into a database to help all members of the team evaluate input from numerous sources before making recommendations and identify trends in the economy before they become government statistics. Such intensive, deep research underlies the stock-picking discipline of the Friess organization, which

Money magazine has characterized as "one of the fastest guns in the business" (Fall 2001).

Doing more and better detective work is crucial for investing "under fire." Continually reevaluating stock holdings through extensive research and homework will keep one invested in the most dynamic, rapidly growing companies. Don't be afraid of stock turnover.

QUESTIONABLE AXIOM #9:
Buy Companies That You Understand, and Know Their Products from Personal Experience

THIS IS A FLAWED AXIOM if investors do not go far enough to investigate the *fundamental underpinnings* of the product they are favoring. So many people will see a product they correctly perceive is "flying off the shelves," but they fail to take the time to assess the myriad of other factors that are critical in driving the price of a company's stock.

It is essential to constantly kick the tires and know your investments. For example, outlined below is a potential research scenario and a variety of suggested questions to ask if you were looking at Varian Medical Systems, a company that produces equipment for radiation therapy, including Intensity Modulated Radiation Therapy (IMRT). IMRT, the most advanced form of radiation therapy, modulates radiation distribution within patients, making it possible to concentrate higher, more effective doses in tumors while sparing more surrounding healthy tissue. Varian's radiation therapy system includes its Acuity hardware and software system that enables clinicians to adjust and verify the accuracy of treatment plans for their patients.

1 Contact the CEOs, CFOs, or heads of oncology at Sloan-Kettering, Johns Hopkins, MD Anderson, and Cleveland Clinic to ascertain profitability of equipment, rate of usage, and maintenance issues, as well as competing equipment they evaluate. Ask:
> ➤ Why did you decide to purchase Varian's IMRT machines?
> ➤ How has Varian's IMRT device affected your profitability?
> ➤ What is happening to insurance reimbursement rates?
> ➤ Since installation, what has been the growth in number of treatments on a monthly basis?

> Have you experienced any maintenance issues or unforeseen costs?
> Does the IMRT system cannibalize sales of chemotherapy or other services?
> In your opinion, is the penetration of IMRT systems still below 30 percent in the United States, as some suggest?

2 Contact Kronos, Elekta, General Electric, and Siemens salespeople to get insights into what they are selling in competition with Varian's product, size and growth of the market, and expected shifts in future technology. Ask:
> What changes do you anticipate in the competitive landscape within the industry?
> What one piece of legislative action or regulation (state, local, or federal) could most negatively and/or positively affect sales?

3 Contact the American Cancer Society and several university research centers as well as centers of alternative approaches to assess the possibility of chemotherapy or other approaches replacing radiation therapy in popularity.

4 Speaking with oncologists, urologists, and pathologists will all be helpful in assessing trends. However, be very sensitive to what their "axe to grind" is, as a practicing surgeon of twenty-five years might have a hard time being objective about the efficacy of the newly competing IMRT technology. Ask:
> Is radiation treatment increasing as a percentage of dollars and treatment time spent on curing various forms of cancer?

5 Contact pathologists at medical testing services such as Dianon Systems or Bostwick Laboratories to assess developments that could positively or negatively affect IMRT.

6 Discuss with the CFO of Varian what information he or she imparts to the investment community. Ask:
> What will be the dilution to earnings per share (EPS) if expensing stock options is required?
> What are unfunded pension liabilities?

➤ What will the impact on 2003 EPS be if long-term rate of return on pension asset assumptions is changed?

➤ What are the current and future trends in prices, labor, raw materials costs, demand, new products, reimbursement rates, currency fluctuations, taxes, and other costs?

➤ Do analysts expect debt or equity financing that could dilute earnings?

➤ What are the economics of one of the IMRT units in terms of sales per unit, capital invested, costs, and profit contribution?

➤ How is revenue recognized — at time of shipment or over a period of time?

➤ What are current margin levels? Are they depressed, improving, flattening, or exceptional (difficult to duplicate)?

➤ Which products or product groups will provide the most impact to the bottom line within the next year?

➤ For each of Varian's main businesses or products, who are the major competitors? Suppliers? Customers? What do critics cite as the company's greatest vulnerabilities?

➤ What is the anticipated pricing, size of the market, growth rate, and payback period for new products going forward?

➤ What shifts are expected in the sales mix and the subsequent impact on earnings?

➤ What are the key components that go into Varian's IMRT radiation oncology device, and how would one characterize availability and pricing?

BOTTOM LINE: Ignore many of the Wall Street axioms and instead target companies that are growing nicely (at least 15 percent year over year) and are selling at reasonable P/Es (under 30 times forward earnings). Then put them under your microscope to make sure the accounting is clean and earnings are real. Although subscribers to this strategy will underperform at times, don't fear, as this strategy will most likely stand the test of time through good and bad markets. You can "invest under fire" with confidence.

Chapter Four

The Search for Value

WILLIAM C. NYGREN
Partner and Portfolio Manager, Harris Associates L.P.

INVESTORS AND PROFESSIONAL portfolio managers who follow a value investment style search for stocks they consider bargains based upon certain criteria. In essence, value investors believe that the true, underlying value of a company is not reflected in its current stock price and that, over time, its price will increase as the market recognizes the overall value of the business.

The investment approach of the Oakmark family of seven funds requires that a stock meet three criteria before Oakmark managers will consider buying it: (1) the stock must sell at less than 60 percent of intrinsic business value, (2) value must grow as time passes, and (3) management must be economically aligned with shareholders.

The Highest Hurdle: Intrinsic Value

OAKMARK'S FIRST investment criterion is to buy stocks selling at a significant discount to intrinsic value—the *estimate* of the price an *all-cash* buyer would be willing to pay *today* to own the *entire company.* Then, fund managers buy the stock only if it is selling at less than 60 percent of that intrinsic value estimate. It's important to focus on the details of this first criterion, as each aspect is important:

Estimate. This isn't an exercise in precision. An estimate of business value between $50 and $60 per share is very useful for a stock trading at $30. However, overly precise value estimates like those published in Wall Street research reports ($54.16, for example) should be viewed cautiously. This degree of precision is impossible to achieve.

Today. Oakmark's analysts want the best estimate of what the business is worth at the time they are assessing it. They do not justify their estimates based on predictions of what *might* happen at the company; therefore, favorable developments are discounted for time value, as well as for the possibility that they will not occur.

In cash. When buyers pay cash, one could assume that they believe what they are purchasing is worth at least what they pay for it. Acquirers using stock, however, may believe an acquisition makes sense because they know their own stock is overvalued. This phenomenon occurred widely in the late 1990s, as more than a few technology company mergers were executed in this manner. The high prices for the target companies made sense only because the acquirers' stocks were incredibly overvalued.

The whole company. Stocks are partial interests in a business, not just pieces of paper. Oakmark's managers are interested in the price someone would logically pay to own the entire business. Therefore, they aren't trying to predict where a stock price might be headed in the next few days, or even the next few months. In the long run, the value of a company and its stock market price must converge. Oakmark's analysts watch acquisitions of companies to determine what rules of thumb acquirers were using when purchases were made. Then, the analysts apply these rules to public companies to assess if they are inexpensive.

Buy below 60 percent of value. Obviously, cheaper is better. The bigger the discount Oakmark demands, the greater the potential return. But that means fewer stocks will qualify. Over time, Oakmark analysts have found that using a "60 percent of value" cutoff affords the opportunity to construct well-diversified portfolios and to stay fully invested through most market environments.

Most stocks fail this criterion because they are usually priced significantly above 60 percent of estimated intrinsic value. Generally, to fall below 60 percent of value requires an overreaction to short-term negative news. For example, after the terrorist attacks in September 2001, expectations for travel fell sharply. As a result, hotel companies' stock prices were cut in half despite expectations that business and vacation travel would return to normal levels within a couple of years. The market frequently treats short-term troubles as if they are long-term problems. However, a steep price decline alone is not sufficient for a stock to meet Oakmark's value criteria. In early 2002, many technology stocks had dropped 50 to 80 percent from their March 2000 highs, yet they did not look cheap. Based on earnings, expected earnings, or even sales, most technology stocks were still priced at very high multiples relative to their historical averages.

Growth—an Important Component

OAKMARK'S SECOND investment criterion is that business value must grow as time passes. Many investors fall prey to the value trap: Stock price and business value both decline at the same rate so that the stock looks too cheap to sell as the price falls. This trap snares many value managers, who then own the statistically cheapest companies that are often the most structurally disadvantaged. Effectively, these stocks trade at low prices because they deserve to. Nothing is worse for a value investor than having declining estimates of value accompanied by a declining stock price. Because Oakmark managers demand that business value must grow as time passes, they can better avoid stocks that are statistically very cheap, but whose value is likely to decline rather than grow.

Free cash flow is an important part of estimating value growth. While the market devotes a great deal of attention to sales growth— and will pay a premium for companies that grow sales at a high rate—Oakmark's managers believe sales growth is only part of the value equation. What sales growth ignores is free cash flow—the increase in cash a company has after financing its operations and investing for its future. Even if a company has slower sales growth compared to a competitor, it could be increasing its value just as rapidly if it generates more free cash flow. That cash can then be used to invest in new businesses, to buy back shares, or to pay off debt. Any of these actions will accelerate per-share value growth. To Oakmark, the growth that comes from investing excess cash is just as valuable as internal sales growth.

So how can investors avoid structurally disadvantaged companies that, on the surface, appear undervalued? Over long periods, the stock market has returned a few percentage points per year above the government bond yield, for total return of approximately 8 to 9 percent. To achieve that return, Oakmark looks for companies where the sum of dividend yield plus value growth at least matches that number. That way, if the stocks start out at 60 percent of value and stay at 60 percent of value, they should produce a return similar to the market. If, as the fund managers expect, the valuation gap narrows, the stock and their portfolios will outperform the market.

Management Working in Shareholders' Best Interest

THE THIRD AND FINAL Oakmark requirement is to invest with management that acts in the interest of outside shareholders. Oakmark managers want to invest in companies whose management is smart, honest, and economically aligned with shareholders. Because most of company managements' important decisions are made behind the scenes, Oakmark wants to have the confidence that these decisions are made with the outside shareholders' best interests in mind. When company management makes capital investment decisions, its sole goal should be to achieve the highest possible risk-adjusted return on that capital. As management considers an array of choices—reinvesting in the business, making acquisitions, paying dividends, paying off debt, or repurchasing stock, Oakmark wants management to make the selection that maximizes per-share business value. It also likes managers who personally invest in the stock of their company and who have options and other incentive packages that reward them for increasing equity values.

If, today, you were offered the opportunity to invest in a private company, you would undoubtedly have many questions about its management. Who is running it? Are they trustworthy? What is their track record? How do they get paid? All are very appropriate questions. For some reason, however, investors often neglect those same questions when purchasing publicly traded stocks. Oakmark's goal is to invest in companies whose management is smart, honest, and acting in the company's interest, so that even if it was an illiquid private company, Oakmark would still be eager to invest.

How does an investor learn about company management? Every

THE SEARCH FOR VALUE   45

public company is required to present brief biographies of top management in its 10K annual report filed with the SEC—available on the Internet. In addition, the Oakmark team assesses how managers are performing in their current company and researches how they performed at previous companies. Oakmark analysts talk to past business associates, current coworkers, customers, and suppliers to determine if this particular management team is smart and trustworthy.

For example, in late 2000 many shareholders thought Oakmark made a mistake in buying J.C. Penney stock. In the two years before their purchase, the stock had fallen from a high of $78 to $12 as Penney's lost market share to discounters like Kohl's and Target and to department stores like Macy's. Oakmark had not had confidence in J.C. Penney management, but in the late summer of 2000 Penney's hired a new CEO, Allen Questrom. Anyone reading Penney's SEC document could have learned of Questrom's success turning around Neiman Marcus, Federated Department Stores, Macy's, and Barney's. Since Oakmark had previously been an investor in Federated, its managers were already very familiar with Questrom's track record. Did they think the new management made a turnaround a sure bet? Of course not—but it certainly changed the odds.

Finally, company management must have vested interests that are aligned with shareholders. Over the several years Oakmark owns a stock, the company will face a handful of major decisions that will strongly influence whether or not the investment is successful. Perhaps management will consider making a large acquisition, or even contemplate selling the company. Oakmark wants to ensure that company management owns enough stock, or has other incentives in place, so that management's personal profit is maximized only if shareholder profit is also maximized. Management should think like owners, not hired hands. By focusing on managements whose compensation and personal wealth are tied directly to the value of the business, Oakmark can generally avoid companies whose managers are more concerned with the longevity of a high salary. Every annual corporate proxy, filed with the SEC and also available on the Internet, tells investors how much stock each company manager owns, how many options, and how that manager's bonus compensation is calculated—everything an investor should want to know.

Taking Advantage of a Long Time Horizon

WHEN ALL THREE of the above investment criteria are met—namely, (1) the stock sells below 60 percent of value, (2) the value grows as time passes, and (3) the company is managed by people who behave like owners, Oakmark managers achieve their greatest competitive advantage—the luxury of a long time horizon. They don't worry about when the market will recognize value, because the longer it takes, the greater the potential return.

In fact, for companies that generate excess cash, an extended period of undervaluation can be used to their advantage. A company might repurchase its own stock at a discount to fair value, which ends up increasing the value of each remaining share. Oakmark has found that, on average, the market takes three to five years to come to Oakmark's estimate of a company's value—the point where stock price and business value inevitably converge. Such lengthy holding periods keep trading costs down and are also beneficial at tax time, as their gains usually end up qualifying for the reduced long-term capital gains rate.

The Oakmark methodology gives little weight to sector allocations or near-term trends. Instead, analysts focus on internal factors, such as a company's potential for improving its operating results. Their stock selections produce a mix that includes companies that are relatively immune to economic cycles and cyclical companies currently out of favor. They purchase stocks with a long-term horizon in mind, and they rarely have a strong enough conviction in short-term events or macro forecasts to influence their opinion. Most of the financial media, as well as individual and professional investors, obsess over monthly economic data and minor deviations from quarterly earnings expectations. However, if an investor were to focus instead on how a company is likely to change over the next five years, the short-term issues become less significant.

The Details Behind Intrinsic Value

THE HEART OF the value investment process—which guides Oakmark in finding undervalued businesses—is identifying a company's intrinsic business value, a measure of the estimated worth of a company. The calculation of intrinsic value is focused on answering a simple question: "What would a rational businessperson pay, in cash, to own the entire business outright?"

Oakmark's stock ideas are subject to a comprehensive analytical process to estimate a company's intrinsic value and to confirm that it may be purchased at a discount. The firm's investment analysts focus on the fundamental ability of the business to generate cash for its owners. A great deal of time is spent meticulously reviewing a company's free cash flow rather than focusing on more traditional value measures such as low price-to-earnings or low price-to-book ratios, because free cash flow ultimately determines how a company builds value for its shareholders.

Deriving its intrinsic value estimate, Oakmark also considers private market values by examining comparable merger transactions and reviewing trading values of similar publicly traded businesses. The entire process is driven by an individual company's fundamental characteristics: How secure is the current and expected competitive position? How does the balance sheet look, and how will it change over time? With each investment under consideration, Oakmark estimates the current per-share business value and also projects how that value will grow over the next five years. Its analysts look at sales and income growth, capital needs, and whether excess cash is generated or cash is consumed. These balance sheet changes are incorporated into the intrinsic value estimate, which is periodically re-evaluated during the holding period.

Avoiding Overdiversification

TIME AND AGAIN, investors are taught the principles of diversification—dividing money among a variety of investments to reduce risk—and its benefit to a portfolio. Since market cycles vary, diversification is designed to reduce overall risk exposure while still allowing for appreciation. Building a well-diversified portfolio—and having *funds* that are diversified—is a mantra of the investment industry. While investors should diversify their assets to reduce risk, the intense focus on this principle has caused another phenomenon: overdiversification.

Overdiversification can happen when an investor buys too many funds that have similar investment styles or objectives. A fund itself can be overdiversified as well. How? According to Morningstar, the average equity mutual fund owns nearly 150 securities; therefore, many managers intentionally or unintentionally mimic an equity index without their shareholders realizing it. Investors may be paying higher fees for actively managed funds while, in fact, they are getting index-like fund portfolios.

Oakmark's managers believe that excessive diversification mathematically leads to average investment performance. Oakmark portfolios are focused—generally holding around 50 stocks, rather than 150. Many funds diversify to the point that mistakes go unnoticed or don't matter. Oakmark creates focused portfolios so that their successes *do* matter. Oakmark's portfolios are designed to maximize the benefit from the firm's stock-picking capabilities—they have larger weightings in companies where analyst confidence and return potential are greatest. In general, the majority of Oakmark's assets are invested in the top fifteen to twenty holdings. Although this strategy may be more volatile over shorter time periods, over a longer time horizon the probability of enhancing return increases due to the focused nature of the portfolio. The historical distribution of stock returns indicates that adequate diversification can be achieved with far fewer holdings than is generally believed. (See Figure 4-1.)

With thousands of mutual funds available, investors should be concerned about holding numerous funds with the same objective—this does little to decrease risk or enhance returns. It simply increases the probability of achieving average returns before subtracting fund expenses and virtually guarantees achieving below-average returns after expenses. Individual investors should focus on decreasing the risk of their overall portfolio by selecting a handful of high-quality equity funds using investment styles that complement each other. It's not necessary, however, that each *fund* itself be fully diversified—by definition, the investor's overall portfolio will be much more diversified than any individual fund.

Selling, Portfolio Turnover, and Taxes

FOR MANY INVESTORS, selling a stock is the hardest decision. One reason may be that most people don't know why they own the stock in the first place. When it comes to selling, the Oakmark approach is very

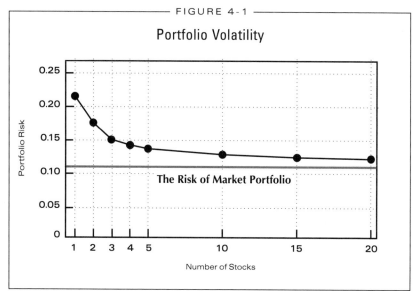

FIGURE 4-1

Portfolio Volatility

The Risk of Market Portfolio

simple: After buying stocks at 60 percent of intrinsic value, fund managers monitor fundamental information to make sure buy and sell targets reflect new information. If the stock gets to 90 percent of its
intrinsic value estimate, they sell it and start the process over again.
Certainly, Oakmark's managers make mistakes. If new information
after a stock's purchase makes them believe that any of their investment criteria were violated—the company lacks value growth or there
is serious concern about company management—they'll sell the stock.

Given Oakmark's disciplined buy and sell process, portfolio
turnover is actually a fallout of the investment process—there is no
set target for turnover or average holding period. The market usually
takes several years to recognize a company's true intrinsic value, and
Oakmark will hold a security, waiting to sell the stock at a proper
price, thus keeping portfolio turnover low. However, sometimes the
market promptly recognizes that a company is "mis-priced" and the
stock quickly reaches 90 percent of value, and it is sold. Obviously,
when that happens, turnover is higher. That may mean paying more
taxes, but it also means higher after-tax returns.

The goal of each fund in the Oakmark Family is to maximize long-
term after-tax returns. This is different from the stated goal of many
"tax-managed" funds, which is to minimize taxes. Oakmark managers
focus first on maximizing pre-tax returns and then seek to protect as

much of that return as possible through sensible tax management. This approach reflects measures including the following:

➤ *Gains on stocks held longer than one year are generally taxed at only half the taxpayer's marginal tax rate.* Because Oakmark's holding period generally exceeds a year, the majority of capital gains distributions usually qualify for this favorable tax treatment.

➤ *When a fund sells part of its position in a stock, it must identify which shares were sold.* Some funds identify those shares sold using the average cost or FIFO (first-in, first-out) method. By going a step further and identifying specific purchase lots, Oakmark attempts to minimize the tax consequence of each share of stock that is sold.

➤ *A portfolio manager can also lower the tax liability of a fund by selling stocks that have declined in price.* Many value managers don't use this technique because they view stocks that have declined in price as more attractive investments. At Oakmark, managers generally try to increase their position when a stock is most attractive, yet still capture the tax loss. Therefore, they often buy and sell partial positions with at least thirty-one-day intervals to avoid violating IRS "wash-sale" rules.

THE PORTFOLIO MANAGERS at Oakmark are focused on a bottom-up, disciplined investment strategy and apply it to all areas of the market—small, medium, and large companies; domestic and international. Through their time-tested, fundamental method of identifying growing companies that are run by managers who behave like owners and buying only when the company is selling at a discount to intrinsic value, Oakmark has achieved excellent long-term investment returns. At a time when stock market fads go in and out of style faster than ever, Oakmark's approach to value investing has proven the rewards of adhering to a disciplined, long-term strategy.

Chapter Five

Technical and Sentiment Analysis—

Timing, Discipline, and Contrary Thinking

BERNIE SCHAEFFER

Chairman and CEO, Schaeffer's Investment Research, Inc.

I N OUR POST-BUBBLE, post-9/11 world, many individual investors are angry and almost all are disappointed. So far in this bear market, the S&P 500 lost as much as 50 percent from its peak levels in March 2000, and the Nasdaq was cut in half twice. These grim statistics are reason enough for disappointment, but there is also a sense of betrayal that begets anger. Just as there was no warning ahead of the 9/11 terrorist attacks, the opinion leaders of Wall Street did little or nothing to warn investors at or near the market peak of the potential dangers of an incipient bear market. Indeed, even at the depths of this bear market the average recommended allocation to stocks by Wall Street strategists had barely budged from its record high levels near the bull market peak.

Much has been made of the sense of betrayal investors feel at the hands of conflicted Wall Street firms and less than forthcoming CEOs. These so-called trust issues are tangential to the two real issues. First, Wall Street is geared to think optimistically, as bull markets are favorable in a highly leveraged manner to its revenues and profits while bear markets are similarly unfavorable. The very idea of deep and protracted bear markets is anathema to Wall Street, so the prospects for such bear markets are routinely dismissed as having such low probability as to be unworthy of consideration. As for Wall Street's "financial consultants" understanding the importance to their clients of preparing for major market downturns, the words of author Upton Sinclair come to mind: "It's difficult to get a man to understand something when his salary depends on not understanding it."

Wall Street's bullish bias over the years has been well documented. Just as it was in evidence at the market top in 2000, it existed at the peak of the market mania in 1929 and was still evident in the throes of the devastating 1929–1932 bear market. What is less understood is how this bullish bias is stoked by the failure of traditional fundamental analysis—as practiced by the major Wall Street firms without exception—to identify bear markets and to preserve investors' capital.

*Wall Street
learns nothing
and forgets everything.*
—BENJAMIN GRAHAM

After explaining why fundamental analysis is incapable of preserving investors' assets during difficult market environments, this chapter presents an approach that is geared toward capital preservation in bear markets and capital growth in bull markets. This approach incorporates technical analysis and the analysis of investor sentiment, and it has been developed over the years by Schaeffer's Investment Research (SIR) into a proprietary discipline known as Expectational Analysis.

Fundamental Flaws

IN HIS TIMELESS work, *The Battle for Investment Survival*, Gerald Loeb stated, "Accepting losses is the most important single investment device to insure safety of capital. It is also the action that most people know the least about and that they are least liable to execute … The most important single thing I learned is that accepting losses promptly is the first key to success." In addition, Loeb said, "The difference between the investor who year in and year out procures for himself a final net profit and the one who is usually in the red is not entirely a question of superior selection of stocks or superior timing. Rather, it is also a case of knowing how to capitalize successes and curtail failures."

The tendency of investors to stick with losing stock positions well beyond rational bounds is well documented. Reporting on a study of 10,000 investors in the July 2002 issue of *Bloomberg Personal Finance* magazine, Terrance Odean, an assistant professor of finance at the University of California at Berkeley, wrote that on any given day the investors were one-and-a-half to two times more likely to sell a stock that had gone up rather than a stock that had gone down. The article went on to report the following in remarks attributed to Peter Bernstein, author of *Against the Gods: the Remarkable Story of Risk:* "What most investors cannot endure is the realization that they did something which kept them from winning. So they do nothing—and sit on dead money. Rather than redeploy, they choose to avoid regret—at all costs."

But this unfortunate tendency of investors to cut profits short and let losses run is aggravated by Wall Street firms, as fundamental analysis is used to develop their "buy lists." The stocks they deem attractive sell for prices they feel do not fully reflect their view of future earnings and cash flow streams. By its very definition and practice, the fundamental approach discourages investors from discarding losing stock positions.

Simply put, if a stock is considered by fundamental analysts to have "value" at $100, it is likely to be deemed to possess yet more value at $75 and even greater "value" at $50, and so on. There is no escaping this potential "death spiral" unless the fundamentals deteriorate to such an extent that analysts might deem the stock no longer attractive. That they are extremely slow to reach such negative conclusions was amply illustrated in 2000 by the fact that few analysts modified their "buy" recommendations on the once-hot dot-com stock leaders even as many plunged by as much as 90 percent from their peak prices. Some blame this woeful performance by analysts in the dot-com bust to a conflicted Wall Street, but the true problem is inherent to the process of fundamental analysis.

Probably the best example outside the dot-com world of the propensity of fundamental analysts to freeze in the wake of a plunging stock price occurred with WorldCom (WCOM), which ultimately entered into bankruptcy. By the mid-1990s this stock had become a darling of the GARP school of fundamental analysis, which looks to buy companies that exhibit profit "growth at a reasonable price" relative to their price/earnings multiples. WCOM shares began to decline steadily from their peak in 1999 near $65 and by October 2000 were trading at about $24, down by more than 60 percent. Yet according to Zacks.com, twenty-two of the twenty-four Wall Street analysts who covered WCOM rated the stock a "strong buy" or a "buy."

With fundamental analysis, there is no viable or consistent exit strategy to forestall bear market losses from becoming so huge as to preclude a portfolio from recovering for many years to come, if ever. For example, if a portfolio is 50 percent invested in stocks that decline an average of 90 percent and 50 percent invested in stocks that decline an average of 10 percent, the total portfolio will lose 50 percent of its value. Should that portfolio proceed to gain 50 percent, it will still be in a 25 percent loss position, as 1.50 times a portfolio value of 0.50 yields a value of 0.75. In fact, this portfolio would need to double to recover to its pre-loss level. Not only is this a daunting task to execute, it can be demoralizing for an investor even to contemplate.

None of this discussion is meant to imply that Wall Street's analysis of company fundamentals is of no value to the investor. Much can be gleaned from fundamental analysis regarding a company's current valuation levels relative to its growth prospects. If current stock valuation levels do not appear to reflect the full extent of a company's growth potential, that stock might represent an attractive buying opportunity. But when and at what price level should this stock be purchased? And once purchased, when and at what price level should it be sold?

Fundamental analysis does not and cannot address the extremely important issue of timing. If an analyst rates a stock a "buy," the implication is that the stock can be purchased right now at its current price level of, say, $50. But it would likely also be fine to buy the stock a week from now at $55 or a month from now at $40. There is little discipline regarding the important decision of when and at what price to buy a stock.

Once a stock is purchased, the results of the fundamental approach are often the precise opposite of Loeb's success formula of "capitalizing successes and curtailing failures." Profits are often curtailed as positions are closed out because the stock reaches some arbitrary "price target" at which valuation levels are supposedly too rich. And losses often become open ended through the "death spiral" process discussed previously.

The question of timing of entry and timing of exit can be properly addressed only through technical analysis—the study of price and volume data.

Technical Tools

IT IS NOT my goal to convert the reader into a technical analyst who forecasts future stock prices based solely on the analysis of past price and volume behavior and patterns on price charts. But even the "pure fundamentalist" should heed the words of pioneering technical analyst Richard Schabacker: "If we grant the hypothesis that prices often move counter to the fundamental suggestions, then we automatically establish the basis for advantage in a consideration of technical factors which may suggest the immediate future trend of prices, and thus aid us in determining when the trend will be with fundamentals and when it will be contrary to them." In other words, technical analysis can provide the timing and the discipline that are so often absent from the fundamental approach.

As stated in "An Overview of Technical Analysis" at Stock Charts.com:

> The price chart is an easy to read historical account of a security's price movement over a period of time ... With this historical picture, it is easy to identify ... reactions prior to and after important events, past and present volatility, historical volume or trading levels and relative strength of a stock versus the overall market.

One need not be a "technician" in order to appreciate the value of this information or to be able to apply it to real-world situations.

A chart serves as a visual representation or map of how investors are collectively viewing the prospects of a company through their daily buying and selling decisions. While the "market" as represented by the collective view of investors is by no means always correct, it is foolish to ignore this collective view in one's investing decisions. Yet the pure fundamental analyst regularly ignores this collective view and judges the market to be "wrong" in many instances, most often when a stock is deemed to be "undervalued."

But the fact that the market is unimpressed with a particular stock is often an indication of one of two situations, neither of which is attractive to the investor. In the first case, there may be developments on the horizon that will adversely effect the stock's fundamentals, and these developments are being reflected or discounted in the stock's current price. We all know that the broad stock market is a "discounting mechanism" that often correctly anticipates future developments in the economy. So it is certainly logical to assume that the market for an individual stock can function in a similar manner. In the second case, the stock or its industry sector may simply be "out of favor" in the current market environment. The "true" fundamentals may ultimately be reflected in the stock price, but for now and the foreseeable future the stock is "dead money."

> *The crowd is most enthusiastic and optimistic when it should be cautious and prudent; and is most fearful when it should be bold.*
> —HUMPHREY B. NEILL

If the poor price action in a stock is an indication of adverse developments in the future, you don't want to own that stock. If it is merely an indication that the stock is currently out of favor and may remain so for an indefinite period, you may want to own the stock at some point but there may well be better current opportunities for deploying your investment capital. The judicious use of technical analysis can help you avoid the stocks that will not recover and purchase those stocks that will recover at a more advantageous time. In addition, by remaining alert to the technical picture once you have purchased a stock, you will capitalize your successes and curtail your failures with much greater frequency.

Technical analysis can hone both your timing and your discipline. Or as it was put far more eloquently by Richard Schabacker: "It is based on objective logic, assuming continuation of the current trend and making provision for rapid shifting of an incorrect forecast, automatically cutting losses short on such improper deductions, and conforming quickly and automatically to the 'judgement of the marketplace' and to the actualities of price movement, rather than trying to fight them or indulging in the human frailties of hope and the pride of personal opinion."

An excellent example of the value that can be added by technical analysis is afforded by the price history of AOL Time Warner (AOL),

Source: Bloomberg L.P.

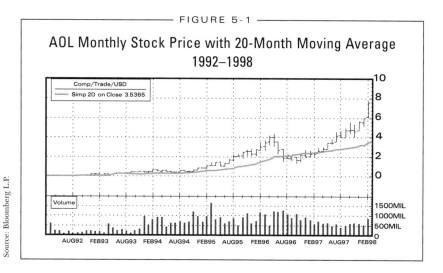

FIGURE 5-1

AOL Monthly Stock Price with 20-Month Moving Average 1992–1998

known as America Online prior to the merger with Time Warner in 2000. The company went public in 1992, and Figure 5-1 tracks the monthly price action of AOL from its inception as a public company through early 1998. Each vertical bar on the chart represents the monthly price range for AOL, with the horizontal line indicating the closing price on the last day of each month. The steadily increasing solid line on the chart is the 20-month moving average, which is simply the average of AOL's closing prices for the twenty most recent months. Moving averages are used by technicians as a technique for smoothing the fluctuations in stock prices in order to obtain a better perspective of the true underlying price action in a stock.

Figure 5-1 reveals several facts about the early days of AOL. First, the share price was rising fairly steadily. This is evident without reference to the moving average line. But the rather smooth rise in the 20-month moving average provides further confirmation of this rising price trend. In fact, SIR uses the 20-month moving average as a line of demarcation between a stock being in a bull market and a stock being in a bear market. A stock trading above its rising 20-month moving average is considered to be a bull market; a stock trading below its declining 20-month moving average is in a bear market. Note in the case of AOL on Figure 5-1 that its 20-month moving average line was in consistently rising mode, and with some brief exceptions in late 1996 and early 1997 the stock closed regularly above the moving average line.

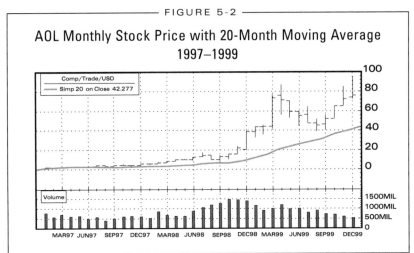

FIGURE 5-2

AOL Monthly Stock Price with 20-Month Moving Average 1997–1999

It is also evident from Figure 5-1 that the bull market in AOL was beginning to accelerate as we moved into 1998. Figure 5-2 displays AOL's price movement into its all-time high of $95.81 in December 1999, a far cry from its early-1998 peak of just $7.81 on Figure 5-1. Note the classic bull market action, with pullbacks and consolidations followed by runs to new highs. And note also how even on the sharpest of the pullbacks AOL's bull market support at the rising 20-month moving average line was never threatened.

But as Figure 5-3 illustrates, all bull markets come to an end. In early 2000, AOL began pulling back from its all-time high levels. But these pullbacks were supported at the moving average line until May 2000, when AOL began closing below the line. In October 2000 the 20-month moving average line began to decline, and AOL had still been unable to hurdle it. At that point a technician could pretty safely declare AOL to be in a bear market.

There are a number of price levels at which a technician might have exited AOL shares on the decline from its peak. Some may have noted the significance of the $75 level and may have chosen to exit in the low $70s after the major breach of $75 in January 2000. A more relaxed exit point that better allowed for the resumption of the rally would have been after the first close by AOL in May 2000 below its 20-month moving average line at $53.37. But recalling the brief weak period in Figure 5-1, one could argue that the line was still rising and that the stock might still rally back to full bull market mode. Another

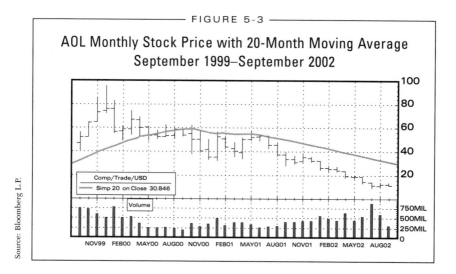

FIGURE 5-3

AOL Monthly Stock Price with 20-Month Moving Average
September 1999–September 2002

Source: Bloomberg L.P.

potential exit point occurred when the stock sank below 50 percent of its all time high of $95.81 at the $47.90 level. Technicians know that once a high-flying stock retreats to less than half its peak it is likely to continue to the downside. The final line in the sand for technicians occurred after the November 2000 close at $40.61, when the 20-month moving average had begun to decline.

A technical analysis of the price action of AOL would have allowed the investor to capture much of the rally into the high at $95.81. Few would have been so lucky as to purchase the shares near their low of $0.08, but there was plenty of opportunity to buy the stock for under $10. Some may have exited before the price peak out of fear that the "parabolic rise" on the chart would end badly. And some may have been fortunate enough to exit near the peak on deteriorating short-term price action. But it's fair to say that technicians would have begun exiting AOL in earnest in the low $70s, and all would have been out by the time the shares were trading in the low $40s.

From Figure 5-4 you can see that by 2002 AOL had ultimately declined to as low as $8.70. At what level did Wall Street's fundamental analysts exit AOL? As of this writing, only two of the twenty-five analysts who cover AOL rated it a "sell," according to Zacks.com. So as many as twenty-three of these twenty-five analysts rode AOL all the way down the "death spiral" from its high at $95.81 to its low at $8.70 without recommending that it be sold. Yes, one could argue, but AOL shares may yet recover to its former levels. This may be

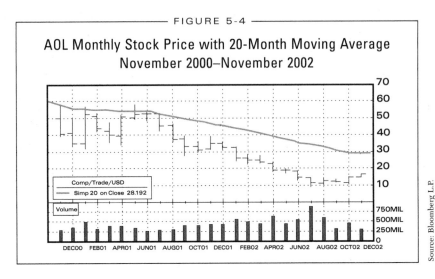

FIGURE 5-4

AOL Monthly Stock Price with 20-Month Moving Average November 2000–November 2002

Source: Bloomberg L.P.

true, but in the course of such a recovery technicians will jump back aboard the stock as it moves above key levels such as the 20-month moving average. And if the shares never do recover, technicians will not burden their capital with a "dead money" stock. As technician Richard Wyckoff wrote in the 1930s: "In Wall Street, it is not what one makes but what one *keeps* that counts."

Investor Sentiment

THE ANALYSTS AT SIR overlay technical analysis with the study of investor sentiment. Technicians often attempt to ride uptrends such as that of AOL in the 1990s as far as possible and then exit once the trend has been invalidated by downside price action. But there are often clues that a rally may be ending well before the stock price has declined much from its peak. In fact, these clues sometimes appear ahead of the price peak, and they emanate from the analysis of investor sentiment.

Investors who are overly optimistic about a stock create an environment of vulnerability. Over optimism is an indication that the vast majority of those who may ultimately commit funds to investing in that stock may already have made their commitment. So the pool of potential buying power may have dwindled to the point that new buyers cannot absorb normal levels of selling. Under these circumstances the shares will fall in accordance with simple supply and demand. And if selling pressure should become greater than normal, the shares may plunge precipitously. In other words, universal optimism and bullish sentiment on a stock that has been in a long bull market sow the seeds for the eventual demise of that bull market through the dissipation of sideline buying power.

It is therefore quite advantageous to combine sentiment analysis that is often early in spotting changes in trends with technical analysis that by definition requires some change in the trend before a position is exited. SIR has developed a number of sophisticated quantitative tools for measuring daily the degree of bullish or bearish sentiment on most of the large-capitalization stocks. Some of these tools are available free at www.SchaeffersResearch.com. Plus, there are some everyday sentiment tools that are fairly easy to interpret, and the best of these is the magazine cover story.

When a company is featured in a magazine cover story, there is a much higher than normal probability that the current trend in the stock is at or near an end. Magazine covers feature stories that have maximum recognition value so as to maximize sales. Maximum recognition value means that the subject is widely known and accepted and has been in place for some time. So if an optimistic cover story is generated about a particular company, you can be fairly certain that the vast majority of investors have been long aware of these bullish facts. Therefore, it is quite possible that the buying power to support further gains in the share price is close to exhaustion, or will be exhausted by the time the late comers commit their funds to the stock as a result of the cover story. And this has proven to be the case in an uncanny number of instances over the years.

My favorite tandem of cover stories each appeared in *Time* magazine and each featured the automobile industry. In November 1992, a *Time* cover story entitled "Can GM Survive in Today's World" painted a very gloomy outlook not just for GM but for the other major U.S. automakers. Just thirteen months later in December 1993, the cover of *Time* featured the smiling visages of the CEOs from each of the Big Three auto companies as background for a bullish article entitled "How Detroit Is Shifting into High Gear." Note from Figure 5-5 that the downtrend in GM's share price ended almost concurrently with the publication of the bearish piece in November 1992 (arrow #1) and that GM's uptrend was nearing an end when the bullish piece was

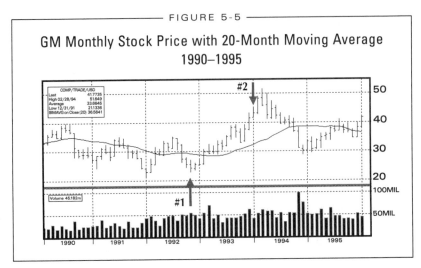

FIGURE 5-5

GM Monthly Stock Price with 20-Month Moving Average
1990–1995

Source: Bloomberg L.P.

published in December 1993 (arrow #2). In other words, the conventional wisdom about the auto stocks was exactly wrong at both points in time. Why? In the first case, the selling pressure had become depleted by the time news of hard times in the auto industry became important enough for a magazine cover story. And in the second case, buying power had become depleted by the time the auto industry turnaround was recognized by the cover story editors.

Now let's return to Figure 5-3 illustrating AOL. The first shot across the bow on the viability of the bull market in AOL was an extremely bullish cover story in the January 24, 2000 issue of *BusinessWeek* that preceded the technical breakdown in the shares. The cover featured AOL executives and was labeled "Deal of the Century" in reference to the upcoming merger with Time Warner. And with AOL still trading at about $45 on April 16, 2001, *Barron's* weighed in with a bullish cover story called "King of all Media," featuring drawings of AOL executives in regal gear. So even as AOL's technical picture was steadily breaking down as previously discussed, the magazine cover backdrop was indicating that investors were over-committed to AOL shares, leaving them vulnerable to further weakening.

Sentiment analysis is useful not only in identifying potential tops and bottoms but in the process of capitalizing successes by avoiding the premature sale of stocks that have been performing well. The danger in holding a stock that has posted big gains is that it is at or near its ultimate price peak, as buying power has been severely depleted. As previously discussed, sentiment is often excessively bullish in such situations. But if there are clear signs of negative or skeptical sentiment on a strong performing stock, you can conclude that sideline buying power remains available to drive the stock to yet higher levels. The skeptical sentiment indicates that analysts, fund managers, and the investing public are holding back on fully committing to this stock, and short sellers may have accumulated large positions. As the sideline money flows into the stock it will continue to move higher. And at some point those who are short the stock will be forced to buy back their shares to preserve capital, thus adding to the buying power "pool."

Overlaying fundamental analysis with basic technical analysis such as charts and moving averages is likely to improve your timing and your ability to let profits run and to cut losses before they become disastrous. Timing, capitalizing successes, and curtailing failures are each extremely important to your ultimate success in investing. Equally important is recognizing that the conventional wisdom regularly pronounced on the covers of business magazines and on financial television is often wrong, and it is often advisable to proceed in the exact opposite direction from that espoused by "expert opinion." In fact, the more in unison and the louder the majority shouts, the more likely are its conclusions to be precisely wrong.

Be a Contrarian

THE VALUE OF thinking in a contrary fashion is not limited to the stock market. In his defining work on contrarianism, *The Art of Contrary Thinking*, Humphrey Neill recalls: "Just before World War II ended, government economists predicted a severe postwar depression. The idea took hold of the public mind, also. 'Everyone' remembered (or had read about) the collapse following the first World War. People jumped to the conclusion that 'it would be the same this time.' As we now know, it was quite different. There was no slump; the opposite occurred." Neill advises the reader to hone the skills of thinking critically and developing a healthy skepticism. He likens contrary thinking not to a forecasting tool but to a tool for checking the accuracy of forecasts. "It is plainly nothing more than developing the habit of doing what every textbook on learning advises," he concludes, "namely, to look at both sides of all questions. Or,

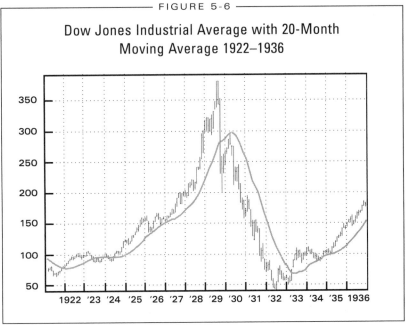

FIGURE 5-6

Dow Jones Industrial Average with 20-Month Moving Average 1922–1936

as Sir Francis Bacon put it: 'Doubt all before you believe ...'"

Technical analysis can often be helpful in providing the objectivity to maintain a view contrary to that of the majority. Figure 5-6 shows the price action in the Dow Jones Industrial Average (DJIA) from 1922–1936 along with a 20-month moving average. Note the similarities during the bull market phase through 1929 between this chart and that of AOL during its bull phase—steadily rising prices with pullbacks invariably contained at the rising 20-month moving average, followed by an accelerated advance into the top. Note the serious breach of the 20-month moving average in the October 1929 plunge, as well as the inability of the DJIA to move back above the moving average on the rally into April 1930. Many at that time were declaring a resumption of the bull market, but a technical view would have been cautious until the 20-month moving average was retaken, and this never occurred. Instead, the DJIA resumed its decline and bottomed in 1932 at more than 75 percent below its April 1930 level. It is clear that a new bull market emerged in 1933, with pullbacks in 1934 and 1935 contained at the rising 20-month moving average. But ironically, the majority of investors were far less enthusiastic as this new bull market unfolded than they were on the rise in early 1930.

Think in Terms of Probabilities

INVESTORS SHOULD DEVELOP one additional skill to successfully confront the uncertainties of the post-9/11 world—the ability to think in terms of probabilities rather than in terms of certainties. Put simply, events that are likely to happen should not be embraced as certain; events that are unlikely to happen should not be dismissed as impossible.

Consider these observations from the September 14, 2002 issue of *The Economist* regarding the various commemorations of the anniversary of the 9/11 terrorist attacks: "Despite the fresh round of warnings this week about the possibility of another attack, many Americans—perhaps most—still seem to treat the attacks as if they were a single, dreadful event, like a natural disaster, or a random crime committed against America ... The current attitude on future attacks seems to be nervous denial; people do not want to think about it."

Denying the possibility of future terrorist attacks may help us make it through the day (and through the night) and may thus serve some pur-

Successful investment is a battle for financial survival.
—GERALD M. LOEB

pose, as long as it does not result in our complacency and lessened vigilance. But the idea of denying this or other low-probability but high-severity events in our approach to investing can poison our ultimate results. As Leon Levy says, as quoted in the November 22, 2002 issue of *Grant's Interest Rate Observer:* "In an uncertain world, governed by probabilities rather than rules, the one constant may be that the more time that passes, the more probable it becomes that you will at some point encounter an improbable event." A rather chilling observation when one considers that the vast majority of improbable world events are negative and that Wall Street has conditioned the vast majority of investors to believe that, in the long run, all will be just fine with their portfolios.

Thinking in terms of probabilities does not necessarily mean adopting a "chicken little" attitude to investing by hoarding cash and gold bars. And it does not mean becoming a pessimist about America's future. But for investing it does mean adopting a skeptical attitude toward the smug assurances afforded by conventional thinkers and Wall Street "hand holders" that all will ultimately be fine. It is likely that all will be fine. But it is possible that all will be less than fine, or even that all will be disastrous, and one's investment approach must take into account this possibility. As stated by Nassem Taleb in *Fooled by Randomness*:

> Rare events are always unexpected, otherwise they would not occur. Rare events exist precisely because they are unexpected. They are generally caused by panics, themselves the results of liquidations (investors rushing out the door simultaneously by dumping anything they can put their hands on as fast as possible). If the fund manager or the trader expected the rare event, he and his like-minded peers would have not been invested and the rare event would not have taken place.

C h a p t e r S i x

Inefficiencies in the Market

LOUIS G. NAVELLIER
President and Chief Investment Officer, Navellier & Associates

S WAYED BY THE argument that the market is efficient and that you can't beat the Standard & Poor's 500 Index over time, many investors buy index funds. But there's no doubt in my mind whatsoever that the stock market is *inefficient*. In fact, I started publishing my first newsletter, *MPT Review,* more than twenty-three years ago to document how truly inefficient the overall stock market is and to identify the stocks with the most potential for appreciation. Since then, I've uncovered many quantitative and fundamental anomalies—or inefficiencies—that are widespread in the stock market.

Quantitative Anomalies

I CAN LITERALLY predict the future by studying the past price and trading patterns of many stocks. According to the efficient market hypothesis that index fund proponents promote, this is theoretically impossible. Let me prove to you why they are wrong. First, let me give you a little history of my background.

I was taught that the stock market was efficient and that it was virtually impossible to outperform the stock market unless an investor incurred excessive risk (for example, by buying high "beta," i.e., volatile stocks). When I was in college in the mid to late 1970s, I was fortunate to be taught by some open-minded professors and have full access to Wells Fargo's mainframe computers, which was a big deal in the pre-personal computer era, to build stock selection models. The first model that I worked on dealt with structuring a portfolio of 332 stocks that would mirror the S&P 500. The reason that I settled on 332 stocks is that that was all I needed to achieve a beta of 1.00 (in other words, the same risk as that of the S&P 500 Index) and to precisely track the exact industry weights of the S&P 500 Index. However, something went horribly wrong with the portfolio of 332 stocks that was designed to precisely track the S&P 500 Index. My returns beat those of the S&P 500 Index!

This was incredibly disturbing to me, because I was taught that it was impossible to beat the stock market over time, so that theoretically all investors must settle for the same returns and buying an index fund was the best option available to achieve this result. I then became suspicious that this view was flawed and that it might be possible to outperform the overall stock market. I investigated why the model of 332 stocks that was designed to beat the S&P 500 actually outperformed the index. Then I stumbled on the secret. There was a select group of stocks that just did not track the S&P 500 very well and instead consistently outperformed the overall stock market!

Today, those select stocks that consistently outperform the overall stock market and do not consistently track the S&P 500 are known as high "alpha" stocks. Mathematically, alpha calculates how much of a stock's return is independent and uncorrelated to a stock market index. This means that the more independent a stock's moves from those of the overall stock market, the more likely it will outperform selected stock market indices. In other words, alpha is the secret ingredient that I came to use to calculate how much a stock is likely to outperform a stock market index.

Alpha is not a perfect indicator, since high alpha stocks sometimes also tend to be associated with high betas—meaning that they tend to outperform the stock market during bull markets but are less predictable during bear markets. However, I figured out a long time ago that if I divided a stock's alpha by its standard deviation (in other words, its volatility based on historical prices) it became more beta-neutral and started to perform much better during bear markets. Today, a stock's alpha divided by its standard deviation is what I call its "reward/risk ratio," which I have been publishing and documenting since my newsletter began.

Figure 6-1 illustrates how the top 5 percent of stocks with the highest reward/risk ratios have performed month by month over twenty-three years. Obviously, the performance has been nothing less than spectacular! That is the good news. The bad news is that if you wanted to invest solely in the top 5 percent of the stocks with the best reward/risk ratios, it requires between 400 percent to 700 percent annual turnover. In the past, such high turnover would have been cost prohibitive. However, since bid/ask spreads and transaction costs have shrunk dramatically during the past few years, Navellier & Associates Inc. has launched cost-efficient management products that are based predominately on my reward/risk ratio analysis and have extremely high portfolio turnover.

Figure 6-2 illustrates how my reward/risk ratio analysis has performed on a trailing three-year and one-year basis for a universe of several thousand stocks. The first bar on the left of each group represents how the top 5 percent of stocks based on my reward/risk ratio analysis have performed during the past three years and one year, respectively. The second bar on each graph represents how the top 6 percent to 10 percent of stocks based on my reward/risk ratio analysis have performed during the past three years and one year, respectively. The third bar graph represents the top 11 percent to 15 percent, and so on. The charts show quite graphically that the

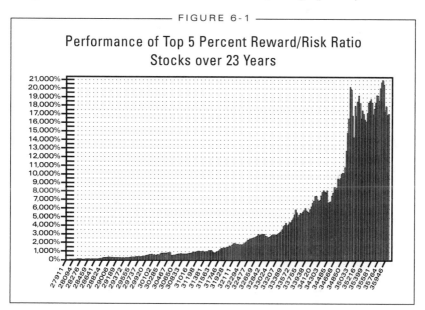

FIGURE 6-1

Performance of Top 5 Percent Reward/Risk Ratio
Stocks over 23 Years

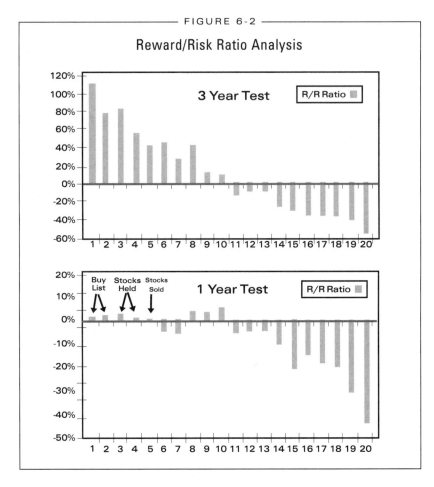

FIGURE 6-2

Reward/Risk Ratio Analysis

reward/risk performance decays in a surprisingly predictable manner.

Obviously, the stock market is not efficient. Otherwise, my reward/risk ratio analysis would not decay in such an orderly, predictable manner. As soon as I discovered how well my reward/risk ratio analysis performed, I knew that the stock market was grossly inefficient, that indexing was not necessary, and that I had been essentially misled during my academic training.

Navellier & Associates Inc. typically buys stocks in the top 10 percent of my reward/risk ratio analysis and sells stocks when they fall below the top 20 percent to 25 percent. The exception would be extremely aggressive accounts that trade by striving to stay always in the top 10 percent of the reward/risk analysis. Overall, my reward/risk ratio analysis has proven to be my best long-term indicator for proving that the stock market is not efficient and that an investor can beat major stock market benchmarks with less volatility. As a result, I believe that active management can substantially outperform most major indices, such as the S&P 500.

Fundamental Anomalies

AFTER UNCOVERING AND documenting quantitative anomalies based on my reward/risk ratio analysis, I later set out to document the "fundamental" force that creates an alpha and causes a stock to move independent of the overall stock market. I found that often alphas are not caused by fundamental factors. Sometimes alphas are caused by "short-covering" rallies, during which fundamentally inferior stocks explode, as they did in April 2001, October 2001, and October 2002, for example. Such seemingly anomalous occurrences, when fundamentally inferior stocks rally so strongly, seem fundamentally disturbing. However, short-covering rallies are often associated with temporary bottoms in the stock market. At other times, alphas are caused by rumors and events such as secondary offerings as underwriters "hype" stocks. Obviously, unscrupulous people who are trying to manipulate certain stocks for their own benefit all too often cause many of the anomalies and inefficiencies in the stock market. As a money manager, I, of course, do not want to buy those high alpha stocks that are performing well due to unscrupulous promotions. Fortunately, fundamental forces also create alphas and cause a stock to move independent of the overall stock market.

What works on Wall Street fundamentally changes from time to time. Sometimes the stock market has an "earnings momentum" bias (as in 1999), sometimes it has a growth at a reasonable price (GARP) bias (2001), or sometimes the market favors smooth, steady growth as it has on multiple occasions. At the end of each quarterly earnings cycle, Navellier & Associates tests more than 100 fundamental variables to determine what fundamental forces have been at play during both the past three years and one year. Experience has shown that many fundamental variables have no predictable value whatever. Often, however, we will stumble onto a fundamental variable that is extremely predictable, as Figure 6-3 illustrates.

The first bar on the left of each graph represents the top 10 per-

FIGURE 6-3

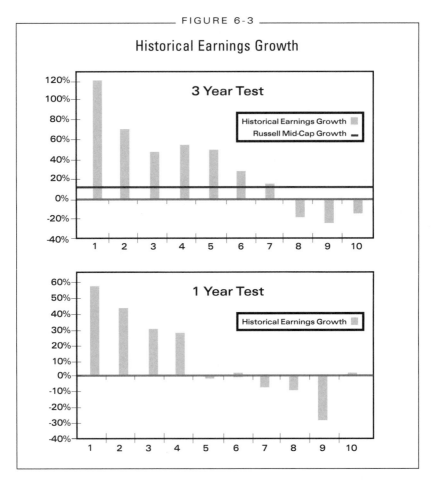

Historical Earnings Growth

3 Year Test

Historical Earnings Growth
Russell Mid-Cap Growth

1 Year Test

Historical Earnings Growth

cent of stocks that have had the strongest historical earnings growth. The second bar on the left of each graph represents the top 11 percent to 20 percent of stocks that have had the strongest historical earnings growth, and so on. The graphs make clear that during the past three years and one year, as historical earnings growth decays, the performance of the underlying stocks also decays in a very orderly, predictable manner.

It's interesting to note that using historical earnings growth as a predicable fundamental indicator was considered by some as entirely ineffective when the stock market was surging in 1999. Back then, Wall Street was much more interested in companies that were new and exciting rather than tried and true. However, ever since the stock market's bubble burst, Wall Street has become increasingly insecure and obsessed with finding companies that have had very predictable earnings growth and very good future earnings visibility. One day, Wall Street will become more speculative again, and historical earnings growth is likely to become increasingly erratic and less predictable as a fundamental stock selection tool.

The moral of the story is that whatever fundamental variables are uncovered, they will not work forever, because as more investors on Wall Street lock in on fundamental variables that work, they ironically become increasingly less effective. As new fundamental stock selection tools emerge, they tend to "regress to the mean" as more institutional investors discover these tools and end up tripping over each other as they try to buy the same stocks. In other words, good fundamental stock selection variables work only until other institutional investors discover the same fundamental variables.

Due to the fact that fundamental variables decay and lose their predictability over time, Navellier & Associates structures "multifactor" fundamental variables that adapt to how well these variables have worked on a trailing three-year and one-year basis. Typically, depending on the stock selection model, the firm will have anywhere from four to eight separate fundamental stock selection variables. Figure 6-4 is an example of one of those stock selection models.

This model is designed to emphasize the most effective variables and deemphasize those fundamental variables that are decaying. Technically, the research team uses an "optimization" model to determine the optimal weight of the fundamental variables that maximizes

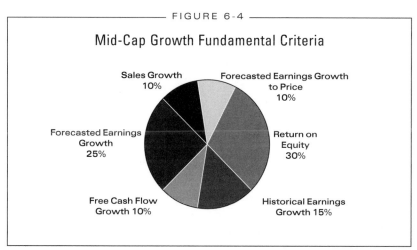

FIGURE 6-4

Mid-Cap Growth Fundamental Criteria

Sales Growth 10%

Forecasted Earnings Growth to Price 10%

Forecasted Earnings Growth 25%

Return on Equity 30%

Free Cash Flow Growth 10%

Historical Earnings Growth 15%

FIGURE 6-5

Fundamental Scoring Process

STOCK	POWER RANKING	FORECASTED EARNINGS GROWTH	HISTORICAL EARNINGS GROWTH	RETURN ON EQUITY (ROE)	FORECASTED EARNINGS GROWTH/ PRICE	SALES GROWTH	FREE CASH FLOW GROWTH
WEIGHT		25%	15%	30%	10%	10%	10%
Coach Inc	(86)	88	(89)	96	51	81	85
Auto Zone	83	88	56	98	82	74	72
Pepsi Bottling Group	79	56	100	92	75	62	85
Outback Steakhouse	76	90	93	65	61	76	68

(Combined score based on optimizing fundamentals)

(Stocks are ranked for each fundamental characteristic with respect to assigned weighting)

return, minimizes beta, and minimizes standard deviation (that is, volatility). Figure 6-5 illustrates how we assign a "score" to selected stocks to rank them in the model.

In this example, Coach Inc. has an extremely high "Power Ranking," with a score in the top 86 percent of all six variables in the Mid-Cap Growth multi-factor fundamental stock selection model. This is based on looking at percentile rankings of stocks in accordance with each of the multi-factor fundamental stock selection models. These models are also tested to make sure that they decay in an orderly, predictable manner, just as with the reward/risk ratio analysis. For example, Figure 6-6 shows how Navellier & Associates' Small- to Mid-Cap Growth multi-factor fundamental stock selection model performed on a trailing three-year and one-year basis.

The graphs in Figure 6-6 illustrate clearly that the stock market is not efficient. If the opposite were true, the Small- to Mid-Cap Growth multi-factor fundamental stock selection model would not decay in such an orderly, predictable manner. Similar to the previous example of reward/risk ratio analysis (Figure 6-2), the first bar on the far left of each graph represents how the top 5 percent of stocks based on my Small- to Mid-Cap Growth multi-factor fundamental stock selection

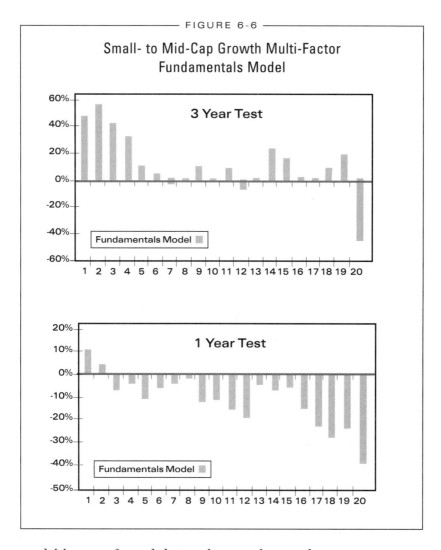

FIGURE 6-6

Small- to Mid-Cap Growth Multi-Factor
Fundamentals Model

model have performed during the past three and one years, respectively. The second bar on the left represents how the top 6 percent to 10 percent of stocks in this multi-factor fundamental stock selection model have performed during the past three years and one year, respectively. The third bar represents the top 11 percent to 15 percent, and so on. The evidence is clear that as the Small- to Mid-Cap Growth multi-factor fundamental stock selection model decays, performance decays in a fairly predictable manner.

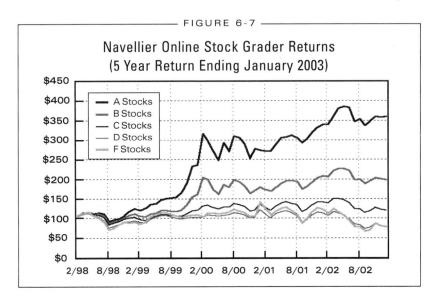

FIGURE 6-7

Navellier Online Stock Grader Returns
(5 Year Return Ending January 2003)

Beating the Index Funds

MY OBSESSION IS documenting anomalies (alpha) in the stock market and trying to profit from them. By far my best stock selection model is Navellier's reward/risk ratio analysis, which has performed well for more than twenty-three years in all kinds of market environments and has proven to be especially predictable.

Although the reward/risk ratio analysis works in almost every market environment, I cannot say the same thing about my multi-factor fundamental stock selection models, which must be continuously tweaked to adapt to various market environments. As a result, these models will vary considerably depending on whether we are in an environment favoring earnings momentum, GARP, historical earning growth, or whatever fundamental variables may be in fashion at the present time.

Navellier's entire database of both quantitative and fundamental research is available online at www.Portfoliograder.com. Updated weekly, this database grades stocks on an easy to understand A, B, C, D, and F scoring system (versus the more complicated percentile ranking that Navellier & Associates uses internally). Figure 6-7 illustrates the historical performance of stocks in this scoring system. Naturally, the A-rated stocks represent the most inefficiently priced stocks and are most likely to beat the overall stock market.

Chapter Seven

Ten Rules for Becoming Wealthy

CRAIG BRIMHALL
Vice President, Wealth Strategies, American Express Funds

I N THE TWENTY-SOME YEARS I have worked for American Express Financial Advisors, I have learned that there are basically only four ways to wealth: You can marry it (don't laugh, some do); you can inherit it (others do that); you can get a windfall (from a lawsuit settlement, lottery, or some other unexpected good fortune); or you can accumulate it.

Most of us are stuck with option #4—accumulate it. To do so, we need to understand how to manage cash flow. First, look at your annual earnings and multiply that figure by your working years. Not counting inflation (that is, pay raises along the way), the result may total several million dollars. Whether you will have that several million dollars by retirement, though, depends on how you manage your cash flow—and how you answer the following questions: What do you *need* now, what do you *want* now, and what can you save and invest for the future?

An old saying goes, "You can't build wealth by buying things you don't need, with money you don't have, to impress people you don't like." So how do you build wealth? Here are ten time-tested rules that can weather the stormiest market cycles.

Rule #1: Live Within Your Means

THIS INCLUDES managing debt and learning to budget. Such boring topics may not be the most exciting things about becoming wealthy, but they may be the most critical.

Our consumer-driven economy is relentlessly hammering away at why we must buy this item or that gadget so we can have the appearance of being successful, happy, and altogether "with it." So it takes financial discipline and good behavior to successfully accumulate money to reach financial independence.

Possibly the biggest trap out there is easy credit, which lets us buy numerous things we might not need. Comedians have pointed out the foolishness: "You buy something that's 10 percent off and charge it on a 20 percent interest credit card!" Benjamin Franklin warned, "He that goes a borrowing goes a sorrowing." And newspaper columnist Earl Wilson opined, "Nowadays there are three classes of people—the Haves, the Have-Nots, and the Have-Not-Paid-For-What-They-Haves."

We all want our lives to be better than those of the previous generation, but too many of us want *now* what it took our parents or grandparents years to get. Learning to live within your means leads to a freer life—debt can be a mean master instead of a worthy servant. So use credit wisely and learn to live within your means. Save first, spend second. If you do so, managing a fixed income in retirement will be a lot easier for you than for those who never learned how to live within their means during their "earning years."

Rule #2: Save Aggressively

THIS DOES *NOT* MEAN "invest aggressively." Rather, it means make it an absolute priority to set aside 10 percent or so of your income right off the top, and even more if your goals tell you to do that. The longer you wait to start saving, the larger the percentage of your current pay you will have to save to reach your goal.

If you can save aggressively, you will be surprised how that "nest egg" will start to compound. Look at any chart of compounding. It has been said that it's the last compounding that makes you wealthy. In other words, $20,000 becoming $40,000 doesn't seem like a lot of headway, but when the $40,000 compounds to $80,000, and the $80,000 to $160,000, and finally the $160,000 to $320,000, we're now talking about some serious money. Two more "doublings" and this account will be worth over $1.2 million. I've found this to be true: Those who spend first and save later inevitably end up working for those who have learned to save first, spend second. Why? Because most successful business owners (the vast majority of millionaires in this country) learned the art and science of financial discipline a long time ago, and all of them that I know understand the need to put aside funds for the future whether it be for future growth of the company or for eventual retirement.

Rule #3: Dollar-Cost Average

REMOVE EMOTIONS from your investing by automatically buying more shares when they are cheap. Emotional investing gets too many people in trouble. Statistics continue to show that we tend to buy when things are going up and sell when they are going down—in other words, we tend to buy high and sell low. Dollar-cost averaging not only removes emotions from investing, but it helps you buy low. Here's how:

By putting a constant dollar amount into a variable market, as the price slips, you buy more and more cheaper shares and thereby reduce your average cost. For example, let's say you are investing $100 a month into a fund in your 401(k). In the first month, the price of the fund is $10 per share and you buy 10 shares. The next month, the price has dropped to $8 per share, so your $100 buys you 12.5 shares. The next month, the price has fallen again, to $5 a share, and you buy 20 shares. In the fourth month, the price ticks back up to $7 per share. Your total investment so far is $400. If you're like most people, though, when you look at your statement and see that by the end of the third month the price has fallen in half, you would probably think you were losing money hand over fist. Especially after a fund continues to decline month after month, investors lose patience and start to bail. They're looking for "better returns," but they don't understand what's going on with the math.

At $5 a share, it feels as though you're down 50 percent (because the price started at $10 per share). However, you own 42.5 shares, which, when multiplied by $5 a share, equals $212.50—and you've invested $300. In the fourth month, the price gets back up to $7 per share. Although it might feel as though you're still down because the price started at $10 per share, you're actually within a couple of dollars of your break-even point. You own 56.79 shares, which when multiplied by $7 equals $397.53, on an investment of $400. And, if you're getting an employer match, the numbers can be even more dramatic. Of course, if the fund or market continues to go down and never comes back up, you can't be guaranteed a profit. Still, dollar-cost averaging—by investing a fixed amount in regular intervals—is the best way to make money in a variable market over time. The most difficult part is having the discipline to keep doing it. Investors should be willing to consider their ability to invest over an extended period of time.

Rule #4: Diversify

NO INVESTMENT is risk free; only a diversified portfolio can mitigate the risks of market cycles. We've all been warned against putting all our eggs in one basket; even Warren Buffett said, "It's better to be approximately right than definitely wrong." By "approximately right," he was referring to diversification.

If one piece of your portfolio is doing substantially better than other parts, the natural inclination is to load up on the part doing the best and forsake those not doing well. But the result will be an under-diversified portfolio that will probably be much more volatile—and the volatility may be on the downward side. Consider the late 1990s when most investors moved substantial assets to large-cap U.S. growth stocks, only to see them decimated in 2000–2002.

Proper diversification does not mean any old bunch of mutual funds or stocks, but a proper allocation among stocks, bonds, real estate, fixed assets, and other investments. It also means diversifying within those investment categories. For example, your stocks should include a mix of midcap, large-, and small-cap stocks as well as growth, blend, and value stocks. You should have bonds that are long, medium, and short term, as well as high grade, mid grade, and low grade.

A mutual fund may offer more diversification than you could afford by owning the same stocks individually. But owning a handful of mutual funds may not offer the diversification you seek unless you research the funds' holdings carefully. That's because many funds have sub-stantial "overlap." In other words, fund A from mutual fund family X may have many of the same stocks as fund B from fund family Y.

Your portfolio should also take into account different kinds of risk: purchasing power (or inflation) risk, interest rate risk, market risk, and investment (or specific) risk. Simply put, different investments can handle different risks. And that is why you need to diversify—to manage the various risks and to reduce overall risk of the portfolio.

Rule #5: Be Patient

WARREN BUFFETT SAID, "The market has a very efficient way of transferring wealth from the impatient to the patient."

But waiting is very hard to do. How long are you willing to hold an asset that is not performing well? One year? Two, three, or four? If you look at the history of asset classes over time, you will see that an asset can be "out of favor" for several years in a row. Here's a recent example: Bonds were perennial underperformers when compared to other financial asset classes in 1993, 1994, 1996, 1997, 1998, and 1999 (when all the money was flowing into U.S. large-growth stocks; how-ever, bonds still had positive returns most of those years, except 1994 and 1999). But when growth stocks tanked in 2000, 2001, and 2002, guess who "overperformed?" Bonds did.

Don't be fooled. Don't think you can time when bonds will per-form and stocks will get hot. If someone really could do that, he would own the world by now. So remember: Time in the market is more important than timing the market. A financial adviser can help you remain patient by reminding you of your goals, how asset classes change over time, and challenging you when you get impatient and want to drastically change what you are doing.

Rule #6: Understand Volatility

VERY FEW PEOPLE understand risk and the volatility baked into every portfolio. See how good your financial adviser is—whenever he rec-ommends an investment, ask what the risk or "standard deviation" is. Risk, or volatility of a portfolio, is measured by a statistic called "stan-dard deviation." Without getting into its complexity, every variable investment has produced a range of returns over its lifetime, and this range, or deviation, can be plotted on a chart. For example, the broad market is measured by the S&P 500 Index. The annual volatility, or standard deviation, of the index is about 16 percent. That means that your "expected return" may be 16 percentage points higher or lower in any year (two-thirds of the time) and up to twice that amount in those exceptional years, or 32 percent higher or lower.

So if the expected return on the S&P is 10 percent, you may see up to a 26 percent return (10 + 16) in good years, or a –6 percent (10 – 16) return in not-so-good times. And in those unusual years (which seem to occur about one-third of the time), you could see returns of up to 42 percent (10 + 16 + 16), or the not-so-enjoyable –22 percent (10 – 16 – 16). (And this range does not change a bit over time.)

Therefore, a portfolio or fund with a standard deviation of greater than 16 would be more volatile than the S&P 500 Index. It is very important that you understand your expected range of returns since it is very likely you won't see the average return occur in any given year, but a wide diversity of returns that, over time, should start to get close to the average you were expecting. The longer your time horizon for reaching your financial goal, the more likely you can tolerate an investment with a higher standard deviation.

Remember, we are assuming mutual fund indexes or broadly diversified accounts, not individual stocks or bonds. When you buy an investment, you are not buying a specific return, but the opportunity to see returns that are likely to fall into the investment's historical range of returns (probably some positive and some negative). Even so, the investment can always break out of that range in the future— the best indicator of future performance is not necessarily past performance. Remember that stocks of small and mid-sized companies may be subject to abrupt or erratic price movements and can therefore be riskier than stocks of larger companies.

Also, always understand what the investment's "average" annual return means, so you can prepare yourself for its volatility. For example, does a 10 percent average mean the investment was up 73 percent and down 30 percent and happened to average 10 percent? Or was it up 15 percent, and then down 5 percent to average 10 percent? Many investors are fooled by averages—they chase the 70 percent return *after* it has happened, when the likelihood of a repeat performance is slim (which we'll discuss more in Rule #7). Yogi Berra is rumored to have said, "Averages don't mean nuthin'. If they did, you could have one foot in the oven and the other in a bucket of ice and feel perfectly comfortable."

Over time investments regress to a mean. "Regression to the mean" simply means that highs and lows will average out so that your return regresses to a certain number or range. Understand an investment's range of returns so you know what to expect annually, and over time. Many people buy an asset when it is doing well (it's above its average), and then sell in disgust when it is doing poorly (now below its average). Behaving that way most assuredly means you will greatly underperform over time. If anything, you should consider buying an asset when its current return is substantially below its long-term average return. But few have the guts to do that. Mutual fund pioneer Sir John Templeton said, "At the point of maximum pessimism, be a buyer."

Remember that markets move from fear to greed, and back to fear. So there are times when the market is "overvalued" and other times when it is "undervalued." Warren Buffett said of the stock buying and selling decisions made at his company, Berkshire Hathaway, "We strive to be fearful when others are greedy, and greedy only when others are fearful."

Rule #7: Don't Chase Returns

IF WE KNOW from Rule #6 that a 10 percent average annual return doesn't really mean a 10 percent return each year, why do we still fall for an ad touting a fund that produces 20 percent annually or some other phenomenal return? Human nature. And maybe we even convince ourselves that for the chance to experience a year or two of 70 percent gains, we're willing to stomach the years of 30 percent losses that also fall within the fund's range of returns.

The trouble is, we probably have to cash out of temporarily slumping funds in order to invest in these volatile funds that may already be at their peak—and headed for a tumble. You may incur some costs.

So before chasing that incredible return, find out how the investment did during the last bad market for that asset class. Find out its risk, and ask yourself whether you can stomach a bumpy ride over the long term. Ask about its standard deviation (see Rule #6) before you buy it. And understand that as prices rise, values may actually be falling. In other words, the pricier an asset gets, the less value you may be getting per dollar spent.

Another Buffettism: "The dumbest reason in the world to buy a stock is because it is going up." So before chasing a return, always consider how likely it is that the investment will continue to produce · that return—and whether it's really worth the cost of cashing out of another, perhaps only temporarily depressed, investment to do so.

Rule #8: Periodically Rebalance Your Portfolio

YOU MAY DECIDE that your asset mix should be, for example, 50 percent growth stocks, 20 percent value stocks, and 30 percent bonds. But asset classes vary in performance over time, so after a year or so, the portfolio balance will start to shift as one asset "overperforms" and another one "underperforms." Emotions would tell you to sell the underperformers and buy the overachievers. If you want to remain adequately diversified, however, you would rebalance by selling some of the overperformers and buying some of the underachievers—probably just the opposite of what your emotions will tell you.

Consider the late 1990s. That period is a textbook case for how it would have been very tough to stick to the discipline of rebalancing, but it would have rewarded you very handsomely by 2001 and 2002. For example, as gains started to build in your large-cap growth stock funds in 1997, 1998, and 1999, it appeared as though the juggernaut might continue—and who would think of selling those hot growth funds? But, if you had been rebalancing, you would have been selling some of your gains and buying the underperformers—bonds, real estate, and value stocks. And we all know how those assets performed from the spring of 2000 through 2002.

So, if you strive to put your portfolio back to its original allocations from time to time (annually, semiannually, or possibly even quarterly), you will be taking gains from the best-performing assets (selling high) and buying those temporarily out of favor (buying low). But it takes discipline to keep your emotions in check.

Rule #9: Manage Your Taxes

TAXES ARE YOUR biggest expense in life—more than mortgage expense, education expense, or any other expense. The average American will work until about mid-May just to pay her annual taxes. So learn how to control your taxes, reduce them, and delay them.

Tax-advantaged investments fall into four buckets: those you buy with after-tax dollars and are taxed annually (CDs, bonds, capital assets, etc.); those that are bought with after-tax dollars and are tax-deferred (non-deductible IRA deposits, tax-deferred annuities, government bonds, etc.); those that are tax-free (municipal bonds, Roth IRAs, some life insurance contracts); and those that are bought with pre-tax dollars and are tax-deferred (deductible IRAs, 401(k) deposits, retirement plans, etc.). Whenever possible, use these tax-sheltered tools. The longer assets can grow without being taxed, the greater the total value when you want to start withdrawing funds. If possible, maximize your 401(k), especially if your employer matches your contributions. Fully fund your IRA, and if you qualify, use a Roth IRA. It is generally a good idea to have assets in all four tax categories, so you will have flexibility should Congress decide to change tax laws in the future (which is a certainty).

Rule #10: Get Advice

NEVER UNDERESTIMATE the value of good advice. Someone who manages investments full time certainly will find things you have overlooked or done wrong. A good financial adviser is like a personal trainer for your finances and can get you on track and keep you there until your goals are met.

Many people preach the "do-it-yourself" approach, but statistics simply don't bear out its success: As a nation, we are undersaving, overspending, and underdiversified, and generally have a tough time becoming (and staying) financially independent. Working with a professional should certainly increase your chances of success. If you have the three Ts—time, temperament, and talent—maybe you can do it yourself, but even those who can could probably benefit from a professional's "second opinion." Financial planning should not cost you—it should make you succeed, if you follow the plan.

That's why even more critical than getting the advice is being sure you follow a game plan. In the end, the only thing that matters is your behavior. *Investor* behavior is more critical to investment success than is *investment* behavior. And the greatest behavior problem for most people is this: procrastination. So get started, get advice, and get going down the road to financial success. If you do, you are already on your way to a better future and to achieving the wealth you desire—just be certain to follow through.

THE MARKETS HAVE BEEN significantly more volatile over the past few years than at any time in the recent past. Uncertainty and volatility seem to drive more and more people to the sidelines, and many become discouraged and abandon their plans.

These ideas can help you reach your financial goals. They are simple, but not necessarily easy. Adopt them, implement them, remain steadfast, and become (or remain) financially independent.

This is not a time for fear, but for discipline. The choice is yours.

Part Two

Key Sectors Driving Market Opportunity

The Unquenchable Thirst for Oil

JAMES T. HACKETT

Chairman, President, and CEO, Ocean Energy, Inc.

A S THE WORLD ENTERS the twenty-first century, the availability of oil and gas is not generally viewed as a challenge for sustaining the world economy. While global consumption continues to increase and the addition of new reserves becomes more challenging, the prevailing attitude is that the situation will have no real long-term impact on the ability to deliver this precious and important commodity at a reasonable price by historical standards. But where are energy prices headed in this millennium? Will the price of fossil fuels follow the low-cost pattern of the 1980s and 1990s, which saw dramatic declines in real prices for oil and gas? Or is the world headed to a return of the 1970s pattern when hydrocarbon prices rose in real terms and set about a wave of conservation, economic malaise, and in some cases, fear about supply availability?

One present-day reality that is not debatable is that the world has an unquenchable thirst for oil. This hunger for energy supplies affects every facet of the world economy. In 2000, the world's daily petroleum consumption reached a new high of more than 75 million barrels a day, according to investment bank Simmons & Company International. Thirty years ago, consumption averaged nearly 50 million barrels per day, which itself represented a four-fold increase over the 12 million barrels per day consumed in 1950. Clearly, the world's dependency on oil is not diminishing in the age of technology. In the United States, where dramatic declines in energy usage per dollar of gross domestic product have occurred, overall consumption has not been reduced. There are definite warning signs that in the next several decades demand for oil will greatly exceed supply, and the resultant price behavior will be more analogous to the 1970s than to recent decades.

This is not necessarily a message of doom and gloom. The world economy is much better able to absorb the higher cost of energy than it was during the 1970s, price shocks should not be as dramatic, and the more free-traded nature of a less regulated industry should allow better supply and demand adjustments. The world economy can still grow at higher oil prices than experienced in the 1980s and 1990s—just not as quickly. One by-product of the higher prices will be the improved ability of the energy sector to more aggressively develop much-needed long-term oil and gas supplies.

Major factors affecting the world's ability to meet the demand for oil include the following:

➤ Excess supply is diminishing and in the control of fewer players.

➤ The world's giant oil fields are maturing, and not enough smaller fields have been discovered to replace them.

➤ Economic advancements, while leading to more energy efficiency, are not leading to reduced overall energy consumption.

➤ Energy demand is growing not just within developed consuming countries but also in current oil-exporting nations.

➤ Investment in areas where the potential exists for large new resource development, such as in the Middle East and Russia, is not occurring rapidly enough because of political and/or infrastructure constraints.

➤ Non-OPEC supplies grew markedly in the 1980s but have since seen only modest growth.

➤ New revolutionary technologies (such as 3-D imaging and horizontal drilling, which were introduced broadly in the 1980s) have yet to surface in a commercial fashion to help with identifying and producing dramatic new sources of hydrocarbons.

Where Has All the Excess Supply Gone?

THE ENERGY BUSINESS is like no other economic activity in the world. It is capital-intensive, essential to the economic well-being of nations, and imbued with political influences. Oil, in particular, in the form of a major supply cartel, is subject to political pressures. The Organization of Petroleum Exporting Countries (OPEC), comprising eleven nations, supplies about 40 percent of the oil used throughout the world each day. During 2001, most estimates placed the group's daily production at roughly 25 million barrels. Saudi Arabia remains the largest producer, accounting for almost 30 percent of OPEC's total annual production.

Analysts disagree on how much OPEC excess capacity currently exists. In late 2002 consensus estimates indicated 4 to 6 million barrels of oil per day, but there is a lack of reliable data. The figure could actually be below 2 million barrels of oil per day. This compares to daily surpluses of 9 million barrels of oil in 1975, according to the Oil and Gas Journal Online Research Center. Not only is the surplus down significantly in absolute terms since 1975, its percentage of worldwide demand is down even more dramatically, given the significant increase in consumption of oil over the past twenty-five years.

Most of this surplus volume is consolidated within the hands of very few Middle Eastern nations. They, along with their Middle Eastern neighbors, control 65 percent of the world's proved reserves, according to the 2002 BP Statistical Review of World Energy. The world's dependency on these limited excess barrels is a significant risk in the coming years. This is especially true in the United States, which now imports 52 percent of its crude oil from OPEC nations and 8 percent from other countries, as it wrestles with the promulgation of some form of meaningful national energy policy.

The ability of OPEC to meet additional demand for energy is critical, because non-OPEC supply is likely to remain flat or grow only slowly in the near term. Over the past decade almost all of the growth in oil consumption has been provided by OPEC supplies. While the OPEC nations are certainly not running out of oil—the Department of Energy estimates that they hold approximately 750 billion barrels of proved reserves—consuming nations are at risk until OPEC and the Caspian Sea countries pursue massive new investments in developing additional production and delivery capabilities.

Before the 9/11 terror attacks, and the resulting heightened unrest in the Middle East, key OPEC countries were in talks with multinational companies to help develop OPEC's hydrocarbon resources. Most of these discussions have broken down or dragged out with current political tensions, but such efforts would suggest that excess supply in the Middle East is dissipating and that foreign capital needs to return to these countries in the future.

In the Oil Patch, Bigger Is Better

A LARGE PORTION of the world's petroleum comes from a small group of giant oil fields. While there are 4,000 actively producing oil fields in the world with almost 1 million wells, the average daily production from each of these fields is less than 20,000 barrels per day, according to a 2000 Simmons & Company International report. On the other hand, approximately 120 fields, only 3 percent of the total number, qualify as "megafields", producing 100,000 or more barrels a day. The big fields are traditionally defined as ones with reserves exceeding a billion barrels, with the rare supergiants having reserves in excess of 5 billion barrels.

The world is highly dependent on these megafields for their daily oil supply because the output from these fields currently accounts for 47 percent of total supply. Not only are there few megafields, but the majority of them are aging. In fact, the fourteen largest fields average forty-three years in age. In the twenty-first century, most of these fields will experience meaningful decline rates as they reach the end of their natural lives.

Replacement of giant oil fields is becoming more difficult. In the 1990s, for example, more than 400 fields were discovered, yet only 2.5 percent now produce more than 100,000 barrels per day, and none produce more than 200,000 barrels per day. Only three oil fields discovered in the 1980s still produce 200,000 barrels or more per day.

For the industry, the twenty-first century will be marked by a significant effort to replace the loss of these megafields. A large part of this endeavor will involve the search for new reserves rather than relying simply upon technological advances to boost production from already discovered reservoirs. Unlike the two preceding decades, there are no new revolutionary technologies on the shelf, such as three-dimensional (3-D) seismic or horizontal drilling, to help pinpoint and produce significant new reserves from old and new fields. The application of both these technologies played an important role—especially in the U.S. industry—in helping to meet increasing demand during the 1980s and 1990s.

For example, according to *Horizontal Drilling—What Have We Found?* by Gary S. Swindell, through 1996, an estimated 285 million barrels of oil equivalent have been produced from Texas and North Dakota, the top two states that use horizontal drilling. This breakthrough also made states such as New Mexico much more productive due to coal seam developments that allowed natural gas to displace oil in the U.S. energy equation. The horizontal drilling technique allows the exploration and production industry to reach reserves from different directions via a single bore hole, minimizing the environmental impact, reducing costs, and/or allowing for better reservoir drainage. The advent of 3-D seismic—the process of using shock wave patterns to develop a detailed model of a geologic structure—has greatly enhanced the accuracy of determining drilling locations. Amoco reports that over a seven-year period from 1990 to 1997, it achieved an approximately 30 percent improvement in its drilling success rate as a result of 3-D seismic alone.

That is not to suggest that the industry will not make strides with continued evolutionary technologies. Improved completion techniques have dramatically benefited reservoir drainage and production capabilities, as drilling fluid design enhancements and downhole tools have improved drilling performance. Also, in the search for oil at ever-increasing water depths, the commerciality of developing deepwater reserves improves with each subsequent design, allowing the industry to develop more reserves in an existing discovered field area, while also encouraging movement into deeper waters.

However, the world will need massive commercialization of new revolutionary technologies—such as GTL, which converts natural gas into a hydrocarbon liquid—to change the supply and demand dynamics for oil in the coming decades.

More Progress, More People, More Demand

THE CURRENT CENTURY promises more economic growth, spurred by population increases that result in a greater demand for oil and gas products. Theoretically, improvements in energy efficiency that the world has made with the advent of computer technology and more energy-efficient conversion and process usage should offset the demand from traditional energy sources. However, over the second half of the twentieth century, at a time when the percentage of energy usage per dollar of gross domestic product dropped in the United States from 22 percent in 1970 to 13 percent in 2000, energy consumption of fossil fuels continued to climb from 65 to almost 90 quadrillion BTUs, according to the DOE/IEA 2000 Energy Review.

These consumption patterns are not restricted only to developed countries like the United States. The rising dependence of western societies on supplies from selected regions of the world to quench the growing thirst for fossil fuels is further complicated by the internal growth of some of the world's largest oil exporters—the so-called swing producers.

A projected population explosion in the twenty-first century could dramatically alter the ability of several oil-exporting nations to meet their growing energy needs without reducing exports. If these countries can no longer meet their own hydrocarbon demand and must seek outside sources, how will nations like the United States, which is highly dependent on imported oil, deal with higher prices and more competition for supplies from even former exporters of oil?

Take Nigeria, Africa's largest country and one of the poorest in the world despite ranking as one of its top ten energy producers. During the 1990s, Nigerian crude oil reserves increased by more than 6.5 billion barrels, climbing to 22.5 billion barrels in 2000, according to a report by Sun Microsystems and Cambridge Energy Research Associates. This country is currently an oil exporter—shipping from its borders 2.1 million barrels of oil equivalent per day in 2000—but over the next several decades, it could actually revert to importing energy to meet its growing consumption needs. Since 1970, Nigeria's population has increased from 51 million to 123 million. Despite its size, the country's average annual internal energy consumption is only a scant 1.3 barrels of oil per person. That number could change dramatically if Nigeria is able to turn around its economy in the twenty-first century. For example, if Nigeria's consumption reaches the level of Mexico—approximately 10 barrels per person—and its population growth rate continues at the same pace for another thirty years, internal energy consumption will grow to more than 8 million barrels of oil equivalent per day versus only 500,000 barrels today. An economy that is now fueled by oil exports would have to quintuple its production of energy in the next thirty years to keep pace with its energy needs. It is much more likely that Nigeria will become a net energy importer between now and then.

All members of OPEC face the same dilemma. Their total population grew from 245 million in 1970 to 524 million in 2000. If that growth rate continues, the population of the OPEC countries could reach 1.1 billion by 2030.

Saudi Arabia is a classic illustration of what OPEC nations face. Considered a rich nation and one of the leaders of the OPEC cartel, the country had only 6 million people in 1970, but by 2000 that number increased to 22 million. If the population growth continues unabated, the country will have 80 million people by 2030. And if Saudi Arabia modernizes its economy to the level of the United States today, its internal energy use would jump from 2.1 million barrels of oil equivalent to over 12 million barrels a day by 2030. A nation once considered a swing producer would have a difficult time simply fulfilling its own demand.

Time Squeeze, Price Squeeze

IN THE QUEST for oil and gas, the industry must overcome a host of complex issues—geological, political, legal, social, and economic. These impediments complicate and prolong the investment process and the desired outcome—the production of new reserves of oil and gas. In the twenty-first century, the industry is confronting a myriad of factors that are delaying high potential projects in areas of the world rich in natural resources. As progress overseas slows, the West may find itself in the next few years dealing with a price squeeze that might have been avoided had investments in new resources and infrastructure been allowed to occur on a more timely basis.

Russia, the world's largest exporter of natural gas and the second-largest exporter of oil after Saudi Arabia, is an excellent example of how slow progress in one nation can affect the rest of the world. Suffering from the effects of the collapse of the Soviet Union, the country's oil production languished from 1992 to 1998 due to a decline in drilling and capital investment. The buoyancy in oil and gas prices from 1999 to 2000 helped ramp up near-term production, but sustaining and increasing Russia's oil production markedly from current levels will require large amounts of capital to develop new fields and to extend the life of existing ones.

In addition to further development of the West Siberia region that comprises the majority of Russian crude output, local oil producers are more aggressively exploring in the Russian sector of the Caspian Sea and teaming with foreign companies to develop oil projects in the Arctic region, Eastern Siberia, and Sakhalin Island in Russia's Far East. But how well Russia will be able to contribute to the twenty-first century energy market will be defined by its ability to develop timely new deposits and invest in massive infrastructure. Yukos, the second-largest Russian oil company, estimates total investments over the next decade by the Russian companies alone will reach $122 billion. Billions more will be needed to increase capacity for transportation to Europe and Asia—and the United States. Tapping Russia's wealth of resources will require incredible investments from around the world, and even more precious than money, lots of time.

Further complicating the supply challenge is the potential growth in domestic demand in Russia and Eastern Europe. The states that comprised the former Soviet Union consumed 300 percent more energy before the breakup than at today's anemic levels. If energy consumption in these states recovers from current rates of two-thirds the rate of Mexico, then Russia's ability to be an exporter to the rest of the world is further in doubt.

Globally, the investment challenge to add oil supplies only escalates. A senior exploration manager with ExxonMobil, quoted in the *Oil and Gas Journal* ("Global LNG Industry Expanding to Meet Heightened Gas-Demand Projections," August 12, 2002), has estimated that half of global oil production will come from new sources by 2010 with commensurate expenditures of nearly $1 trillion.

Alternate fuels are not projected to replace oil's importance in the early part of this century, but natural gas will continue to make gradual inroads.

Liquefied natural gas (LNG) has gained increased visibility as a resource that could help augment energy supply shortfalls in the future, especially in the United States, by allowing gas supplies to continue to substitute for oil supplies. However, security concerns and continued price volatility have slowed the investment plans for this alternate fuel source. Ten countries currently import LNG, with Japan being by far the greatest user. In 2002, the United States' portion of this market represented only 1 percent of the total LNG demand, and Morgan Stanley forecasts it to rise to 5 percent by

2005. The country's import capacity has grown in recent years due to the opening of two closed facilities and the expansion of an existing terminal. By the end of 2003, U.S. capacity is estimated to rise to 3 billion cubic feet per day from 1.1 billion cubic feet per day in 2001.

This LNG capacity growth represents progress in a long lead-time industry, but sustained investment in LNG is only economical in the United States at prices above $3.00 to $4.00 per million cubic feet. The gas market remains volatile with prices often falling into the $2.50 range. This price unpredictability makes long-term planning difficult. Seventeen regasification facilities are currently proposed in the United States and Canada that could add more than 10 billion cubic feet per day of capacity. The reality is that less than half of them will be completed without higher normalized prices and without many more years of site selection, regulatory approvals, construction, and supply contracting.

Price instability, politics, and economics are also affecting the development in North America of Arctic natural gas supplies that could help offset increased oil demand in the United States and Canada. The tight market of 2000 and early 2001 renewed some interest in Arctic gas development, both in Alaska and the Mackenzie Delta of Canada, according to CERA Advisory Services. But with a projected price tag from $17 to $20 billion dollars for an Alaskan pipeline and $3 billion dollars for a project to reach the McKenzie Delta, plans have remained in the study stage. ConocoPhillips estimated that sustained prices above $3.50 would be required for the economic success of any Alaskan route. With approximately 218 trillion cubic feet of potential gas reserves in Alaska alone, this is a huge resource that remains relatively unavailable in the near term.

Gas supply availability throughout the world is large. However, the infrastructure constraints, investment requirements, and long lead times for development will still provide major constraints in meeting the challenge of its substitutability for oil, regardless of whether gas prices strengthen, as they did in late 2002.

Nowhere but Up

WITH ALL OF THESE FACTORS at play—a diminishing excess oil supply cushion, dwindling giant oil fields, meager non-OPEC supply growth, rising consumption, and the need for huge capital investments—it seems inevitable that higher energy prices will play a part in the economy of the early decades of this millennium. The thirst for oil and other fossil fuels appears to remain unquenchable given the lack of readily identifiable and commercially viable replacements for these products in the approaching decades. An industry that is often considered past its prime and noticed only for its environmental aspects will confront a whole new series of challenges complicated by the pressures of society and the limitations of natural resources in the 21st century. What we took for granted in the 1980s and 1990s can no longer be assured. The world will once again be galvanized by the critical role that energy performs in the world economy. The search for, and development of, oil and gas remains a vital mission in the support and improvement of a global society, and we cannot fail in the task ahead to secure more hydrocarbon supplies for a thirsting world.

C h a p t e r 9 *N i n e*

The Predictive Power
of the Bond Market

ANTHONY CRESCENZI
Chief Bond Market Strategist, Miller Tabak & Company

T HE BOND MARKET probably affects you more than you know. Its influence stretches well beyond most people's awareness of it. But in fact, the bond market is immensely important to the national standard of living.

Yet when most people think about the bond market, it's more as an afterthought. Bonds are not very sexy to the average investor, and the bond market itself is either too complex or seems too uninteresting for most individuals to consider giving it much of their attention. This may not be too surprising in this era of abundant financial products considering the complacency engendered by the twenty-year run-up in the stock market and the accompanying long period of economic prosperity.

But this is where reality and perceptions clash, for the bond market is really the dog that wags the tail. The bond market, and interest rate levels more specifically, significantly influence the behavior of the stock market and the economy, not vice versa.

Unfortunately, many individuals miss this point and therefore miss the many signals that the bond market emits for the astute investor. These signals can present opportunities or serve as warnings in a wide variety of personal financial matters, ranging from home mortgages, home equity loans, credit cards, personal loans and car loans to the stock market, interest-bearing assets such as certificates of deposits and money market funds, or international investments, and even extending to implications in politics.

Interest Rates and Personal Finance

THE BOND MARKET is the place where interest rates are set, so the interest rate levels you see quoted on loans, credit cards, savings accounts, money market funds, and the like are all linked in one way or another to the bond market. Most of these interest rate levels are linked to the U.S. Treasury market, the most actively traded debt securities in the bond market. Mortgage rates, for example, are tightly correlated to the yield on the 10-year U.S. Treasury note. Just take a look at Figure 9-1.

As you can see from the chart, the yields on the 10-year U.S. Treasury note and 30-year fixed-rate mortgages basically move in lockstep with each other, with the 10-year T-note leading a bit. The tight correlation between the two illustrates the reality that interest rates are set in the bond market and shows the potential importance of following movements in the bond market even for individual investors, especially when obtaining a home mortgage, for example.

The reason that so many interest rate instruments are linked to the bond market is that the bond market serves as a reference, or benchmark, for where investors believe interest rates should be.

For most households, interest rate levels have a big impact on everyday finances. In the United States, where debt is a big part of

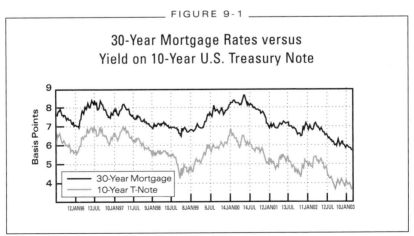

FIGURE 9-1

30-Year Mortgage Rates versus
Yield on 10-Year U.S. Treasury Note

Source: Bloomberg L.P.

Source: Federal Reserve

FIGURE 9-2

Liabilities of the Personal Sector (in Billions of Dollars)

TYPE OF DEBT	Q3 2002
Mortgage debt	$6,229.0
Revolving debt	$ 723.7
Nonrevolving debt	$1,000.3
Other liabilities	$2,023.9

the way people live, this impact is largely manifested in a household's monthly bills and the debt load people carry.

The explosion in debt has resulted from the increased availability of credit to consumers. Demographically, it is especially the baby boomers—those born between 1946 to 1964—who have increased their use of debt to tap into every possible means to finance their consumption of goods and services. Figure 9-2 highlights the enormous amount of household debt outstanding in its various forms.

Profound Impact on the Stock Market

THE IMPACT OF interest rates on your personal finances extends well beyond your debts: Interest rates can affect your equity portfolio, too. Indeed, history has proven that interest rates can have a profound impact on the stock market. As a result, the stock market watches the bond market like a hawk. Stock market professionals respond predictably to the Fed's periodic raising or lowering of interest rates, making one of the most famous adages in the stock market "Don't fight the Fed."

By gaining a better understanding of the bond market, you can recognize the potential risks and opportunities that the gyrations of the bond market present to the stock market each and every day. Your goal should be to become less of a casual observer of the goings-on in the bond market and more of a strategic thinker with respect to how the bond market's fluctuations might affect the stocks that you own, and how the bond market's behavior should be integrated into your investment decisions. This needn't mean that you become an investor in bonds; it merely means that you should incorporate your understanding of how the bond market affects the stock market into your investment decision-making process.

Consider a few examples dating back to 1998, when the world was gripped in a wrenching series of financial crises that began in Asia and spread throughout the rest of the world, including the United States. The financial contagion caused markets to swoon, and foreign currency and debt markets began to seize up. A liquidity crisis developed as investors shunned foreign markets and avoided financial securities that were not actively traded. Even U.S. Treasuries, for example, considered the safest financial securities in the world, were partly shunned as older, less active maturities, called off-the-run issues, performed poorly compared to actively traded maturities. For the U.S. Treasury market to have experienced price anomalies was an extraordinary event, and it highlighted the state of crisis that the markets were in at the time.

Enter the Federal Reserve. On September 29, 1998, the Fed responded to the crisis with the first of three rate cuts that year. In the policy statement that accompanied that first cut, the Fed explained that it decided to lower interest rates "to cushion the effects on prospective economic growth in the United States of increasing weakness in foreign economies and of less accommodative financial conditions domestically." The Fed clearly recognized the deleterious impact that dysfunctional financial markets could ultimately have on the U.S. economy. In addition, the Fed knew that it could use the power of interest rates to help restore investor confidence, which was shattered throughout the world.

The Fed's interest rate tonic worked its usual magic, as the global markets staged a substantial recovery. The Dow Jones Industrial Average, for example, which had fallen from an all-time high of 9367.84 just two months prior to the Fed's rate cut, to a low of 7400.03 on September 1, roared back to a new all-time high two months after the rate cut. The recovery once again illustrated the powerful impact of interest rates.

While there's no question that the Fed's rate cuts were needed to help restore stability to the financial markets in 1998, the rate cuts arguably sowed the seeds for one of the most explosive and, ultimately, harrowing periods in economic and financial history.

The problem was that the rate cuts became a classic case of too much of a good thing or, put another way, a double-edged sword. Arguably, the rate cuts were meant to address a market problem, not an economic one, so the Fed should have reversed its rate cuts once the crisis was over. It didn't, however. What followed in 1999 was a bubble both in the economy and in the stock market. The Fed tried to arrest the bubble in June 1999 with the first of six interest rate increases, but the Fed responded too slowly and the bubble grew. The stock market was caught in a euphoric mood—a mania, in fact—and turned a blind eye to the Fed. The stock market had also turned its back on a critical development in the bond market—an inversion of the yield curve, a development normally considered an ominous signal for both the economy and the stock market (more on the yield curve later). But the equity market continued to plow ahead and chose to ignore historical precedent. For many investors, it would turn out to be a disastrous mistake.

When 2000 began, it was the same old story. The Fed was still raising interest rates, yet the equity market was caught in dot-com mania. It was a bubble that was about to burst, and it was the Fed and the bond market that would burst it.

The Fed continued raising interest rates until May 16, 2000, when it decided to increase the size of its rate hikes from a quarter of a percentage point at a time to a half point. The Fed did this to ensure that the stock market, which had started to slip, would stay down for the count. It did. Like many other eras before, the stock market finally succumbed to the powerful influence of interest rates. And so did the economy.

By the end of 2000, signs of an economic slowdown and talk of recession abounded. The exuberant, free-spending consumer gave way to a more cautious, tepid one. Spending during the 2000 holiday season, in fact, was dreadfully weak and the worst since the last recession in 1990–1991. Businesses responded to the weakness in the economy by cutting production and shedding workers. Businesses also began to curtail their capital spending by cutting spending on new plants and equipment and by cutting back heavily on technology spending. This contributed to the battering of the technology-laden Nasdaq index.

In 2001, the Federal Reserve faced virtually unprecedented challenges, having to battle not only the burst bubble and the ensuing economic recession that began in March, but also the economic effects of the tragic events of September 11. As Federal Reserve Chairman Alan Greenspan put it in his February 2002 testimony before Congress, "If ever a situation existed in which the fabric of business and consumer confidence, both here and abroad, was vulnerable to being torn, the shock of September 11 was surely it."

Led by Chairman Greenspan, the Fed met the unprecedented challenges of 2001 by aggressively lowering interest rates, cutting the Federal Funds rate eleven times to a forty-year low of 1.75 percent at year's end from 6.50 percent at the start of that year. In 2002, the Fed lowered interest rates further, to 1.25 percent. The Fed's interest rate cuts helped to lift key interest-sensitive sectors of the economy, chiefly the housing and automobile sectors, which both grew strongly at the end of 2001. In addition, the Fed's rate cuts spurred a massive wave of mortgage refinancing activity, with nearly $1 trillion of mortgages refinanced in 2001 and an additional $1.2 trillion in 2002, thereby helping millions of households. In these and other ways, the Fed's cuts helped the economy to recover in short order. While the indomitable spirit of Americans was no doubt as good a reason as any for the economic rebound, the Federal Reserve's interest rate reduction played an immense role. The rebound helped to buffer the U.S. equity market against the possibility of even deeper weakness than occurred and helped to lift shares in economically sensitive companies relative to other industries.

These recent episodes in the financial markets demonstrate that when it comes to investing in the stock market, the bond market is a power to be reckoned with. If you can learn to read the bond market's signals you can sharply improve your investment performance. You can learn, for example, how to know when to increase or decrease your risk taking, and where you should put your money during the different stages of the economic cycle.

Yield Curve as Crystal Ball

ONE OF THE BEST SIGNALS emanating from the bond market is the yield curve. The indicator that many investors put ahead of all the rest, it is the closest thing that the bond market has to a crystal ball. For decades it has reliably foreshadowed major events and turning points in both the financial markets and the economy, and it is one of the most closely watched financial indicators. This is because there is significant historical evidence proving that the yield curve is one of the best forecasting tools available.

The yield curve is a chart that plots the yield on bonds against their maturities. The shape of the yield curve is generally upward sloping, with yields increasing in ascending order as the maturities lengthen. In other words, a "normal" yield curve is one in which the yields on long-term maturities are higher than the yields on short-term maturities. The maturities generally included in yield curve graphs usually range from 3 months to 30 years.

Market observers focus on the shape of the yield curve as a barometer of the U.S. economy. The focus is generally on the yield spreads between various combinations of short- and long-term maturities. The two most commonly watched spreads are the spread between 3-month T-bills and 10-year T-notes (see Figure 9-3), and the spread between 2-year T-notes and 30-year T-bonds. Both of these spreads have shown strong historical correlation to the behavior of the economy.

Over the years, as noted previously, the yield curve has proven to be one of the best economic indicators among the plethora that exist. The yield curve is thought to be a better predictor of the economy than the stock market, for instance. Indeed, studies have shown that the yield curve predicts economic events roughly twelve months or more in advance, while the stock market is considered a useful predictor only six to nine months in advance.

The shape of the yield curve can mean a variety of things to bond investors, but there are two basic ways of looking at it. First, a yield

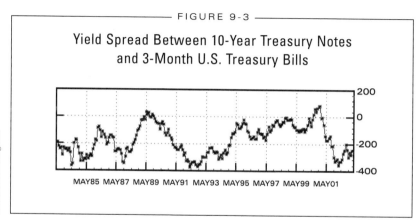

FIGURE 9-3

Yield Spread Between 10-Year Treasury Notes
and 3-Month U.S. Treasury Bills

200
0
-200
-400

MAY85 MAY87 MAY89 MAY91 MAY93 MAY95 MAY97 MAY99 MAY01

Source: Bloomberg L.P.

curve that is "positively sloped," or steep, is usually seen as an indication that short-term interest rates are relatively low and can be expected to remain low as a result of an accommodating stance on monetary policy by the Federal Reserve. When the Fed lowers short-term interest rates, its monetary policy is considered friendly, which is usually good news for bonds, stocks, and the economy because it lowers the cost of borrowing. A steep yield curve, therefore, generally foretells good times for investors over a several-quarter horizon.

On the other hand, a "negatively sloped," or inverted, yield curve is usually seen as an indication that short-term interest rates are relatively high and can be expected to remain high, with the Fed engaged in a strategy to slow the economy by raising short-term interest rates. This, of course, generally portends a gloomier set of conditions for bonds, stocks, and the economy because it raises the cost of borrowing. In fact, since 1970 every inverted yield curve has been followed by a period in which S&P 500 earnings growth was negative and has almost always preceded either an economic slowdown or a recession.

The yield curve's powerful predictive value was clearly illustrated in 2000 when the events of that year were forewarned by the inversion of the yield curve that began in January 2000. Investors who heeded the yield curve's warnings at the start of that year by diversifying their investments out of stocks are now sitting on a pot of gold. Almost everyone else, who held their stocks, got caught like deer in headlights.

Interest Rates and Politics

THE POWERFUL INFLUENCE of interest rates may well have repercussions beyond economic spheres. Compelling evidence exists to suggest that the influence extends to the political arena, too. While there's no doubt that many issues can shape the outcome of an election, the impact of interest rates has historically been quite palpable.

President Jimmy Carter, for instance, was saddled by high interest rates throughout much of his administration in the late 1970s. Interest rates were high at that time due to rampant inflation rates. Republicans, led by Ronald Reagan, seized upon interest rates as a campaign issue, and in 1980 Carter lost his reelection bid partly because of the public's discontent with soaring interest rates.

Reagan benefited from a steady decline in interest rates that occurred throughout his administration. The decline helped to contribute to perceptions that Reagan restored and revitalized the nation, a perception that continues to this day. In fact, many agree that the bull market witnessed in the late 1990s actually got its start in 1982 under Reagan's watch.

Similar to Carter, President George Bush Sr.'s bid for reelection was stymied by high interest rates. Early in Bush's term, the Fed had raised interest rates in an effort to slow the economy and reduce inflation. The Fed's rate hikes eventually slowed the economy significantly and, combined with other factors, led to the recession of 1990–1991. To Bush's dismay, the Fed was slow to respond to the recession and lowered interest rates slowly and in small increments. The poor state of the economy became a campaign issue for the Democrats and helped sweep Bill Clinton into the presidency in 1992.

Bill Clinton, for his part, masterfully used the powerful influence of interest rates as the centerpiece of his economic strategy. He accomplished this by adopting strategies on fiscal policy, developed by Treasury Secretary Robert Rubin, that encouraged low interest rates and hence strong economic growth. The result was a historic shift in the government's yearly fiscal balance, from deficit to surplus. What followed was an extraordinary drop in interest rates and a virtually unprecedented period of economic prosperity. Likewise, President George W. Bush may yet benefit from the extraordinary rate cuts implemented by the Federal Reserve in 2001 and 2002.

It is unconventional to think about the impact of interest rates on politics. But the evidence clearly suggests that the bond market can play a major role in shaping the political landscape.

Keeping an Eye on Bonds

WHEN INVESTING IN uncertain times, investors should integrate the bond market into their investment decision-making process in the following way:

> ➤ Remember, even if you don't own a single bond, trends in the bond market—where interest rates are set—can still have an immense impact on your personal finances, from the interest rates you pay on your home mortgage and car loans to your credit card rates.

➤ For equity investors, the impact of interest rates on the economy, and hence the stock market, has historically been quite large. This is why the saying, "Don't fight the Fed," is a credo on Wall Street. Let this adage guide your investment decisions.
➤ Use the yield curve as a predictor of the economy and the stock market. History has proven the yield curve to be one of the best forecasting tools available. Put it in your toolbox.
➤ Be aware of the impact that interest rates can have on the political landscape, which can materially affect your investments.

Do these things, and you will begin to unlock the power of the bond market.

Gold and Monetary Disorder:
Three Bullish Gold Price Scenarios

J O H N   C .   V A N   E C K

Chief Gold Strategist and Chairman, Van Eck Associates
and Van Eck Funds

THE UNITED STATES, as well as other countries, may face a double-dip or prolonged recession in order to correct the remaining market imbalances arising from the boom of the 1990s. The monetary authorities' attempt to contain the recession by low interest rates and fiscal deficits may only prolong the needed correction. Short-term creditors, suffering from low and even negative returns, may seek gold as an alternative investment to protect their wealth.

Diversifying portfolios into gold may indeed be wise over the next few years. Diversification may protect wealth and reduce risks arising from (1) a possible deflationary adjustment of the imbalances of the great boom of the 1990s, (2) a possible period of stagflation, and (3) a possible eventual period of accelerating inflation, monetary disorder, and a crisis of confidence. There is no assurance that these risks will materialize, but if and when they do, the growing prudence and popularity of gold portfolio diversification and consequent gold investment demand could result in an upward trend in the price of gold, a profitable investment opportunity, and an improvement in portfolio performance.

A Brief History of U.S. Monetary Policy

THE FEDERAL RESERVE ACT in 1913 provided for the dollar being convertible into gold and for limited credit expansion. It reflected classical economic theory, which was built on the concept of a harmonious free market balance of interests among savers, investors, and producers. As a result of the Great Depression, however, the world lost confidence in free economy policies.

Economist John Maynard Keynes developed a theory that assumed there was a conflict between the interests of savers and investors. He believed that cheap credit should be used to encourage business to invest and consumers to spend. During the 1930s, a shift in political attitudes took place as governments actively intervened in the economy and assumed responsibility for full employment, economic growth, and social programs. Stable international money, meaning currencies that were convertible into gold, was abandoned in favor of national monetary management. Policy makers' judgments in setting interest rates were substituted for the combined wisdom of the free market. The legislative mandate under which the Federal Reserve operated was revised to establish the dual objectives of full employment and price stability.

The Federal Open Market Committee adopted the policy of setting federal interest rates with an eye toward controlling inflation. Government policy accommodated bank demand by consistently maintaining positive "free reserves" in the banking system. The government always met the demand for currency in circulation and lowered bank reserve requirements. The government sought maximum sustainable output and employment by stimulating business and household loan demand by lowering interest rates so that aggregate demand would meet "potential output." The rate of potential output itself was boosted by relatively cheap credit. Monetary policy and political pressures kept market interest rates relatively low, which tended to enrich debtors and to reduce creditors' ability to obtain a fair return.

As a result of this policy, economic growth since World War II has been accompanied by a huge credit expansion, inflation, and imbalances. The Open Market Committee increased the adjusted monetary base at an average annual 8 percent rate since 1973. This rate of growth was well above the real GDP growth rate averaging 3.5 percent during this period. With each slowdown in spending, the committee added liquidity to the economy, which was not fully withdrawn when spending improved, thus giving an additional long-term inflationary bias to monetary policy. Commercial banks and non-bank intermediaries took advantage of the higher reserves and expanded credit accordingly. Credit expansion became an important "engine of growth." Outstanding business and household debt climbed from $973 billion (93 percent of GDP) at the end of 1970 to $15.3 trillion (146 percent of GDP) at the end of September 2002, up an average annual compound rate of 9.1 percent. Outstanding domestic financial sector debt soared from $128 billion at the end of 1970 to $10.0 trillion at the end of September 2002, up an average annual rate of 14.7 percent.

Price stability gave way to inflation rates of more than 10 percent in 1974 and again in 1979–1981. More recently, they have declined to approximately 2 percent. The purchasing power of the dollar declined more than 90 percent since World War II. Monetary policy in the last half of the 1990s focused on a "low and stable" inflation rate, not on the growing asset, credit, and other imbalances.

Current Economic and Financial Risks

THE UNAVOIDABLE CONSEQUENCES of rapid business, household, and speculative credit expansions are economic and financial imbalances in consumption, investment, labor, and price-setting decisions and periodic recessions to correct the imbalances. Classical and "Austrian School" economic theories state, and the history of business cycles confirms, that the length and severity of recessions depend on the magnitude of the imbalances and maladjustments that have accumulated during the preceding boom. Credit excesses may have their most dangerous effects not in rising prices but in these maladjustments and imbalances. The longer the boom lasts, the harder is the market resolution of the imbalances and maladjustments. "Growth" recessions in the United States since World War II took place in 1954, 1958, 1961, 1970, 1974, 1982, and 1990. Severe financial and business contractions and depressions followed past global "new era" booms in 1720, 1772, 1825, 1873, and 1929.

The bursting of the high-technology bubble in 2000 began a correction of the imbalances resulting from the 1991–2000 boom. Stocks collapsed. Business profits fell rapidly. The 57 percent fall in the manufacturing profits sector from 1997 to the first quarter of 2002 was one of the worst declines since 1930. Capital spending suffered a sharp downturn.

Economic weakness could lead to a double-dip and even multi-year recession and deflation. Macroeconomists believe that deflation can be overcome and a new business cycle started by lowering interest rates, stimulating further borrowing, and increasing fiscal deficits. On the other hand, low interest rates may not succeed in increasing aggregate domestic demand to meet potential output. The continuous growth and leveraging of private debt may be close to reaching a limit. Businesses may not have sufficient profitable investment opportunities. Microeconomic contractionary forces may be strong enough to make macroeconomic expansionary monetary and fiscal policies ineffective, as in Japan.

The economy could be vulnerable to further risks and shocks in the postbubble adjustment process as follows:

➤ *Risk #1.* In September 2002, the managing director of the International Monetary Fund warned that there were increased risks to the global economic outlook. The Fund stated that the global current account imbalances were unlikely to be sustained over the medium term and that the world should worry about a rapid correction. A likely scenario would be that revised expectations of U.S. growth prospects would cause lower U.S. consumption, imports, and growth. A sharply lower dollar would export some of the pain to Europe and Japan. The U.S. current account deficit, which was in surplus in 1990, has gradually grown and reached a record 5 percent of GDP. The dollar rose from a low in 1995 to a peak in January 2002, due to capital inflows, but by February 4, 2003 it had declined approximately 21 percent in terms of the euro.

➤ *Risk #2.* The risk of financial distress may grow further. The past growth of business, household, and speculative debt in excess of the economy's growth raised the risk level higher than at any time in history. The value of corporate bond defaults in 2002 hit a record, surpassing 2001's record. A possible measure of risk, the gross credit exposure of the public's share of the global over-the-counter derivatives market (after taking into account legally enforceable bilateral netting agreements), rose 12 percent from the end of 2001 to $1.3 trillion on June 30, 2002. Record-high debt levels, credit rating downgrades, deteriorating equity values, economic weakness, a record number of loans in foreclosure, and climbing delinquencies are weighing on the market. A weak economy may be unable to service the huge debt, burdened by compounding interest costs and a decline in the overall economy's rate of return. The size of the debt may become a serious financial imbalance that could require a long period of debt deleveraging. The ultimate risk is the possibility of a chain reaction, a cascading sequence of defaults that will culminate in a financial implosion. The ratio of the price of gold to the price of silver, a characteristic of the credit spread anticipating developing distress, rose from a low of 62.5 in July 2002 to 79.7 on February 7, 2003.

➤ *Risk #3.* Optimistic expectations of a stock market rebound may be delayed. Assumptions of future long-term equity returns may be scaled down, which could reduce current relatively high valuations. The squeeze on profits may continue in spite of current recovery hopes. Current overcapacity could grow if real economic growth remains below potential growth and leads to a growing negative output gap. Fiercer foreign and domestic competition could put more pressure on business pricing power and lead to falling unit prices. In 2002 core CPI goods prices declined approximately 1.5 percent over the prior year's level. A lag in lower unit labor costs in spite of increased productivity could mean lower unit profits. Also, underfunded pension plans and rising insurance premiums could further add to costs.

➤ *Risk #4.* Consumer spending and the strong housing and car markets, supported by low interest rates, maintained economic growth in 2002. That year's lowest mortgage interest rates since the mid-1960s contributed to record home building and mortgage refinancing, which strengthened consumer spending. However, the risk is that the housing and car markets may reach saturation levels, especially if and when long-term interest rates rise. The aggregate household debt service burden as a percent of disposable personal income has grown close to peak 1986 levels. Consumers may spend less and save more, raising the personal savings rate from approximately 4 percent to its former 8 to 9 percent.

The Japanese Experience—Failure of Macroeconomic
Policies to Prevent Deflation

JAPAN, THE WORLD'S second-largest economy, is facing a financial crisis that could have dire consequences not only for Japan but for the rest of the world as well. The Japanese face a dilemma in that they cannot fund huge budget deficits forever, and the government cannot possibly stop spending abruptly without driving the economy into deep recession. Japan's stock market bubble burst in 1990. Rather than allow the market promptly but painfully to correct the resulting microeconomic financial and economic imbalances, the government intervened and adopted macroeconomic easy money and government debt-financing policies to prevent its economy from turning into recession.

The Japanese government currently runs a fiscal deficit of about 7 percent of GDP. Deficit spending raised the gross public debt from approximately 60 percent of GDP in 1990 to a forecast 155 percent of GDP in 2003. The Bank of Japan conducted drastic monetary easing, unprecedented in the history of central banking. Short-term interest rates were reduced to zero. In the spring of 2002, the growth rate of its monetary base was raised to an annual rate of 20 to 30 percent.

In spite of these policies, the consequences have been economic stagnation, a four-year deflation, and a build-up of nonperforming bank loans. Japan's Financial Services Agency estimates the business, household, and speculative bad loans at the equivalent of approximately $390 billion, about 13 percent of GDP, but they could be much higher. The nonperforming loans have kept many unprofitable companies in business. Since 1990, new nonperforming loans have exceeded write-offs and reserves against old loans. The Bank of Japan has promised to keep zero interest rates and to flood the market with liquidity until prices rise. If and when inflationary pressures build up, the banks' bad debt problems might ease, but long-term interest rates could rise. This, in effect, would lower the values of the debt held by the banks, substantially raise the government's interest cost burden, and make it harder for companies to meet interest payments—potentially driving up default rates and pushing more companies into bankruptcy. Part of the equivalent of approximately $10 trillion of financial assets saved by Japanese households could be at risk of becoming gradually worthless in terms of purchasing power. Moody's Investors Service downgraded Japan's sovereign credit rating from Aa3 to A2 in April 2002, because a debt trap might become inevitable. Fitch Ratings cut Japan's credit rating to AA- in November 2002, because of Japan's apparent failure to control its debt and revive its economy. The Nikkei stock market average in October 2002 slumped to a twenty-two-year low, down 79 percent from its 1990 high.

As confidence in financial conditions fell, Japanese investors further diversified their portfolios into gold. Net retail gold investment demand had a substantial number of first-time buyers.

Gold as a Monetary Asset

GOLD HAS BEEN VALUED from the early Bronze Age. The first known gold objects, dating possibly as far back as 5000 B.C., were Egyptian ornaments, ritual vessels, and personal jewelry, symbolizing power and luxury. Gold's high melting point and resistance to corrosion made these objects indestructible. Although China may have used gold coins earlier, King Croesus of Lydia around 550 B.C. has been credited with minting the first coins in the West containing gold (and silver) in a small convenient form of standard weight, purity, and authenticity. They were accepted by the Mediterranean market and used as money as the Greeks depreciated their silver coins. Since then, gold coins and bars have served from time to time as a stable, universally accepted "standard of value," what many consider the ultimate geopolitical and financial safe-haven asset.

Goldsmiths in the seventeenth century issued certificates representing gold on deposit, which were among the earliest forms of gold-backed paper notes. Created in 1694, the Bank of England mainly financed government debt by issuing these notes. Banks also used them to finance business loans. Credit thus created from time to time became issued at excessive rates and resulted in business cycles. In many cases, paper notes became worthless.

The gold standard was first put into operation in 1821 in Great Britain when the Coinage Act declared the new gold sovereign as the sole standard of value and unlimited legal tender. Before that date the weight of gold was tied to silver, which was England's money, at a defined rate. Gold was a genuinely rare metal. World gold production from 1800 to 1850 totaled only around 1,200 metric tons.

The gold standard was a monetary system in which the monetary unit was a fixed weight of gold. The monetary authorities would buy or sell the metal at a fixed price in convertible paper money per unit weight of the metal. Convertible paper currency gradually supplemented the use of coined gold. The Bank of England regulated the money supply by expanding or contracting its assets.

Outside of Great Britain, a bimetallic standard of gold and silver prevailed. World gold production expanded, propelled by discoveries in the United States, Australia, and South Africa, to almost 10,400 metric tons from 1850 to 1900. A monometallic gold standard was adopted by Germany in 1871, followed by France, and then by the United States in 1900. Thus, gold became the single standard to which all other forms of money were coordinated, the international medium of exchange and unit of account. Price levels of gold standard countries were kept in constant relationship with one another and were determined according to the world supply of gold. This supply was limited by nature and so provided a global regime of stable prices that creditors could trust. For instance, the annual mined output of gold increased the total stock ever mined at a rate of about 1.6 percent a year during the past fifty years, which was close to the global productivity growth rate.

The gold standard was suspended in Britain in 1931, in France in 1936, and finally, in the United States in 1971, but gold remained a monetary asset.

Why Invest in Gold?

GOLD HISTORICALLY has provided a low, and even at times a negative, correlation with most other asset classes, especially U.S. stocks. Thus, gold has proven to be a good portfolio diversifier by reducing the overall level of risk (volatility). The World Gold Council has issued several reports pointing out gold's advantages over stocks, Treasury Bills, and Treasury Inflation Protected Securities (TIPS), and demonstrating that even a small allocation of a portfolio to gold significantly improves the consistency of portfolio performance during stable and unstable financial periods.

Gold was a very profitable portfolio diversifier in the 1970s when its price soared exponentially from $35 an ounce (the official price in 1970 when central banks stopped controlling its price) to a peak of $850 an ounce in 1980. (See Figure 10-1.) The monetary disorder of that period, when business and household credit expanded at average annual rates of more than 11 percent from 1970 to 1980, included inflation rates of over 12 percent in 1974 and again in 1979–1980. Investment demand for gold was strong, as investors partially diversified their portfolios into this asset class as a "store of value and wealth" to reduce risk and unjust impoverishment from negative real short-term interest rates of around 5 percent. (See Figure 10-2.)

Subsequently, gold's performance was poor as monetary order was restored, as its price corrected its great bull market of the 1970s, as the economy and traditional and speculative stocks soared, and as some central banks reduced their holdings of gold.

Gold regained its position in 2002 as an important and accepted risk-reduction asset class and safe haven during times of uncertainty and concern. From its cyclical low of $255 an ounce in April 2001, the price of gold rose to a high of $384 an ounce on February 5, 2003, up 50 percent from its low. Technically, its price broke out of a five and one-half year trading "bottom" on the upside in December 2002

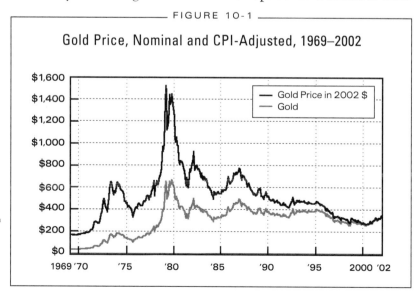

FIGURE 10-1

Gold Price, Nominal and CPI-Adjusted, 1969–2002

Source: Bloomberg L.P.

when it burst through $330 an ounce. It may have resumed its historic long-term uptrend and begun a new cyclical uptrend. Its price is well below its 1980 high of $850 an ounce, suggesting the possibility of attractive potential gains.

The rise in the price of gold was due in large part to increased investment demand and lower supply. Dollar and global weaknesses; doubts about the strength and profitability of a U.S. recovery; pervasive corporate governance, accounting, and auditing scandals; and continued strife in the Middle East reduced confidence in and prices of traditional stocks. Gold Fields Mineral Services Ltd. reported that world gold investment demand more than doubled during 2002 over 2001. In particular, Japanese investment demand was strong due to fears of banking and economic instability and "zero" interest rates. Falling jewelry demand due to the fragile global economy was more than offset by rising investment demand. Gold supply was reduced by mine deliveries into outstanding forward-sold positions rather than into the market.

Heightened uncertainty and risks in North Korea, in India-Pakistan, and in the Middle East and fear over global security could increase gold's safe-haven appeal. Furthermore, a war in Iraq could result in reducing the supply of oil to the Western world. Energy rationing could magnify the depth of a double-dip recession.

Gold Supply

THE SUPPLY OF GOLD to the fabrication and investment markets, which rose to peaks in 2000 and 2001, began to decline in 2002. Gold Fields Mineral Services Ltd. reported that supply of 3,665 metric tons in 2001 fell 4 percent in 2002. The supply of newly mined gold, which had more than doubled from the early 1980s, is expected to decline slowly in the near future. (See Figure 10-3.)

Due to relatively low gold prices, gold mining exploration expenditures have declined sharply since 1997. Ore reserves have not been replenished at the same rate that they have been depleted. The industry eventually may need much higher prices to finance the cost of finding new ore reserves that are necessary in the long run to replace the existing low-cost reserves. It may take approximately eight years to bring new mines into production.

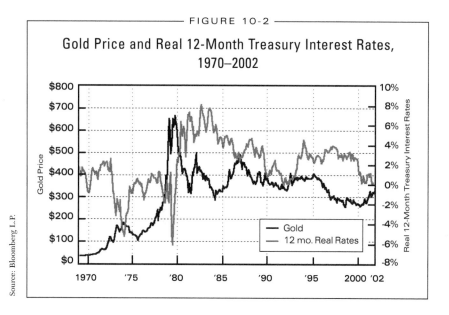

FIGURE 10-2

Gold Price and Real 12-Month Treasury Interest Rates, 1970–2002

Source: Bloomberg L.P.

The principal reason for a lower supply in 2002 was a reduction in the amount of net producer hedge books. A more benign sentiment in the gold market and the reduction in interest, gold leasing, and contango rates made forward sales unprofitable for the gold mines. When gold prices were declining or stable, it became profitable for gold bullion banks and speculators to borrow gold from central banks, which wished to obtain a return on their gold reserves, at very low gold leasing rates, sell the gold on the market, invest the proceeds at the higher prevailing Libor interest rates, and buy the gold forward from the mines at higher contango prices. The mines obtained higher future prices, but in effect sold future output "short." Central banks, largely European, rapidly increased their loans (leases) of gold from an estimated 900 metric tons in 1990, to 2,100 tons in 1995, and to 4,700 tons in 1999. In 2001 and in 2002, there was an unwinding of net producer hedged positions. The net amount of the producer hedge book at the end of 2002 was estimated at about 2,700 tons. The natural delivery of mined gold into expiring forward contracts by the gold mines could create a solid support for the gold price.

During the nineteenth century, central banks slowly built up their gold reserves. By 1905, they held more gold than the private sector. The banks saw a gold reserve essentially as a guarantee of their note issue. In the 1990s, some banks began to reduce their reserves and to

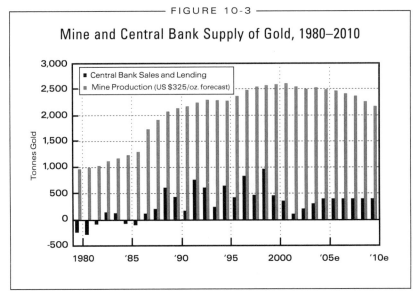

FIGURE 10-3

Mine and Central Bank Supply of Gold, 1980–2010

Source: Gold Fields Mineral Services, Beacon Group Advisors
(April 2002 Mine Supply Study), Van Eck Global

increase their gold loans with a depressing effect on the gold price. Gold as a percent of total central bank reserves declined from 44 percent in 1970 to 12.6 percent in July 2002. The September 1999 Central Bank Gold Agreement put limits on the signatory central bank gold transactions and contributed to stabilizing the market. (The Agreement stated, "Gold will remain an important element of monetary reserves.") The United Kingdom's program, announced in May 1999, of selling 395 metric tons to restructure its official reserves was completed in March 2002 at an average price of $275 an ounce. The Bank of Switzerland is currently the main central bank seller. No major change in the rate of net official sector sales is expected until the Agreement expires in September 2004.

Gold Demand

FABRICATION DEMAND was 82 percent of supply in 2002. Jewelry demand, in turn, made up 85 percent of fabrication demand. The remaining portion generally consists of demand for electronics, dentistry, medals, and imitation coins, as well as other industrial and decorative applications. This demand is elastic and varies with economic conditions.

Overall investment demand, only 4.4 percent of supply in 2001,

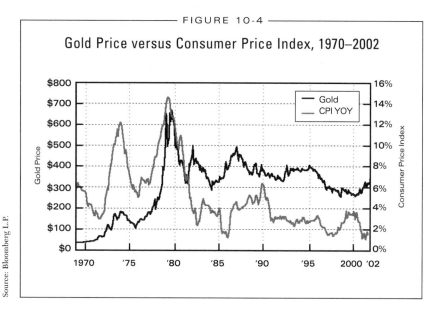

FIGURE 10-4

Gold Price versus Consumer Price Index, 1970–2002

Source: Bloomberg L.P.

more than doubled to 10.8 percent of supply in 2002 and is the main variable in the price of gold. Gold is a credit default risk-free and currency devaluation risk-free monetary asset. It is a "cash" supranational alternative asset, a global safe haven, and risk-averse investment. Its demand is inelastic and is closely related to confidence in economic conditions and in the quality of credit and currencies, especially the dollar. Its demand rises in times of fear and monetary disorder. In Europe and North America, gold has been used as a portfolio inflation hedge, especially since 1970. (See Figure 10-4.)

However, gold has historically been a deflation hedge as well as inflation hedge. During recessions, stocks have underperformed and financial defaults have increased. Investors then became more risk- and loss-averse and sought to preserve rather than grow wealth. Portfolios were reallocated toward cash and gold. The investment demand for gold rose with each widespread financial and business contraction. Historian Bob Hoye has stated that in the five previous major financial bubbles (1720, 1772, 1825, 1873, and 1929), the real price of gold climbed for three or four years on average after the bubbles burst. Following the last bubbles in London in 1873 and New York in 1929, gold's real price doubled in both cases. It rose at a progressive rate after each bubble burst.

Global private investment stocks of gold bars and coins are estimated to have doubled since 1950 to 22,000 metric tons, around 15 percent of total above-ground stocks of gold, and are currently valued at approximately $250 billion. In normal times, growth of investment demand has been concentrated in Asia and the Middle East, where gold investment has always played an important role in personal wealth accumulation. The October 2002 opening of the Shanghai Gold Exchange and the exemption of gold investment from the 17 percent value-added tax by the Chinese authorities could boost Chinese demand. Total aboveground stocks of gold are estimated at approximately 143,000 metric tons, currently valued at approximately $1.6 trillion. The stocks of jewelry have grown rapidly to 71,000 metric tons (51 percent of total stocks), and of other fabrication to 16,100 metric tons (11 percent of total stocks), while official stocks have declined to 30,000 metric tons (21 percent of total stocks).

Three Bullish Gold Price Scenarios

THERE ARE, OF COURSE, innumerable gold price scenarios. No one knows the future. The scenarios described below are based on the possibility that Keynesian policies are not sustainable forever and that a major correction will take place in the current business cycle.

Scenario #1: Deflation. The correction of the remaining microeconomic imbalances from the 1990s boom could continue. The dollar, economic, financial, and geopolitical risks listed above may become real and result in a longer recession and deflation in spite of low interest rates and growing Federal deficits. Real economic growth of less than potential trend capacity growth could mean rising excess capacity and downward pressure on prices, wages, and profitability. Consumers may save more and spend less of their incomes. The rate of unemployment may grow. Earnings disappointments and lower market valuations may weaken stock prices further. More defaults and a steepening of the yield curve may weaken long-term bond prices. The dollar could weaken further.

Investors may lose more confidence in traditional investments, become more risk-averse, and seek to protect their wealth. Under these conditions, they may diversify into stronger currencies, cash, and gold, an alternative safe-haven investment. In addition, there may well be a further reduction in the mines' net producer hedge positions. Accordingly, gold investment demand and prices may be expected to trend upwards.

Scenario #2: Stagflation. To prevent the correction of the remaining microeconomic imbalances from causing a deflationary spiral, the monetary authorities may keep interest rates very low. After the intended Fed funds rate was reduced to 1.25 percent in November 2002, the annual rate of increase for the adjusted monetary base was raised to 16.7 percent (mid-December 2002 to February 5, 2003) from approximately 7 percent for the prior twelve months. Political pressures may force the Federal government to increase its spending and deficits further to offset low aggregate private demand. State and local deficits are also expected to grow. The widening deficits run the risk of reducing net national savings, the driver of capital formation and growth. Private foreign capital may no longer flow to the United States although foreign central banks may support a falling dollar. These policies may delay but not avoid the excess capacity adjustment that may be necessary to revive profitability and to start a new business expansion. Government full employment policies could contribute to relatively high wage costs, which could put pressure on profit margins and capital expenditures. Consumer spending could be weak. Macroeconomic monetary and fiscal policies may not be strong enough to offset microeconomic deflationary policies. The consequence may be a prolonged period of uncertainty and economic stagnation.

The anticreditor bias of monetary policy in the United States has reached the stage where short-term investments again have discriminatingly low and even punitive negative real yields. (See Figure 10-2.) For instance, 3-month Treasury bills yield 1.2 percent and 2-year notes yield 1.5 percent (February 18, 2003). The Labor Department's CPI year-to-year increase for December 2002 was 2.4 percent. The Federal Reserve Bank of Cleveland's twelve-month median consumer price index in December rose 3.1 percent. Core CPI services prices have risen at an annualized rate of about 4 percent. Investors who put their savings in T-Bills or savings deposits are being impoverished. Trillions of dollar's worth of retirement savings are subject to the risk of deteriorating purchasing power. As long as the public believes that low and even negative real yields are a short-term condition and that consumer prices may fall, expansionary monetary and fiscal policies may be continued.

Under these circumstances, investors could become more defensive. Also, as the Fed may continue to maintain negative real short-term yields to stimulate the economy, investors may increasingly turn to gold investments for a real positive return as the probability of rising gold prices outweighed the disadvantages of gold's volatility. Gold diversification may again become an accepted and prudent risk-management policy and have a place in diversified portfolios. Investors could again adopt a policy of allocating 5 to 15 percent of their portfolios to gold-oriented assets, as some Swiss banks recommended from the 1960s to the mid-1980s. The ensuing investment demand may well be substantial and positive for the gold market.

Scenario #3: Accelerating Inflation (Currency Debasement). A long-lasting overly expansionary monetary policy could eventually result in an accelerating and onerous inflation. The needed pain of raising short-term interest rates and slowing monetary growth may be delayed due to the fear of spoiling a fragile economic recovery and of incurring an even greater recession. The larger and the longer the government debt grows, the greater the probability that it may eventually prove to be too burdensome. Total outstanding U.S. debt has grown 4.6 fold from $4.4 trillion (135 percent of GDP) in 1981 to $20.3 trillion (193 percent of GDP) by the end of September 2002. In addition, the net present value of unfunded government obligations for healthcare and retirement is approximately $20 trillion. Some of the world's leading monetary authorities have already adopted an official policy of gradually "inflating" the debt away by targeting approximately 2 percent rates of inflation. As the debt becomes more burdensome, policymakers may attempt to raise the rate of inflation further to reduce the rising cost of servicing it, historically the favorite way for governments to rescind old debt.

If creditors and investors become convinced that low or negative real interest rates and resulting impoverishment may continue forever, and doubt the Fed's commitment to price stability, confidence in economic policies, in financial assets, and in the dollar may be shaken. They may seek to preserve wealth by investing in tangible real assets and by further diversifying into gold. The ratio of the Dow Jones Industrial Average to the price of gold, which rose from a low of 1 in 1980 to a peak of 44 in 1999 and is now in a downward trend, may once again return to a ratio of 1. This ratio shows gold's relative per-

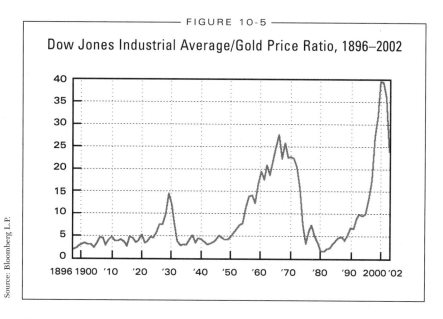

FIGURE 10-5

Dow Jones Industrial Average/Gold Price Ratio, 1896–2002

Source: Bloomberg L.P.

formance in past periods of monetary disorder—the deflation of the 1930s and the inflation of the 1970s. (See Figure 10-5.)

The dollar and gold today are the world's primary safe-haven investments. If confidence in the dollar collapses, gold may become the world's last safe-haven investment. Its demand and price may soar exponentially. A currency reform to reestablish monetary confidence may then be necessary. It could be based on a return to the dollar's convertibility into gold, as provided in the U.S. Constitution and in the original Federal Reserve Act. Historically, after past periods of inflation and monetary disorder, such as with America's Continental currency in 1781, the French assignats in 1796, the German mark in 1923, and the U.S. Civil War greenbacks, the monetary authorities returned to a gold-backed currency. If and when this occurs again, the price of gold would be federally fixed in terms of a defined weight of the metal. As a result, such convertibility would end gold's bull market. The stage would then be set for a new central bank credit expansion. On the other hand, hopefully for creditors and others in the future, sustainable full employment, labor compensation and interest rate levels, and profits and economic growth will be sought by a return to real price stability and neoclassical free market policies. "In God We Trust."

Chapter Eleven

Gold's Precious Secret: It's Money

JAMES TURK
Founder, GoldMoney

SCHOOLBOOK ACCOUNTS HAVE it that President Nixon demonetized gold more than thirty years ago, in 1971. With the stroke of his pen, he took the dollar off the gold standard and hundreds of years of gold's history as money came to an end. Or did it? Here's some food for thought that challenges conventional wisdom but will nevertheless prove useful as you evaluate your investment portfolio.

The dollar price of crude oil has been rising for decades, as Figure 11-1 shows. Beginning at $1.17 in December 1945, the upward trend in price—illustrated by the arrow in the chart—has been rising consistently for fifty-eight years, notwithstanding some recurring price fluctuations both up and down on either side of the arrow.

In contrast, Figure 11-2 presents a very different picture. Again, there have been price fluctuations around the arrow, which are the result of routine supply-demand changes. But the arrow illustrating the trend in price is moving sideways. This chart shows that the price of crude oil today is not out of line with past experience, provided it is measured in terms so-called of goldgrams—an online currency that is one gram of gold. By presenting its goldgram price, we can see that crude oil today costs not much more than it did in the 1950s, and in recent years it frequently cost a lot less.

These two charts are surprisingly different. Why has the price of the same commodity taken two separate paths so unexpectedly

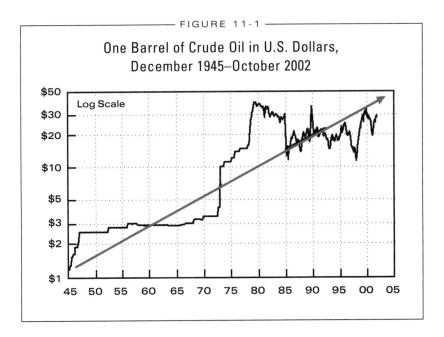

FIGURE 11-1

One Barrel of Crude Oil in U.S. Dollars,
December 1945–October 2002

divergent? Clearly, the answer lies in the money used to calculate crude oil's price.

We can see that the price fluctuates in both charts, rising above and falling below the arrow in each. After all, nothing in our world is static, and we clearly see in these charts an example of that reality. Supply and demand changes cause prices to fluctuate, which over time self-adjust. As the price rises, demand declines, and supply tends to increase. These factors together limit the price rise, and then a new cycle begins. In this new cycle, prices fall until they become too cheap. At that point, supply becomes limited because oil producers cannot make money at the new low price, so they cut back their production. At the same time, demand tends to be very strong as people take advantage of the low price. They buy and use more, perhaps consuming crude oil as a substitute for more expensive energy. Consequently, in both charts the price repeatedly rises above the arrow and then falls below the arrow, only to again in time repeat this cycle.

This interaction between supply and demand is basic economics, but this fundamental principle is distorted and therefore difficult to assess over long periods of time because the dollar and other national currencies do not provide an accurate, consistent measure of purchasing power. In other words, because the dollar is being inflated,

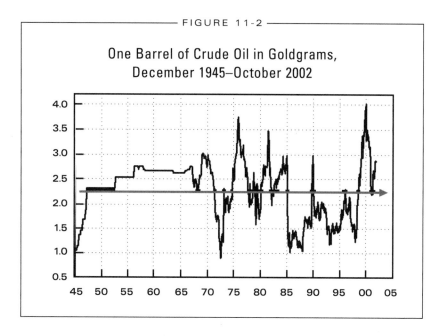

FIGURE 11-2

One Barrel of Crude Oil in Goldgrams,
December 1945–October 2002

the arrow denoting the crude oil price trend in Figure 11-1 is rising. But goldgrams are not being inflated, so the arrow in the second chart points sideways.

Dollars Lose Purchasing Power to Inflation, Gold Does Not

THE DIRECTION OF the arrow in each chart illustrates the outcome of money; namely, that dollars lose purchasing power from inflation and goldgrams do not. National currencies in this regard come up short when compared to the goldgram, which is gold's precious secret. Gold is still a useful tool to determine the price of any good or service. In other words, it is money.

At times crude oil was very cheap when it cost only about one goldgram (gg) per barrel. In December 2000 crude oil was very expensive when it cost about 3.989gg per barrel, which was well above the 2.255gg per barrel average price during these fifty-six years. But these price fluctuations occurred as a result of changing supply and demand, not because of factors that can be traced back to the actions of national monetary authorities.

In contrast to the dollar, gold is not being debased by inflation, which is the reason the above two charts are so very different. It's not that crude oil is becoming dearer and therefore more expensive, because we can see that its goldgram price is in fact fairly consistent over these past fifty-two years. Rather, the price of crude oil is rising in dollar terms only because the dollar is losing purchasing power— the dollar is being debased.

The purchasing power of gold cannot be diminished by the inflationary woes that plague the dollar and other national currencies for one simple reason. Dollars, euros, pounds, and all the other currencies are created by bookkeeping entries, which can be generated at will and with essentially no cost, but gold cannot be created this way. It is a tangible asset produced by mining, a process that is arduous and sometimes even dangerous. Mining is also the result of sober study and many months—some times even many years—of advance planning and research to determine the economic viability of a mine. The decision to build a mine to produce gold is purposeful and thoughtful. So the production of gold contrasts markedly to the way national currencies are created. Further, the management of currencies is often buffeted by political expediency that undermines the soundness of the currency, but gold is not impeded in this way. Gold is a result of the free-market process, not political actions.

So the conventional wisdom that gold has been demonetized is— like many conventional "wisdoms"—incorrect, because gold is still useful in economic calculation. Gold is money, so it can therefore be used effectively to gauge prices, and not just crude oil and other tangible assets. goldgrams can be used to measure financial assets as well.

Gold as a Means to Measure Wealth

FIGURE 11-3 PRESENTS the Dow Jones Industrial Average in dollars and goldgrams, based on 100 in January 1945. The annual rate of return in dollars has been 7.2 percent, compared to only 3.2 percent in goldgrams. The marked difference is again explained by the loss of purchasing power of the dollar from inflation.

The price of crude oil or any asset can be measured in terms of gold in order to provide a perspective on what is happening to a currency's purchasing power. But this insight is not new. Consider this

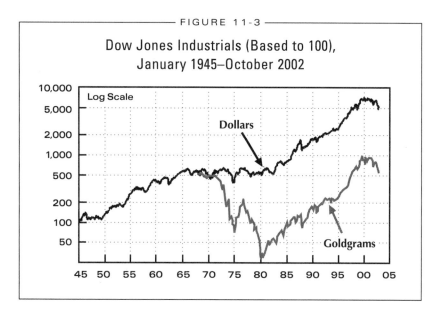

FIGURE 11-3

Dow Jones Industrials (Based to 100),
January 1945–October 2002

quote from *An Enquiry into the Paper Credit of Great Britain,* a won-
derful book penned in 1802 by Henry Thornton, an economist and
governor of the Bank of England: "We assume that the currency
which is in all our hands is fixed, and that the price of bullion moves;
whereas in truth, it is the currency of each nation that moves, and it
is bullion which is the more fixed."

By "fixed" in the vernacular of 200 years ago, Thornton means
having a stable purchasing power. And his use of the word "moves"
means the opposite, to lose purchasing power. He used "moves" back
then to describe what we today call inflation.

Thornton provides some valuable insight. The price of goods or
services cannot be adequately expressed in terms of a national currency only. In other words, by thinking only in terms of dollars and
not gold, we place upon ourselves a severe limitation in the understanding and measuring of purchasing power and therefore our
wealth. So just as the business person who speaks several languages
has a competitive edge, the international investor who performs economic calculation in several monies also has an edge. This foresighted
and adaptable investor who is comfortable in using multicurrencies to
gauge performance achieves a different perspective on what is happening to his wealth.

For example, let's assume that in one year your portfolio gains 10 percent, which by any measure is a healthy rate of return. However, if you calculate that gain in terms of dollars, and the dollar during that same year lost 10 percent of its exchange value to the euro, did your wealth really increase by 10 percent? And what if the euro in that same year lost 5 percent of its value compared to the goldgram? Clearly, your 10 percent nominal gain in dollars is illusory.

In short, money is important to your financial health. We therefore need to take care in understanding and determining what is happening to the purchasing power of different currencies. As the world economy becomes more global, and as the players within it gain greater choice to participate and invest in cross-border opportunities, it is becoming less wise to take a one-dimensional view of one's portfolio. Assets should be measured in terms of goldgrams as well as one or more national currencies in order to address the reality so clearly explained by Thornton—that national currencies "move."

We are today wrestling with some of the monetary problems that Britain faced in the early 1800s. The pound was losing purchasing power year after year. And gold in any form had disappeared from circulation within Britain because it was worth more than the depreciated British currency, which was nominally defined as a weight of gold. So the great minds of that day set out to answer a basic question: Why was the pound buying less and less?

Henry Thornton came up with the answer that still rings true today. It is "the currency of each nation" that loses purchasing power. These changes in a national currency distort prices and therefore make all types of economic calculation—including investment decisions—more difficult.

Fortunately, there is a remedy. Gold is an aid to investors. Its use in economic calculation provides a time-tested and proven way to measure wealth, an important task in a world becoming increasingly complex.

In recent years, gold has largely fallen out of favor in the Western world. Although it is still acquired, held, and used for money throughout Asia, North Americans and Europeans have generally shied away from gold. Because the goldgram's rate of exchange to the dollar and other national currencies has been subdued, gold has not attracted the attention it would have done if its price were rising. Many view this result to mean that they do not need gold.

It would be comforting to think that the price of gold is still doing its time-proven job of straightforwardly communicating purchasing power and that its current lackluster price is signaling that there is minimal inflationary threat. However, while that interpretation may be comforting, it doesn't jibe with some important facts. For example, the uptrend in the Employment Cost Index (ECI)—which many experts consider to be one of the economic reports most closely watched at the Federal Reserve—is well established. Although the quarterly rises in the ECI have recently slowed along with the economy, it remains in the uptrend that actually began in the mid-1990s.

Another concern is rising commodity prices. Crude oil prices, though down from their recent peak, are up substantially from two years ago. The Commodity Research Bureau (CRB) Index in early 2003 was up 25 percent from its February 1999 low, even though it had backed off from a three-year high. Because this index of seventeen different commodities is broad-based, the run-up in the CRB cannot easily be blamed on bad weather, poor crops, or a jump in energy prices. The consistent rise in this index for more than three years can mean only one thing—the dollar is being inflated.

Sure enough, a quick glance at monetary and credit indicators shows rapid expansion. Bank credit in 2002 grew at an 8.0 percent annualized rate, and M3 (a Federal Reserve calculation of the quantity of dollars in circulation) growth remained brisk into 2003, even though it had been cooling off from the prior year's torrid pace that produced some double-digit annualized growth rates. Both of these measures show that the quantity of dollars was growing more rapidly than economic activity, a sure sign that the dollar is being debased.

So it is understandable that there is concern about rising inflationary pressures. But why has there been so little response from gold? Is inflation a threat, or isn't it?

When it comes to markets, no indicator is infallible. Consider also that gold itself can become overvalued—as it obviously was at its $850 per ounce peak in 1980—or undervalued—like the $35 price prevailing in the late 1960s or even the $100 low it touched in 1976. But the *price* of gold is not the same thing as the *value* of gold. Consequently, it is incorrect to look at the price of gold without also considering whether it is relatively cheap or expensive in dollar terms. Adjustments to the dollar price of gold are needed to establish a consistent measure that transcends time. So it is not the "price" of gold that is a good inflation measure. It is the "real price" of gold that is useful in determining whether the dollar is being inflated.

The Real Price of Gold

FIGURE 11-4 PRESENTS the real price of gold, as determined by the Consumer Price Index. There are two different starting points. The dollar/gold exchange rate was $20.67 per ounce in December 1933, and then $35 in January 1934 after the 69 percent devaluation of the dollar by President Roosevelt. The goldgram rate is presented on the right side of the chart. Given the flow of gold out of the Federal Reserve before the devaluation and the reversal of this flow after the devaluation, it is clear that gold was undervalued at $20.67 and over-valued at $35.

Adjusting with the CPI, in 2003 it took $480 to purchase what one ounce of gold bought in 1934 or $283 to purchase what one ounce bought in 1933. Which of these two measures of the real price of gold is more useful? I recommend using both of them.

Referring again to Figure 11-4, it is obvious that when gold falls to or below the bottom line of the channel, gold is a very good value, even undervalued. When gold rises to or above the upper line, it is becoming overvalued. Right now this chart is saying that gold is a good value and should therefore be accumulated. But what does this chart say about inflation?

The current price of gold can be misleading. Look at where the price of gold should be as determined by the CPI. Just as $20.67 was too cheap and unsustainable in the early 1930s, so too is the gold price unsustainable at a $283 CPI-adjusted price. But if $480 seems high to you, then a mid-range price of $381 is arguably a reasonable measure of inflation-adjusted purchasing power. The fact that gold in early 2003 had been below this $381 price for several years is only an indication that gold has been out of favor and/or other factors have been affecting its price—it is not a signal that inflation is under control.

One can use this insight to add new perspective to the once-popular axiom that investors should put 5 percent to 10 percent of their portfolio in gold. The reason for this policy was clear in Thornton's day, but less so after 1971. Since the time Nixon's pen weighed in

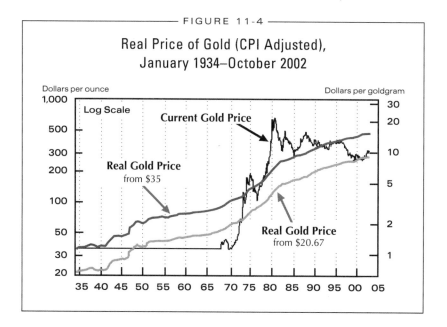

FIGURE 11-4

**Real Price of Gold (CPI Adjusted),
January 1934–October 2002**

heavily, various reasons to meet this gold percentage hurdle have been offered. They range from gold is an investment at one end of the spectrum, to gold provides disaster insurance at the other, but these attempts to explain gold's usefulness have muddied the water. The real reason is much simpler.

Gold should be held in a portfolio because it is money. In other words, a well-balanced portfolio consists of stocks, bonds, and cash, and gold fits precisely into this last category. Because it is money, gold is part of the cash component of your portfolio. When gold is at the bottom trend channel, 10 percent of your portfolio should be in gold-grams. When gold is at the top trend channel, these overvalued gold-grams should be exchanged for undervalued assets to reduce your gold component to 5 percent of your portfolio.

The conclusion is clear. By accurately measuring purchasing power over long periods of time, goldgrams can make economic calculation more useful and insightful. Gold is money, but it seems logical to go even further than that. This analysis shows that gold is much better money than the dollar.

For hundreds of years, gold had always been the center of international commerce. That role changed not too long ago. In the 1944 Bretton Woods Agreement, the dollar and not gold was made the center of global commerce, but placing the dollar at center stage happened only because the dollar was tied to gold. Had the dollar not been so closely identified with gold—"as good as gold" was the saying used back then—the dollar would never have ascended to that important role.

Because the dollar stayed linked to gold until 1971, the present monetary regime is only some thirty years old. It is not much of a track record compared to gold's long history. And given that big rise in the dollar price of crude oil so clearly seen in Figure 11-1, it is clear that even in this very short history as the currency of global commerce, the dollar has failed to match the quality of gold to handily convey an accurate measure of purchasing power.

It is generally accepted that two factors needed for successful investing are to keep better informed and to stay ahead of the crowd. In this context, one last point about gold needs mention. People over the years have lost sight of gold's usefulness in economic calculation because gold stopped circulating as currency. But perhaps not for much longer. We are witnessing a profound revolution in technology and global communications. These advancements make it possible to overcome those factors that have impeded gold's ability to circulate as currency in years gone by. Gold remains useful in economic calculation. And now technology is again making gold useful as currency, which is gold's other precious secret.

Chapter Twelve

Small-Cap Stocks in an All-Weather Portfolio

J A M E S   D .   A W A D

Chairman, Awad Asset Management

S MALL-CAP STOCKS, those whose companies have a market capital-ization of $1.5 billion or less, tend to be more volatile than larger cap stocks. But because they don't get as much publicity and cover-age from the large brokerage houses as the large-cap stocks do, you can often find among them many diamonds in the rough.

Although many investors with a high tolerance for risk seek out small-cap growth stocks to exploit their volatility, small-cap value stocks have a place in any well-balanced portfolio. Awad Asset Management is on the conservative end of small-cap investing. Among our goals in managing money is, first and foremost, preserva-tion of capital. Second, we try to minimize volatility. We realize that our clients would rather be up 12 percent two years in a row rather than be up 70 percent one year and down 30 percent the next. Our third goal is to provide a real return over a market cycle that is a mul-tiple of risk-free returns (meaning the return provided by a one-year Treasury instrument). Goal number four is to beat the Russell 2000, the major index of small-cap stocks, while having built a portfolio that has less risk than a Russell Index fund.

They say the most important three things in real estate are loca-tion, location, and location. For us, the most important things are research, research, and research. We visit a half-dozen companies a week personally, either in the office or on the road. We try to identify companies that are going to show consistent earnings growth, that dominate their market or market niches, that have good balance sheets, and that generate excess cash flow. We also prefer companies whose management owns a lot of the company stock. We then try to buy these stocks at a P/E ratio materially lower than that of the Russell 2000 and below book value or strategic acquisition value.

Sell Discipline

KNOWING WHICH STOCKS to buy is only half the battle. Knowing when to sell them is just as important. There are two reasons we sell a stock. The happy reason is that we've made our money. Ideally we buy a stock that has very little Wall Street coverage. It may be covered by one or two regional brokers, then somebody like Merrill Lynch or Morgan Stanley picks it up and recommends it, and then Fidelity starts buying it. Pretty soon it goes up to a point where its P/E ratio is equal to that of the Russell 2000. That's where we start to sell. We finish selling when it gets to a 25 percent premium to the Russell. We're then handing it off to the growth momentum players.

The unhappy reason we sell a stock is that we've realized we were wrong about it. Our indication that we were wrong is a second disappointing quarter. Because we talk to the companies we invest in continually, we should not be negatively surprised by a quarter. If one quarter proves disappointing and the reason seems valid, we'll hold the stock. If there's any hint of a second disappointing quarter, however, we're going to sell the stock. That's telling us either that our analysis is wrong, that management is not telling the truth, or that management is not executing its stated strategy. We don't want to let a cancer grow. We'll sell the stock, then revisit it at a later date.

Our selling discipline tends to leave us with a portfolio of companies with above-average earnings growth, above-average consistency of earnings growth, and below-average metrics such as P/E ratios and price-to-acquisition-value ratios. We want enough concentration of winners so they count, but enough diversity so that our losers don't kill us. With the research staff we have and the amount of money we manage, we've averaged about thirty-five positions per portfolio. So we will own thirty-five stocks and probably be monitoring another thirty-five to forty at any given time.

The Economy and Small Cap

WHEN INVESTORS LIKE small caps they love them, and when they don't like them, they hate them. It's like an elephant getting in and out of a tub—small-cap mutual funds tend to experience large inflows of money when small cap is outperforming the S&P and large outflows of money when small cap is underperforming the S&P.

Large-cap stocks outperformed small-cap stocks from the end of 1993 through the end of the first quarter in 1999. During those six years money flooded into technology, communications, and Internet stocks. Small-cap stocks were not viewed as sexy enough, and were shunned for not providing enough action. Within the small-cap universe, those stocks that did best, ironically, were the companies that lost money. This was the period when people were infatuated with getting into Internet stocks. The saying during the dot-com boom was, "Get eyeballs, not earnings."

The four quarters ending March 1999 were particularly painful for small-cap stocks. The stocks of companies that lost money—large caps—did better than the stocks of companies that made money—small caps. The highest P/E stocks did the best, and the lowest P/E stocks did the worst. During that fourth quarter about 80 percent of small-cap stocks declined, and most by about 40 percent. Meanwhile, the Dow, Nasdaq, and S&P were all hitting new highs, driven by a small number of technology, communication, and Internet stocks. Not only was small cap underperforming, but small-cap value was the worst place to be.

From March 1999 through the end of 2002, however, the Russell 2000 outperformed the S&P by about 35 percent, so having some percentage of your portfolio in small caps certainly softened the blow.

After such a big market boom and then a devastating market bust, it's important to have realistic long-term expectations. Over the long term, you're entitled to only 10 to 12 percent a year investing in equities. If you start to shoot for more, you're going to be sorry. So have a realistic goal. Think long term.

Just as important, diversify your asset classes. In other words, have some large-cap growth, some large-cap value, some small-cap growth, and some small-cap value. Rebalance your portfolio annually, so the percentages remain the same. That's a very difficult thing to do, emotionally, because it means taking some money out of what's doing well and putting it into something that's not. As hard as that may be, that's exactly what you want to do to avoid a dramatic, negative shock, even though you may be sacrificing some short-term returns in the process.

Politics and Picks?

AT AWAD ASSET MANAGEMENT we are "bottom-up" stock pickers. We generally don't look at what's going on in the world and say, because of these headlines we must have X percent in energy, X percent in defense, and X percent in a cyclical sector. That's what the top-down manager would do. We'd rather build portfolios from the bottom up.

That said, no investor should operate in a vacuum. You must be aware of what's going on politically and economically to some degree, so you can gauge news trends' effects on the market and adjust your portfolio according to your personal tolerance for risk.

Here are two recent headline topics no investor could ignore:

➤ *9/11.* After 9/11 we've all realized that terrorism is a significant geopolitical risk that is going to have at least intermediate effects on our economy and maybe long-term effects. So monitor how the American versus radical Muslim conflict progresses and its effects on the U.S. economy and on the prospects for individual companies. One wants to own companies that control their own destinies in an uncertain geopolitical world.

➤ *Enron and Tyco.* In light of recent corporate governance scandals, investors are going to want to own companies whose business models and balance sheets they can understand, and which can grow organically, internally, rather than through acquisition and financial engineering. That trend is going to favor small-cap companies because those characteristics are more frequently found among them than among large-cap companies.

Are You a Bull or a Bear?

IN THE LONG term you have to be a bull if you live and work in America. History has been strewn with the economic corpses of those who've been too bearish on America for too long. We have the most powerful economy in the world, we have the most efficient corporations in the world, and we've got the most powerful military.

That said, you also must realize that there will be periods when the stock market overshoots itself, and you've got to be willing to take money out of the market when things are getting "too easy."

Similarly, you must be willing to put money back into the market when there's blood in the streets. In other words, have greed when others have fear, and always have fear when others have greed. You should become increasingly cautious when the game gets easy and increasingly optimistic when no one wants to play. If you can do that over the long term you'll get sound returns. Even though you may not be the hottest kid on the block in hot markets, over time you'll end up with steady returns.

What investors have just gone through since the late '90s in the markets is very similar to the bull/bear markets in the '60s and '70s. For those who lived through those tumultuous periods, the parallels were very apparent, enabling some to see the risk in the huge speculation that went on in the technology, communication, and Internet momentum phenomenon.

What's important is not to get too bullish or too bearish during any given period. To be an optimist when things aren't going well and to be humble and cautious when things are going well yields the steady, steady kind of performance, which, while not always glamorous, will get an investor to the goal line over the long term.

Companies in It for the Long Haul

THE MARKET IS currently in the "capitulation stage" as investors are, en masse, throwing the babies out with the bath water. If you buy the right stocks during this period and if you measure your investment results in terms of years, not months, you're going to end up making good money.

Currently, we are easily able to find small-cap stocks below book value, with no debt, with several dollars a share in cash, and with attractive long-term projected growth rates. They epitomize good value investments. By contrast, you don't want to buy some of the Nasdaq leaders of the last bull cycle that are down 70 to 80 percent just because they're down a lot. They never should have been as high as they were. Some of them are going to fall to zero. Some of them have valuation problems; some of them have business model problems.

The last time we went through this type of boom-bust cycle, it was 1972 and the "Nifty Fifty" were all the rage. Some of those stocks that crashed in 1972, like Merck, didn't see their 1972 prices again until 1982. Merck did turn out to be a growth company, but it took ten years to get back to its old peak. On the other hand, Polaroid sold at 149 in 1972. In 1979 it sold at 20 and kept falling. Last year it went bankrupt. So some of the old leaders are never coming back.

Here are several small-cap stocks Awad Asset Management likes for the long term:

➤ Barra (BARZ) is a company that helps institutions to minimize their trading risks and improve their ability to trade easily and in a more cost-effective way and to control risk management in portfolios; they are expanding their business overseas, and it is a 20 percent grower selling at an attractive valuation.

➤ John Wiley (JW), whose stock I've owned for twenty years, is a publisher of scientific, technical, and educational materials.

➤ In the financial area, the regional bank North Fork Bancorp (NFB) has an outstanding long-term growth record, is attractively priced, and has good long-term growth projections.

➤ In technology, Tech Data is a good long-term growth company selling below book value and at ten times earnings.

Chapter Thirteen

The Bright, the Brave, the Biotech

MARK MONANE, M.D., M.S.
Principal, Equity Research, Needham and Company

A
CCORDING TO THE *Bloomsbury Guide to Human Thought* (1993), biotechnology (Greek for "the science of the manipulation of life") is the application and exploitation of biological processes or organisms to man's own ends. The word itself may be a comparatively recent innovation, but the practice of biotechnology began some 10,000 years ago, with the first domestications of plants and animals as well as the start of agricultural systems. A more modern reference is often attributed to the ancient Sumerians, who, in 1750 B.C.E., used yeast cells to break down starch and sugars in order to make beer.

It wasn't until the twentieth century that the term "biotechnology" was coined. In 1919, Karl Ereky, a Hungarian engineer, used this term to describe all efforts to produce goods from raw materials with the aid of living organisms. Throughout the recent history of science, there have been significant milestones, like Gregor Mendel's pioneering work on plant genetics. A pivotal breakthrough for the industry came in 1953 when James Watson and Francis Crick discovered the self-replicating structure of DNA. The 1970s and 1980s put biotech on the map for good. In 1982, the Food and Drug Administration (FDA) approved the first biotech drug, Humulin® (genetically engineered insulin) for diabetes management.

More recently, we biotech analysts at Needham and Company

―――――――――――――――――― FIGURE 13-1 ――――――――

Performance of Major Indices for 2000–2002
Were Good, Bad, and Ugly

	2000	2001	2002	3-Year Total Loss
DJIA	-6%	-7%	-17%	-27%
SPX	-10%	-13%	-23%	-40%
NASDAQ	-39%	-21%	-32%	-67%
BTK	62%	-9%	-42%	-14%
DRG	28%	-15%	-22%	-15%

Source: Reuters BridgePartner and Needham & Company

characterize the years 2000, 2001, and 2002 of the biotechnology industry as "The Good, The Bad, and The Ugly," respectively. In 2000, biotechnology stocks, with a gain of 62 percent, significantly outperformed the broader market, whereas in 2001, biotechnology stocks ended in negative territory along with traditional stocks. Although 2002 was quite disappointing in terms of performance, we point out that, for a three-year total loss, biotech's 14 percent loss fared better than that of the broader market (see Figure 13-1).

Rapid scientific advances in a wide range of biomedical areas such as biochemistry, molecular biology, cell biology, immunology, genetics, high throughput screening, combinatorial chemistry, and information technology are transforming drug discovery and development, paving the way for unprecedented progress in developing new medicines to ameliorate the effects of disease. The new biotechnology may make it possible to (1) manage and cure more diseases than is possible with current traditional therapies, (2) develop more targeted and effective new medicines with fewer side effects, and (3) anticipate and prevent disease rather than just simply react to existing disease symptoms.

Could biotechnology be the next revolution, like the miniaturization and mainstreaming of the computer, the invention of the printing press, and the availability of ice, salt, and other staples of today? The most successful segment of biotechnology today is the development of therapies in a wide variety of forms and functions to improve health and save lives. A recent survey by PhRMA noted that there are 371 biotechnology medicines in development by 144 companies for nearly 200 diseases. These potential medicines, all of which are either

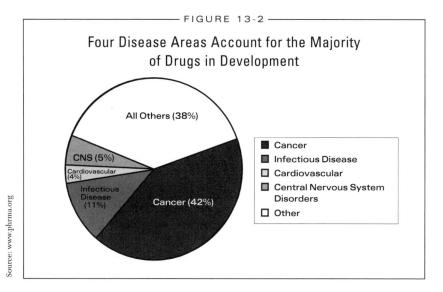

FIGURE 13-2

Four Disease Areas Account for the Majority of Drugs in Development

All Others (38%)

CNS (5%)

Cardiovascular (4%)

Infectious Disease (11%)

Cancer (42%)

- Cancer
- Infectious Disease
- Cardiovascular
- Central Nervous System Disorders
- Other

Source: www.phrma.org

in human clinical trials or under review by the FDA, may build on the list of 95 biotechnology medicines already approved and available to patients. The vast majority is geared toward the management of chronic diseases such as cardiovascular disorders and cancer, as well as acute illnesses such as infectious diseases (see Figure 13-2).

Driving Forces Affecting Biotechnology Stocks

WE BELIEVE THAT biotechnology represents a pivotal holding for a growth strategy portfolio. As mentioned above, the biotechnology pipeline appears rich, with more than 100 medications and vaccines currently in the market, greater than 300 molecules in late-phase testing, and almost 1,000 products in preclinical and clinical testing. According to the PhRMA organization, biotechnology-derived medications are expected to increase to more than 15 percent of all medications by the year 2005, targeting the biggest diseases in terms of prevalence and human suffering.

In our opinion, in the coming years the most compelling opportunities for the $1.2 trillion health care market as a whole, and biotechnology in particular, relate to the management of chronic diseases. The demographics behind these opportunities are staggering, the commercial opportunity is huge, and biotechnology's answers to those human dilemmas are emerging rapidly.

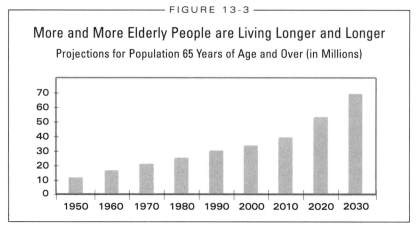

FIGURE 13-3

More and More Elderly People are Living Longer and Longer

Projections for Population 65 Years of Age and Over (in Millions)

Source: CDC, 1999.

Figure 13-3 exhibits how the elderly portion of the population is expected to increase over time. In 1920, life expectancy at birth was fifty-four years. By 1965, life expectancy had increased to seventy years. The average American born today can expect to live more than seventy-six years, and life expectancy has risen dramatically for all age groups. Every five years since 1965, roughly one additional year has been added to life expectancy at birth.

As the baby boom population of the United States ages, the number of people potentially at risk for chronic diseases will increase

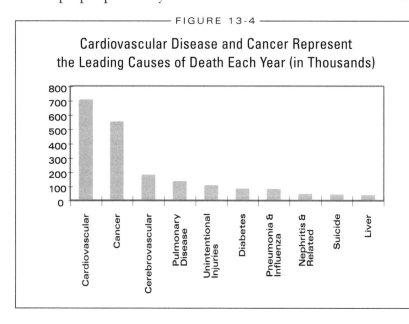

FIGURE 13-4

Cardiovascular Disease and Cancer Represent the Leading Causes of Death Each Year (in Thousands)

Source: National Vital Statistics System, United States, 2000.

dramatically. For example, about 70 percent of Americans over 65—or about 24 million people—now suffer from cardiovascular disease. Demographic trends indicate that this number could exceed 50 million by 2050. Cancer, a term for various diseases in which abnormal cells divide without control, is a disease correlated with advancing age, with 50 percent of those affected over the age of 50 and 75 percent of those affected over 75. Thus, we expect the prevalence of cancer, the number-two cause of death in the United States (see Figure 13-4), to increase with the aging of the baby boomers.

Four Major Areas of Drug Development

JUST FOUR AREAS—cancer, infectious disease, central nervous system disorders, and cardiovascular medicine—make up the focus of more than 60 percent of all drugs under development (see Figure 13-2). Drug spending in the United States is also concentrated in these large areas of unmet needs. As the bank robber Willie Sutton said about banks, drug companies focus on these areas because that's "where the money is."

The market for cancer therapies is currently a $15 billion opportunity, although this figure underestimates the total market potential because there is a large unmet need in the management of this disease. Cancer currently affects 1.2 million new patients each year, with 75 percent of those affected over the age of 55. Cancer is the second leading cause of death, second only to cardiovascular disease. In 2002, the American Cancer Society estimated that 555,500 people would die of cancer in the United States, at a rate of more than 1,500 deaths per day. To date, there remains a large unmet need in the management of this disorder, because treatments for many cancer types offer patients only marginal or no survival benefit. The number of cancer cases will continue to grow, spurred by the aging population. By 2009, this patient group could total 8.4 million. In 1997, about 6.3 million people worldwide died from some form of cancer, and most major international cancer agencies expect this number to double by 2022.

Anti-infectives (antibiotics, antifungals, and antivirals) represent the third-largest pharmaceutical market, with worldwide sales of approximately $25 billion in 2001. According to the Centers for Disease Control and Prevention (CDC), anti-infectives are the second most frequently prescribed class of drugs, and infectious disease accounts for 25 percent of all visits to physicians each year. Since pathogens become resistant over time to the drugs they encounter, the necessity to develop new classes of anti-infectives is a self-renewing process. From the pharmaceutical development standpoint, we think that anti-infectives are an attractive market because of the following facts:

> This therapeutic area is in need of new, improved therapies, due primarily to increasing resistance.

> There is a large market potential for products with differentiating characteristics.

> Anti-infectives have clearly defined clinical study endpoints.

> These drugs have relatively short clinical development timelines (five years for anti-infectives versus seven years for cancer therapeutics).

> This drug class has a low development risk profile (*in vitro* and preliminary animal data are highly suggestive of clinical outcome).

About 70 percent of Americans over 65—or about 24 million people—now suffer from cardiovascular disease. Demographic trends indicate that this number could exceed 50 million by 2050. Direct and indirect costs for the management of cardiovascular disorders in the United States were estimated at $329 billion in 2002, according to the American Heart Association. While drug spending accounts for only 10 percent of this figure, medication use is integrally tied not only to the prevention and treatment of overall cardiovascular morbidity and mortality, but also to downstream spending on interventions such as procedures and hospitalization. For this reason, we expect the therapeutics area for cardiovascular medication will be growing at a rate closer to 25 to 33 percent per year over the next three to five years. This fact underscores the role of medication as paramount therapy for the overall management of these disorders.

Diseases of the central nervous system include a wide variety of disorders affecting persons of all ages. Affective disorders such as depression are present in as many as one in four Americans, and while drug therapy is available, most patients remain undertreated. Chronic neurological diseases such as multiple sclerosis affect 350,000 to 500,000 Americans, and Parkinson's disease inflicts 1.5 million Americans, mostly over the age of 60. New therapies in this area focus on maximizing benefit and also decreasing the side effect profile associated with medications currently in use. Geriatric syndromes such as Alzheimer's dementia have increasing prevalence with advancing age, and currently there are 4 million people in the United States with this diagnosis; therapy to date has provided only mild success, mostly in controlling symptoms of the disease. Drug spending for CNS disorders is number two among all categories, with approximately $25–30 billion per year in the United States alone. Given the increasing prevalence of older patients as well as the need for more cost-effective and better-tolerated drugs, we expect this area of therapeutics to be a major area of growth and development within the biotechnology sector.

Principles of Stock Selection in Biotechnology

IT IS IMPORTANT to take a systematic approach when evaluating a biotech company. In general, we believe that an investor should look for at least one drug in a Phase 3 clinical trial, several other drugs in early Phases 1 and 2, and other products in preclinical testing. The company should also have well-thought-out plans for partnerships and for the marketing of these new drugs, as well as a defined timeline for expected revenues and cash flows. Despite the gloomy fact that 2002 was the worst year in recent memory for the industry, the biotechnology fundamentals still remain intact. In fact, biotech companies have the healthiest pipelines ever. The key factors of good biotechnology investments are outlined below.

Profitable Biotechnology Companies

Based on Thomson First Call estimates, in the twelve months through the first quarter of 2004, we expect earnings of top-tier profitable biotechnology companies to grow 27 percent versus 8 percent for pharmaceutical companies and 11 percent for S&P 500 companies. Although biotech stocks appear to be overvalued on a price to 2003's estimated earnings basis (29x for biotech versus 18x for pharmaceuticals and 18x for the S&P), it is our view that given their higher growth rates than those of traditional companies, biotech stocks merit some valuation premium. Moreover, we point out that on a P/E to growth (PEG) basis, biotech stocks are trading at 11 percent and 37 percent discounts compared to pharmaceutical companies and S&P 500 companies, respectively. The PEG for biotechnology now stands at 1 for

2004 estimated earnings, suggesting an attractive value opportunity versus previous years. Going further, there is a potential for 100 profitable biotech companies by 2006. Even if 25 percent, that is, 25 companies, are indeed profitable, the number of profitable companies will double from the current situation.

Yet-to-Be Profitable (Developmental Stage) Biotech Companies

We believe that there are a number of good, solid companies that have experienced significant stock value depreciation mostly because of market conditions or sector scares, rather than because of shaky fundamentals. For this reason, we recommend investors to look to yet-to-be-profitable companies with strong fundamentals, including:

➤ *Promising late-stage products, which are likely to drive companies to profitability within the next three years.* Three major drivers of value are innovation, innovation, and innovation. Pricing power has been eliminated given the advent of generics and strong competition in several overcrowded drug classes. Biotechnology specializes in creating value through innovation, with different dosing options as well as novel targets. The big pharmaceutical companies are looking for new and innovative products for further top-line and bottom-line growth, thus creating the environment for future biotechnology and drug company partnerships. Approximately 50 percent of all new drugs approved in recent years come from biotechnology companies, a large achievement considering the maturity of the industry as well as the smaller market capitalization versus the big drug companies.

Products (e.g., drugs, vaccines) over platform technology (e.g., genomic sequencing) are preferable today. The Internet of health care—the genomic companies—has peaked. On the rise are companies with an eye toward product development and commercialization. In addition, not just any product will do. There has been an increasing shift toward safety over efficacy. The old paradigm of efficacy at a high price—that is, with numerous or serious side effects—is no longer in favor as physicians, patients, and insurance companies want safe drugs.

➤ *Multiple near-term events, to provide "news flow" and potentially lead to share price appreciation.* In biotechnology, the calendar of scientific presentations is the equivalent of earnings season, a regular check-up on progress. Stocks in the biotechnology sector are driven by (1) the speed of the clinical trial testing, (2) the success or failure of their therapies in clinical trials, and (3) the role of these new therapies versus existing therapies for the same disease process.

➤ *Strong management teams, with experience in biotech as well as in big pharmaceutical company management, academia, and finance.* Big pharmaceutical companies have amassed large research and development teams to adequately address a given issue. Their management teams are robust and full of well-educated and informed decision makers. Given the relative lack of development of the biotech sector as a whole, such decision makers are not necessarily present. Furthermore, biotech companies do not have the budgets for large management teams, and the fates of many companies rest in the hands of a few decision makers. A good management team will include members with experience in biotech as well as at big pharma companies, especially in the areas of drug development and marketing. Academic experience is desirable, yet there is an underlying trap that separates a company with a glorified and expensive research department from a company devoted to drug development. While Fidelity is correct in its statement, "past performance is not a predictor of future success," the successful biotechnology companies of today feature one or more members of management teams that have been in successful biotech or big drug companies in the past.

➤ *Stable financial underpinnings, which may help the company stay liquid in a difficult financing environment.* Resource use is essential, as biotechnology companies live and die by the motto, "cash is king." These companies are not well capitalized compared to big drug companies. Generally, we favor companies that have two years of cash on their balance sheets, given the expected "operating burn" associated with biotech development. In the absence of two years' cash, if the company's near-term outlook is positive, and investors believe news will be positive for the company and the stock, then buying "ahead of news" is important: Companies with recent good news are in a position of strength to engage in further partnering or financing opportunities.

➤ *A strong pipeline, with multiple products under development.* While one-hit wonders do occur, we believe that the better chance of success favors those companies that leverage products with multiple indications (in other words, applications) and have several products in development. For example, the cancer drug Rituxan® was developed for the lymphoma market but is now being tested for a variety of cancers. We favor those companies with a sound clinical and mechanistic rationale to develop a given drug for a variety of related conditions. This "multiple-shots-on-goal" approach increases the odds of developmental success.

> *Solid clinical trial design, with a reasonable means to an end.* Clinical trial design is a subtle but equally important aspect of the company evaluation and ultimately of stock selection. We favor the boring, plain vanilla study design. Glamour is for the big screen: For the small screen of biotechnology, we recommend attention to those companies with more concrete endpoints. The study should be designed to answer an unambiguous question—for example, does the drug improve survival, or does the drug improve quality of life? The study design should show the independent effect of the drug if possible, versus the drug used in combination with a variety of other agents. The study should have enough patients in order to answer the proper question; insufficient study sample size may yield a positive effect of the drug, but it may also lead to a statistical miss. We therefore favor trials of 80 percent or greater. Also, we believe the more variable the outcome, the more patients are needed in the study due to the possibility of a statistical type 2 error (i.e., one which rejects a positive answer when indeed the answer is positive).

> *Attention to seasonal trends, in the weather and the news flow.* Biotechnology stocks are generally driven by news flow, not the traditional earnings flow. Presentations of company data from clinical trials at scientific meetings, non–road show company visits to investors, company talks at investor conferences, and announcements of clinical trial results are the major drivers of biotechnology stock prices. Therefore, at the time of this writing, we expected the biotechnology stocks we cover to gain momentum in the second quarter and the fourth quarter periods of the year, in which there are the highest variety and number of conferences. We view the fourth quarter in particular as "The Season of Biotech™," which starts in October with the ICACC (Interscience Conference on Antimicrobial Agents and Chemicals) meeting and ends in December with the ASH (American Society of Hematology) meeting. The "Spring Fling in Biotech" is a second season of note, and begins in March with the ACC (American College of Cardiology) meeting and ends in May with the ASCO (American Society of Clinical Oncology) meeting.

The Bright

THE THREE MOST important areas of focus of a potential biotech investment are products, products, and products. We believe that the era and hype surrounding genomics is over. Although the advances in genomics and specifically pharmacogenomics will continue to develop over the decade, and may well lead to better targeted drugs with improved benefit-to-risk profiles, we believe that the products in late-stage testing today will remain the focus for today's investor. While tool companies, those companies developing improved research techniques and applications, will continue to grow, the growth of the sector overall will be limited to the research and development budgets of biotechnology and pharmaceutical companies.

In our view, products remain the brightest area of focus now and in the near future. The best product-based companies include those developing therapeutics (in other words, drugs) in the forms of oral medications, subcutaneous injections, intravenous infusions, transdermal patches, and inhalable powders. Investment in product companies represents solid areas because of the following drug attributes:

➤ high price
➤ high margin
➤ high barrier to entry
➤ high barriers to competition
➤ high visibility to competition
➤ high numbers of customers
➤ high technical life

The Brave

ALMOST BY DEFINITION, the biotechnology world is a petri dish for volatility. This fact is accentuated by the uncertainty in the clinical trial process. Uncertainty and long waiting periods are inherent in biotechnology. The clinical trial business is a long and laborious one. Risks here, risks there, risks everywhere. Biotechnology investment makes sense when the rewards are greater than the risks, a similar guideline physicians use when prescribing a medication or performing a surgical procedure.

Furthermore, throughout a trial incomplete information exists, making stock selection even more challenging. Final results of clinical trials, a definite mover of biotechnology stocks, are often presented on a day difficult to predict: Interim looks are rarely allowed by study design, and provide only piecemeal information. Finally, most events in biotechnology end as binary, pass/fail events: survival improved or not improved, heart failure treated with a change in pulmonary symptoms, blood pressure reduced by 5 mm Hg or more, and so on.

The Biotech

WE VIEW THE health care sector as an area with solid fundamentals, as overall heath care spending hit a 10-year high in 2002. We expect this trend to continue and favor those companies focused on therapeutics among the fastest-growing sector in health care. Biotechnology companies have been the home of innovation for drug development.

Yet biotechnology development as well as stock selection is risky, and investing under fire presents enough risks on its own. We believe that the rewards of biotechnology outstrip the risks over the long run, but investors may lose faith in these not-yet-profitable companies. Investors may avoid risk overall, with appetite for only profitable companies with their presumed lower developmental, clinical, and regulatory risks.

Yet investing involves not only finding good companies but also finding good stocks. Given the periods of heavy news flow as described above, stocks may "front-run" themselves based on this news flow and gain in anticipation of good news. This gain may often be followed by rapid selling on the news release. In addition, "the basket of goods" approach, whereby one picks ten stocks and hopes that the basket will produce two or three winners, is not in favor. The random basket is less likely to procure a higher proportion of winners, given the odds and challenges in clinical development: An informed basket of stocks is in favor.

Biotech runs in cycles, given that product development is longer than in other sectors and the predictability of success is conversely low. Bad news begets bad stock performance and diffuses interest away from the sector. Good news implies good news for the sector, reminding the investor of the potential upside associated with the innovative therapies for large areas of unmet need.

Chapter 14 *Fourteen*

Foreign Direct Investment in Emerging Market Countries:
A Calculated Risk

VLADIMIR L. KVINT
Professor of Management Systems and International Business,
Fordham University Graduate School of Business

IN THE LAST two decades of the twentieth century, watershed political changes rocked five continents and, as a result, broke open scores of countries that had never before been an integral part of the global market. The historic political and economic demise of the Soviet Union, the collapse of apartheid in South Africa, and the dismantling of military and personal dictatorships in Latin America, Pacific Asia, and the Indian subcontinent increased the global business world to a size five times bigger than what it had been prior to the 1980s. This process, which is still very much underway, marks the second time in the past 500 years that geopolitical events have so dramatically remapped the global commercial landscape. The first time was when Christopher Columbus and the other great explorers introduced the riches of the new world to Europe's most powerful nation-states.

Prior to these changes sweeping the business climate since 1980, about 90 percent of all legitimate, profit-generating, cross-border commercial transactions took place among the developed world—North America, Europe, Japan, and Australia. The rest of the world was divided into two parts—the so-called developing nations and countries under various forms of dictatorship. As military dictatorships in Argentina, Brazil, Turkey, and Greece and personal dictatorships in the Philippines, Indonesia, Paraguay, and numerous countries in the Middle East fell apart, embryonic free markets took the place of command economics in Europe. The death of these regimes prompted an unprecedented demand for foreign direct investment (FDI), a phenomenon that opened the doors for international business in these countries. The result was the birth of the global emerging market (GEM).

Global Trends

IN THE PAST two decades, the global emerging market spearheaded certain worldwide trends and has greatly influenced business transactions across the entire globe. In fact, it was the trigger for the most powerful trend on the eve of the new millennium—globalization. The GEM is made up of about fifty countries in Latin America, Pacific Asia, and the Indian subcontinent; the fifteen newly independent countries of the former Soviet Union; and ten more states in central and eastern Europe. Since the 1980s, the GEM has become a partner and a competitor for well-developed nations and, simultaneously, a model for the remaining developing and underdeveloped countries. The contribution of emerging market countries to global output equals that of all Western Europe and slightly less than that of the United States. The contribution from the GEM constitutes 30 percent of total global output.

One major global trend has been the redistribution of executive federal power into the hands of regional and local authorities, a legacy that stems from the death of most centralized economies. Regional governments inherited some economic responsibilities that were previously the eminent domain of dictators.

The world has also witnessed an unprecedented number of privatizations as another global trend, as well as the drying up of capital available for foreign direct investment. As opportunities for investment multiplied, investors found themselves having to make more difficult decisions about where to put their money, and potential host countries had to become more competitive in an effort to attract multinational corporations and other investors. Although privatization actually began in well-developed capitalist nations such as Great Britain, it became globally prominent with the death of centralized command economies. The new, democratically elected federal and regional governments of these countries knew that they lacked the expertise and capital necessary to make their state-owned industries profitable. These governments realized it would be unwise to try to retain managerial control of these vast industrial and commercial holdings. Consequently, they put forth formal offers to sell stakes in their prized stated-owned industries, mainly to American, Western European, and Japanese investors. What happened next was an immediate and acute shortage of foreign direct investment for those firms that so badly needed it.

In order to protect their power and privilege during their reign, dictators had in the past invested significantly in the production of weapons and military might. With the departure of these dictators and their regimes, we began to see the global trend of demilitarization and the partial conversion of the military-industrial complex into civilian production. The conversion was another invitation for international capital to participate in privatization, with respect to these former military production plants.

In emerging market countries, economic stability has led to a higher standard of living and less transitory political leadership. Unfortunately, macroeconomic stability continues to coexist with high unemployment and widespread poverty. This is the reason why, in countries like Bulgaria, Albania, Romania, Ukraine, Uruguay, Indonesia, India, and the Philippines, we can identify rapid changes in the political fortunes of different governing parties.

A problematic by-product of globalization has been an influx of people from emerging market countries into highly developed economies such as Germany, the United States, and the United Kingdom. This exodus of people in search of economic opportunity has created serious social welfare budgeting problems in well-developed nations. For example, in Germany, France, Italy, Greece, and even the United States, the number of illegal immigrants in search of a better standard of living has skyrocketed in recent years. In the United States alone, there are some 13 million illegal immigrants.

Democratization of former communist countries, the failure of the dictatorships in many other countries, and the low efficiency of command economics, fostered another global trend that can be described as "political disintegration." The embers of nationalism, fueled by minorities previously suppressed by totalitarian regimes, burned fiercely in former Yugoslavia during the 1990s, and the ensuing bloody conflict spawned five newly independent states. The Soviet Union's disintegration resulted in fifteen newly independent states. The 1989–90 "Velvet Revolution" and the 1993 "Velvet Divorce" of Czechoslovakia resulted in the Czech and Slovak Republics. In Indonesia, we witnessed the birth of an independent East Timor. Eritrea split off from Ethiopia in east Africa. And far from finished, this global trend of political disintegration, which in some countries takes on the characteristics of "Balkanization," percolates around the globe. You see it in Canada where you have the Quebec separatist movement; in Belgium, with the Flemish autarky, now separate from the Walloonians; in Spain with its Basque independence movement; as well as between the rich northern and poor southern states of Italy, among many others.

On the flip side, regional economic integration has been another trend to influence foreign direct investment. It affects not only the well-developed countries, which belong to the European Union or NAFTA, but emerging market countries as well, including MERCOSUR (the common market of Latin America's southern cone); the ANDEAN Pact (the free trade pact among Peru, Columbia, Venezuela, Bolivia, and Ecuador); ASEAN (the trade association of ten Southeast Asian nations); the CIS (the commonwealth of twelve former Soviet states); the Baltic Union of Latvia, Lithuania, and Estonia; the BSEC (the Black Sea Economic Cooperation Pact); the CARICOM (the Caribbean Community and Common Market); and ECOWAS (Economic Community of West African States).

FDI as a Factor of Economic Development

HUNGARY, THANKS IN PART to the approach of its government and new legislation, has secured the highest level of FDI per capita among all emerging countries. But in absolute numbers, the largest FDI recipient in the emerging markets of Europe is Poland. At the start of the year 2002, Poland had attracted $60 billion in total FDI capital. The leading recipient, globally, among all emerging market countries is China. China has even overtaken the United States as the ultimate recipient of FDI.

The reason why some countries attract so much more foreign direct investment than others is due to a variety of factors. Take Russia, for example. Why would a country with such vast natural resources, a highly educated, hardworking population, a tradition of great scientific achievements, and a developed infrastructure fail to attract an enormous amount of FDI? In fact, Russia in the past decade attracted less cumulative FDI than either Brazil or China attracted in only one year.

In order to answer this question about Russia, consider Slovakia, where the attitude toward foreign investors was once the same as Russia's is today. Slovakia was, until 1999, the lowest recipient of foreign direct investment in Eastern Europe. A government practice of political isolation; artificial barriers toward foreign participation in privatization; restrictions on foreign investment over a wide spectrum of corporate sectors, particularly banking and insurance; and voucher privatization schemes, with vouchers distributed only among Slovak citizens, made it practically impossible for foreign companies to make investments. But in 1999, under the leadership of newly elected Prime Minister Mikula Dzurinda, the Slovak government began to do away with these restrictions and adopted a more hospitable approach to foreign companies. The country subsequently experienced an influx of foreign direct investment, thanks to its new outward-reaching policy. In the year 2000 Slovakia attracted more foreign investors than ever before, and by 2002 annual inflow of FDI was equal to 10 percent of the nation's GDP. This country of 5.4 million people surpassed its neighbors in the percentage of increase in foreign investment. Behind Slovakia came its neighbor, the Czech Republic, with an increase of FDI inflow that was equal to 8 percent of its GDP, and then Poland, with a jump of 3 percent.

The problems that had daunted Slovakia prior to 1999 still discourage foreign direct investment from flowing into Russia, Ukraine, and Bulgaria. In these countries, lobbyists of local moguls who operate on the basis of seemingly incurably corrupt systems succeed in keeping out foreign corporations.

In general, we can speak about FDI as a factor of economic growth if this investment reaches a level of $1,000 per person in that specific country. If the amount is lower than that, then FDI as a phenomenon doesn't really change the economic landscape of a particular country. Very few countries in the world, however, can boast of reaching a level of FDI of $1,000 per capita. It is important to understand that a high level of FDI does not necessarily correlate with a nation's natural resources, general education levels, or national transportation infrastructure. All this is secondary to what outsiders perceive as the political risks of investing in a particular country and the agenda of its current regime with regard to economic development.

Look at what is going on in the six independent countries that used to make up the Federal Socialist Republic of Yugoslavia. The best example of the high political risk of investment is found in the Republic of Serbia. Serbia used to be the most economically developed state within the Yugoslav federation—and the largest market, with 10 million citizens. But the isolationist policies of former Serbian strongman Slobodan Milosevic bankrupted the country and turned it into the lowest recipient of foreign investment dollars. For example, until 2002, the total, cumulative amount of all FDI in Serbia came to $1.25 billion. That means that Serbia attracted only $125 of FDI per capita, the lowest in all of Central and Eastern Europe. Croatia, on the other hand, its much smaller and far less economically developed neighbor at the time of the breakup of the socialist Yugoslavia, had attracted more than $5.4 billion.

Different industries within emerging market nations attract different levels of foreign money, with the most attractive being the banking and financial services sector. On average, this sector attracts about 23 percent of FDI in global emerging markets. The trade and hospitality industry sector trails in second place, with about 20 percent. Next is the manufacturing sector, followed by the energy, water supply, and transportation sectors.

One of the best ways to attract foreign direct investment is to set up dedicated economic development zones that give tax breaks and other inducements to investors. Ireland is perhaps the most spectacular case of a country that has used such an approach successfully. Ireland has done so well recently in its efforts that it has been able to stem the flow of young talent out of Ireland and woo back some of those professionals who had gone in search of high-paying jobs in the United Kingdom and elsewhere.

The amount of global foreign direct investment has been decreasing since 2000, when FDI reached its peak of $1.3 trillion. In 2001 it fell to $725 billion, and in 2002 it was only about $585 billion—but the amount of FDI going to emerging market countries did not fall drastically. In 2000 it was $240 billion, in 2001 it was $225 billion, and it is estimated to have been $220 billion in 2002, which is still a tremendous amount of money for emerging market countries where job creation costs much less than in developed nations.

FDI in Emerging Markets Needs Economic Freedom

ANY INVESTOR OR company executive putting together a strategy for entering an emerging market must weigh the problems and opportunities brought on by the various aforementioned recent, influential global trends. But still an even more pressing problem exists: How does one define an emerging market? The International Finance Corporation, a division of the World Bank Group, differentiates markets based on gross domestic product per capita (GDP/capita). However, in my view, any indicator that could bunch together India and China, with a GDP barely reaching $450 per capita; Ukraine, Albania, and Moldova, with less than $800 per capita; and Singapore with almost $28,000 per capita, is not useful when making investment decisions. Singapore, still deemed an emerging market by the IFC, has a per capita that is much higher than the majority of well-developed nations. Therefore, making a decision based on just one such indicator is foolish.

Due to the complexity of both the risk and the level of development of national economies, the current business world cannot be broken down into only two categories, developed countries and emerging markets. The world is far too complicated for such simplistic classification. Instead, the following categories work well to illustrate the stages of economic development in various nations.

❑ *Developed countries*
  ➤ Super economies (The United States, Germany)
  ➤ Modern economies (Canada, Denmark, Switzerland)
  ➤ Industrialized nations (Japan, Australia, Italy)
❑ *Emerging markets countries*
  ➤ Economies in transition (Romania, Argentina, Brazil)
  ➤ Oligarchic markets (Russia, Ukraine, Indonesia)

➤ Emerging market dictatorships (Bahrain, China, Vietnam, Turkmenistan)

➤ Pre-emerging markets (Georgia, Sri Lanka, Tunisia)

❑ *Developing national economies* (Pakistan, Caribbean island countries)

❑ *Underdeveloped economies* (Afghanistan, Sudan, Haiti)

The level of political risk of investment does not necessarily correlate to a country's level of democracy. When investing in reasonably democratic countries such as Ukraine, Argentina, and India, the investor is still faced with a significant level of political risk, while countries ruled by dictatorships such as China and Brunei have stable political climates with acceptable risk levels. This helps to explain why among all emerging market countries, China attracts the greatest amount of foreign direct investment. Even nations ruled by oppressive regimes are able to obtain FDI. In 2001 Zimbabwe lured more FDI per capita than the United States or Australia. Democratic societies like Greece, Argentina, Brazil, Romania, Hungary, and the Czech Republic are also still seen as emerging markets, as well as communist dictatorships such as China, Vietnam, and Belarus, the only remaining dictatorship in Europe.

In many countries in the global emerging market, we have seen a paradoxical situation develop in which a government welcomes foreign investment but doesn't give investors the leeway that they need to make their projects successful. In countries like Bulgaria, China, Russia, Argentina, Pakistan, and Egypt, foreign investors still experience strong intervention on the part of the national government in their business ventures. Often this intervention translates into corruption and nepotism. This is common in Azerbaijan, Russia, Brazil, and Bulgaria.

Likewise, countries whose governments rarely intervene in business ventures funded by foreign investors, for example, Bahrain, do not necessarily operate on a democratic system of rule. In its Index of Economic Freedom, the *Wall Street Journal* and the Heritage Foundation ranked the top six countries for freedom from government intervention: not the United States or France, but instead Hong Kong, Singapore, New Zealand, Estonia, Ireland, and Luxembourg. The countries ranked at the bottom were more obvious: Iran, Laos, Cuba, Libya, Iraq, North Korea, Burundi, Sierra Leone, and Sudan.

Strategic Thinking and Risk Management
in the "New World" of FDI

THE BIRTH OF emerging market countries altered in a fundamental manner the approach of top executives in categorizing and analyzing political and economic risk. Some twenty years ago, the idea was that political risk was to be avoided outright, although some firms dared to invest in areas that were deemed questionable on this front. In traditional markets, foreign investors gained an edge due to lower production costs and prices, the original impetus that drove American, European, and Japanese firms into developing nations. Participation in these markets was not only a key success factor, but it was also essential to the continued existence of traditional competitors from highly developed postindustrial nations. The birth of emerging markets forced industry leaders to create systems that would pinpoint risk and development through more sophisticated, multifaceted risk-management strategies. These systems, of course, must constantly be updated, in order to incorporate adjustments in risk due to changing geopolitical factors.

A key factor to consider when evaluating business risk overseas, particularly in developing countries, is the development stage of a nation's business infrastructure. Although this may seem contradictory to a traditional evaluation of business risk, which typically is a sum of product and financial risk, incorporating an assessment of the level of business infrastructure gives one a more realistic picture of the true business risk inherent in a particular country.

Typically, investors enter emerging market countries with capital borrowed from other investors, venture capitalists, commercial banks, and other sources. Experienced creditors would never put up significant amounts of money for investors without some evidence of insurance against political risk. Such insurance is obtained easily enough through agencies and companies with representatives in countries targeted for such types of investments. For example, if one approaches the U.S.–based insurance giant, AIG, formally known as the American International Group, you can procure insurance on more favorable terms in countries where AIG has branch offices, such as Argentina and Egypt, versus countries with lower political risk such as Albania, but where there is no local AIG operation. In short, AIG is more willing to insure investors in regions where it has a presence and some expertise, despite the particular level of political risk in those countries.

Financing can generally be secured on more favorable terms if an investor chooses to work with an investment bank that has a presence in the country in which he is planning to invest. If targeting Bulgaria, better to approach ING Barings, which has an office in Sofia. If interested in Argentina and Russia, contact Citibank. In the case of the Czech Republic, the German banks are a good bet, as is JPMorgan Chase. Regarding insurance and loans, investors should open accounts with commercial banks, preferably ones that can be trusted in the investor's home country.

The next requirement is an accurate valuation of any property that a strategic investor may purchase or any state-owned property up on the privatization sale block. A Big Four auditing firm is critical in such a situation because otherwise the investor has to depend on the quality of due diligence work done by unknown local auditors, who must be investigated. The same goes for the law firms that an investor employs to file the corporation registration and other key documents with the government. Choose firms that have a deep-seated knowledge of the local law and enforcement regimes when looking to build an international joint venture or to execute an acquisition.

The conclusion of this point is that investors need the presence of major capitalist institutions—insurers, investment banks, commercial banks, accounting firms, and law firms—that are recognized internationally within the country in which they wish to invest. Only then can the investor start to evaluate the product and financial risk in more traditional ways.

Quite often the strategies and processes that go along with foreign direct investment in different emerging market countries share mutual characteristics, regardless of geographical differences. For example, unlike the stability of Western Europe and North American countries, there are high levels of political risk. Many emerging market countries have inchoate legal frameworks, although the laws on the books do reflect some general ideas about protection of foreign investors' property rights. These nations generally have undeveloped business infrastructures and ambiguous capital market institutions.

These factors boost significantly the levels of political, economic, and business risk associated with foreign direct investments.

This consideration does not specifically include the technological risks because this is not a homogeneous characteristic throughout the emerging market countries. Eastern Europe consistently graduates university students with an extremely high standard of technological education and practice, so much so that these students often rival their counterparts in the United States. This is particularly true in the Czech Republic, Hungary, Poland, and Russia. Hungary, for example, has always enjoyed a tradition of producing world-class scientists and mathematicians. The Czechs are well known for their high standard of engineering education and achievements. This is not the case, however, in many Latin American and Southeast Asian countries, where the level of technological education and practice is quite low.

A choice to invest abroad, particularly into an emerging market country, always reflects a tough trade-off made between the scale and type of risk that a firm can manage and the profits it expects to reap as a result of the venture. Prior to 1980 when business leaders heard about risk, they would often dismiss a project altogether. Very quickly, these same leaders learned the hard way that they would lose out to competitors who took the risk and set up operations in developing nations, enjoying much cheaper labor, richer natural resources, a bigger market for sales, and lower production costs. Companies generated profits directly in those developing nations, as well as money made from selling those goods back in their home countries. During the 1980s, large companies from well-developed nations exported their competition to emerging market countries and began to create risk-management systems. Now these firms know how to measure risk accurately, to evaluate the types of risk they can tolerate, and the way they can adjust their operations to manage the risk they take on.

In emerging market countries, companies deal with many types of risk, as has been noted: traditional business risk like product risk and financial risk; political risk such as the expropriation and nationalization of foreign properties and physical damage to property due to political unrest; as well as the risk of being unable to convert soft currency back into hard currency. Many firms built strong risk-management systems, such as those of the Canadian Imperial Bank of Commerce (CIBC), European engineering giant Asea Brown Boveri (ABB),

The Walt Disney Co., and McDonald's Corp., among many others.

Sovereign governments of emerging market countries are the only ones who can manage the systematic risk in their nations. No single corporation or foreign investor can do this. When General Electric Co. came to Hungary in the late 1980s, under the leadership of CEO Jack Welch, the company knew it could not handle the systematic risk that it faced in this environment. But the Hungarian government, similar to others in emerging market countries, had created its own risk-management systems designed to attract and protect foreign investment. Other nations that made a similar effort were Poland, Brazil, China, Taiwan, and, more recently, Croatia.

FDI: A Weapon Against Poverty

PRIVATE WESTERN INVESTORS who took on unfamiliar risks to move into these emerging market countries also ran up against massive social problems—poverty, intense corruption, high unemployment during uncertain periods of transition, and record high emigration rates to well-developed countries. These problems substantially changed the nature of private investment that flowed to emerging markets.

In January 1999 at the World Economic Forum in Davos, Switzerland, newly elected Secretary General of the United Nations Kofi Annan called for a new partnership between multilateral organizations, governments of sovereign nations, and private capital to fight worldwide poverty, unemployment, and mass migration. It has now become clear that multilateral organizations and governments do not have the necessary capital to fight poverty and thereby stabilize developing economies and bolster their transitions into free-market economies without the participation of private corporations. Before, private investors who acted in response to the social needs of the populations in their investment regions would, at best, make occasional monetary donations as a form of public relations. Now, the game had changed. Investors have a personal interest in solving these problems: Investment requires stability. Investment requires customers who can afford to buy products and services. A safe haven for investment cannot exist when social problems impede sustainable development. Private capital began a process of peaceful and, in many respects, irreversible, change. These partnerships, which also involve local authorities, have become a formidable weapon against poverty, a situation that investors never encountered in their home countries.

FDI and the Threat of Terrorism

AN EFFECT OF globalization that has had both positive and negative consequences has been the dismantling of decades-old geopolitical and national borders, such as the Iron Curtain. From the positive angle, the failure of the dictatorships and the ensuing democratization process brought down the Berlin Wall in 1989 as well as many other artificial and detrimental divides. This made it possible to execute cross-border investing more efficiently and cheaply. It also brought with it a new threat that was clearly underestimated until the tragic events took place in the United States on September 11, 2001: terrorism. One of the by-products of globalization is the threat of terrorism, particularly from some groups within the Islamic world.

At the end of the twentieth century, the Muslim world was very much a divided one, philosophically and economically. Some nations had opted for democratic change and economic freedom such as Turkey, Uzbekistan, Kazakhstan, Jordan, Tunisia, Morocco, Bahrain, and even Indonesia, while others were still floundering without developmental direction. These nations include Egypt, Lebanon, Algeria, Iran, and Malaysia. In fact, a substantial number of Muslim countries such as Syria, Libya, and Sudan remain in the hands of dictators who have no interest in democracy and harbor pockets of well-established, well-funded extremists who pose a threat to mankind in general, be it in the developed, developing, or emerging market countries. The development of private business in Arab nations and the integration of these businesses in the global market will undoubtedly play an important role in the fight against terrorism.

FDI and the Obstacle of Corruption

ANOTHER ISSUE THAT must be combated is that of corruption, as it remains one of the major obstacles to investing in emerging market countries. Research shows that the lower the level of corruption in a particular country, the higher the level of foreign direct investment per capita in the country. Transparency International, a think tank that operates out of Berlin, Germany, suggests that the following countries have the lowest of level of corruption: Singapore, Hong Kong, Chile, Taiwan, and Hungary. On the other hand, Bangladesh, Indonesia, Venezuela, Pakistan, India, Russia, and Argentina are plagued by corruption. The World Bank names Azerbaijan as the most corrupt country, with Turkmenistan also high on the list.

Corruption not only dissuades FDI in a lot of instances, but it also works to keep a country rooted in poverty. There is scant evidence that the well-meaning programs of multilateral institutions such as those sponsored by the United Nations and World Bank have done much to improve living conditions of the poor in the developing world. What economists have instead credited is the creation of jobs associated with FDI.

FOREIGN DIRECT INVESTMENT can be expected to continue to grow at levels of 15 to 18 percent annually into the next decade, particularly given that the emerging market will only increase in size, as underdeveloped nations move up the socioeconomic ladder to fit into the developing nation category. This will continue to ensure that we will see great progress in emerging market countries in the next twenty years.

Chapter Fifteen

The Changing Spectrum in Asia

ROBERT D. HORMATS
Vice Chairman, Goldman Sachs International

M UCH OF EAST ASIA experienced a period of remarkable economic growth in the early and mid-1990s. That growth was
interrupted by the financial crisis of 1997–1998. Growth is now
resuming, albeit at a more modest pace, in most countries of the
region. But the character and product composition of that growth is
changing along with the dynamics of trade within the region.

The central factor in Asia's growth going forward can be summed
up in one word: China. Its increasingly important role in the region
is based not only on its continued robust growth but also on the kinds
of industries and investments that are thriving there and the changing nature of its trading relations with its Asian neighbors. Although
Japan's economy is still considerably larger than that of China, and it
still accounts for a much larger share of regional trade and financial
activity, its weak economic performance over the past decade has
diminished the perception, if not the reality, of its future role as an
economic powerhouse in Asia—whereas China's economic role and
economic power in the region are growing rapidly. Japan's Koizumi
government has sought to undertake a series of reforms to address
the problems of nonperforming loans and excessive corporate debt,
which are weighing down the economy, but the outcome of these
efforts remains unclear.

Underlying Dynamic and Regional Interplay

MUCH OF CHINA'S trade and inward investment to date has been centered on processing and assembly. The most recent figures indicate that over half of China's exports came from these activities; it imports raw materials, semiprocessed goods, and intermediate products, mostly from other Asian countries, and exports assembled goods to much of the rest of the world. This is particularly true in the electronics sector and information technology (IT) sectors. China's imports and exports in these areas track one another almost exactly. Far from showing a growing surplus in these areas, Mainland China continues to be a net importer. Mainland processing adds only 5 to 10 percent to the total value of its gross technology imports. (See Jonathan Anderson, "The Great Myth Part 2, China Will Take Over Asia," Goldman Sachs Research Publication, January 30, 2002.) Most of the remainder of China's net exports continue to be low-wage products such as apparel and toys. But all this is changing.

While China is likely to remain a powerful force in many of these sectors, it is determined to move up the value-added chain and realize greater efficiencies in manufacturing, agriculture, and services. All sectors of its economy will need to become more competitive in the face of the rising foreign competition within China, much of it brought about by World Trade Organization (WTO) membership. Foreign direct investment is likely to be concentrated to an increasing degree in services and advanced technology, as well as in fast-growing areas such as autos. The bulk of new foreign direct investment of late has been aimed at sales in the domestic market and value added exports. What sustains such investment is the prospect of continued robust growth in domestic demand and increased, higher processed exports. Moreover, repatriated returns on investment in China amount to a healthy 8 percent.

Much of the rest of Asia is caught between a growing and more competitive China and concerns about excessive dependence on the United States. While the formidable competitive challenge posed by China has been seen as a threat by some in the region, many Asian industries have come to see China as a strong market for their products and raw materials. It is interesting to note that between 1993 and 2001 China's gross industrial output rose from 2.4 percent of estimated global industrial production to 4.2 percent, while its gross manufactured goods imports rose from roughly 2.5 percent of world industrial production to 4.1 percent.

As a whole, ASEAN (an acronym for the Association of South East Asian Nations, encompassing Malaysia, Indonesia, Thailand, Singapore, the Philippines, Brunei, Vietnam, Laos, Cambodia, and Burma) has had a substantial trade surplus with China, as does South Korea. Taiwan, a source of substantial investment to the mainland, also has enjoyed a large trade surplus with it. Much of this is in the IT sector. Indeed for most, writes Anderson, "the decline in traditional industries ... was more than offset by the rise of higher value-added IT electronics sectors, with other manufacturing industries remaining broadly consistent in share terms. Rather than a source of concern, the structural change over the last decade is testimony to the flexibility ... of these economies."

Most of China's neighbors are now engaging Beijing in a dialogue on ways to sustain regional economic cooperation so that China's growth will benefit them. Beijing, for its part, has been making a considerable effort to improve regional economic relations, in part because of a desire to increase exports to the area, to maintain stable economic relations with its neighbors who constitute important suppliers of components and raw materials, as well as to reinforce positive political relations.

Many East Asian countries, most notably Singapore, Malaysia, and Thailand, have become concerned that over half of their overall exports outside the region consist of information technology and other electronics products and that much of this goes to the American market. This was formerly seen as a source of economic strength and robust exports, until recently when weaker economic growth in the United States, and especially in this sector, negatively affected most of these economies. Very few of the smaller Asian economies have been able to generate sufficient domestic demand to offset slower exports to the U.S., Europe, or Japan. Korea, and to a degree, Malaysia, have succeeded better than most in mitigating the fall in electronics exports to the United States, in part because of effective fiscal policy and in part because reforms in their banking systems since 1997 have enabled their banks to expand credit to small and medium-sized domestic industries, and to mortgages for homeowners, creating a source of domestic demand not dependent on exports.

What, then, lies ahead for Asia in coming years? How should investors approach a region that has experienced in rapid succession a boom and then a bust? Will another bust occur—and should investors anticipate that and shy away from the region? Can China's boom continue, and will it be the same as in the past, or will it present new opportunities as well as new risks? What economies and sectors are likely to thrive in the coming years? Will the powerful growth of China benefit or harm the rest of the region? And how can investors take advantage of the future growth of China and other nations of the region?

In an attempt to answer at least some of these questions, it is useful to start with an assessment of some of the trends at work in China, then assess how other nations of the region will relate to them, and finally suggest a few of the changes that investors should heed to make wise investment decisions in coming years. It is also worth injecting a note of caution here that a series of geopolitical issues can overturn even the most rational of economic projections; the dangers of additional terrorism following the Bali bombings, continued insurrections in areas of the Philippines, concerns about future instability in Indonesia and its impact on the region, and menacing revelations about North Korea's nuclear program all foreshadow the potential for surprises that could produce economic and market disruptions. Instability in the Middle East that disrupts oil supplies could also have a major adverse impact on the many nations of the region that require substantial amounts of oil imports.

The New Dynamics in China

CHINA, AS DISCUSSED above, has been one of the world's most dynamic economies for the past two decades. That performance is likely to continue in this decade as well—accelerated further by the phasing in of Beijing's commitments under the WTO agreement. Important sectors are being liberalized at a rapid pace. The kinds of investment coming into the country are changing. Many Chinese companies are seeking to increase the value added to their products and to establish powerful global brands. At the same time, concerns are growing over unemployment. The prospect of higher unemployment introduces more than a little caution and restraint when it comes to restructuring, or closing, inefficient companies, particularly those that employ a large number of people or are responsible for important social services in a particular city or region. This means also that a large number of nonperforming bank loans cannot be resolved as easily as authorities would like, lest big companies be forced to close and add new workers to the ranks of the unemployed.

Over time the goal is to shift capital away from inefficient industries, most of which are now in the government sector—forcing such companies to reform or perish and to make greater financing available to the growing number of small and medium-sized private enterprises and to the rising corps of entrepreneurs, many of whom are starved for bank capital and cannot easily raise funds in capital markets. The speed and effectiveness of this shift, whether it can be done without producing excessively high unemployment or social instability, will be an important indicator of how dynamic the Chinese economy will be later in the decade. If the Chinese government provides more support and encouragement for these newer and more efficient companies, foreign investors will also see them as potentially profitable opportunities. And over time they will form a larger component of local stock markets and be permitted to issue shares on global markets.

Where are profitable investment opportunities likely to emerge? One area is services—including distribution, banking, and telecommunications. In some cases the benefits will accrue to domestic companies, in others to foreign ones. To date only a fraction of foreign or domestic private investment has gone into service sectors because of government limitations and regulations; this is destined to change under the WTO agreement. As it does, domestic industries such as banking will make great efforts to improve their own competitiveness, and foreign institutions will play an increased role. The combined impact will produce greater efficiency throughout the economy—from which other industries also will benefit. The risk is that the state monopolies will not go easily or quietly, and various provinces and authorities might seek to slow the process to permit more time for local industries to adjust. But in time opportunities for investment in services will grow steadily.

A second area where good investment opportunities might emerge is in the automobile industry. Total car sales in China in 2001 were about 2.3 million—a figure expected to rise to as much as 6 million in 2010. To put that in perspective, every year in this decade new sales in China will be equivalent to the entire stock of cars in Australia. Virtually every major car company in the world is now in China, investing in partnerships with the big three Chinese automakers. These joint ventures are likely to grow despite a considerable amount of intervention by the federal and local governments in the form of licensing requirements, often-heavy administrative guidance, and difficulty in working with partners who might have different priorities.

Increasing auto sales raise another issue for China, and a third area for potentially high returns: energy. China's appetite for energy is likely to increase rapidly in the coming years, largely due to stronger industrial demand plus added demand from a growing auto fleet. That means that Chinese energy companies will be importing a lot more and investing in production overseas, particularly in Southeast Asia and the Middle East. A swelling appetite for energy will engage China to a greater degree in Middle East politics and increase the country's vulnerability to destabilizing events there. It will also mean that China will invest more in domestic sources of energy and new transport systems to move gas and oil from other parts of China, and from neighboring regions such as Central Asia and Siberia, to coastal China. Foreign capital and expertise is likely to be useful and needed here.

A fourth potentially profitable investment area is in information technology. China is turning out a large number of well-trained scientists and engineers—well equipped to support high-technology manufacturing and research facilities. And these are coming to China through investment by many of the foremost technology companies of the world, such as Microsoft and IBM. As China moves up the skill ladder it will produce increasingly high value-added goods; some of these it will export, others it will adapt to the domestic market to fill the growing internal demand for higher-quality goods in ever greater amounts.

A major test in many areas of the Chinese economy will be how well and how quickly China's corporate sector can compete head to head with the large multinational corporations, as some certainly hope to do not only in their own market but also in world markets. China aspires to move from being a large platform for subcontracting to a world-class exporter of high-value brands. Moving up the technology ladder on the basis of partnerships is a preferred strategy for most Chinese companies today. Currently roughly half of China's exports come from joint ventures, most with Asian companies that have relocated production there because the labor-intensive character of that production made it uncompetitive at home. Whether China's companies can move from this dependence on large joint ventures to stand-alone manufacturing and master the all-important global distribution and marketing skills that many multinationals bring to these joint ventures will be a key factor in their future success. Those that can will be potential economic powerhouses for decades to come.

But China must still address formidable challenges. Large numbers of nonperforming loans continue to tie up capital in inefficient companies. Unemployment is a big and growing problem, risking potential economic and social instability in both rural and urban China. Pressure on older industries, banks, state monopolies, and agriculture from foreign competition under the WTO will be strong and could lead to pushback and uneven implementation. But if China can address these issues constructively, as I believe it will, it has the talent, the vision, and the political consensus to sustain the reform and growth process.

China's Neighbors

WHAT DOES THIS ongoing change in China mean for other emerging economies of East Asia? The initial answer is that in many sectors China will be a growing competitive challenge. Particularly in the electronics and IT sectors, China is moving into the kinds of products that heretofore have been produced in many of its Asian neighbors. And China is seeking to export such products to the same regions as they currently do—North America, Japan, and Western Europe. In fact, China is becoming more competitive in these sectors in Asian domestic markets; almost half of China's exports to ASEAN countries are electronics.

But in many sectors it will also provide a robust market. One hope for nations in ASEAN is that they can increase exports of agricultural goods and raw materials to China. A China-ASEAN Free Trade Area could be a way of increasing agricultural sales to China. Although sales to Japan are inhibited by import restrictions—sometimes, especially where rice is concerned, politically sensitive—Japan is also pursuing the notion of a free trade agreement (FTA) with ASEAN. In 2002, China's Premier Zhu Rongi also suggested the notion of an FTA composed of China, South Korea, and Japan. These proposals all pose formidable complications that will be difficult to negotiate in the near term, but represent a regional desire to reduce dependence on exports to the United States and, to a lesser degree, Europe.

Most nations of the area will not be content with merely exporting agricultural goods, energy, or raw materials, however. They also want to continue to move up the technology ladder. The ability of regional economies such as ASEAN, South Korea, and Taiwan to compete with China in technology products and other types of more sophisticated goods will depend on several factors. These are key considerations investors should take into account when evaluating the prospects of nations and companies in the area.

First among these factors, do they have the flexibility to move to higher and higher value-added production, in goods as well as services? India is an interesting example of a country that has gained considerably from the export of high value-added, but low-cost, accounting, software, architectural, and other services. Its companies are innovative, global, and highly networked, and it is attracting a lot of foreign investment in these areas. In high value-added industries throughout the region, success will depend not only on providing low-cost products but also on the agility of corporate management, the quality and level of education of the workforce, and the skill of the management and workers in adapting to new technologies to raise product quality and market to foreign tastes. South Korea has demonstrated the ability to do just this in electronics, IT, and autos.

Many countries of the region are managing to substantially increase sales to China. Recognizing that no country can have a comparative advantage in everything—not even China—the test for other Asian nations will be whether their economies, their forms of corporate governance, and their workforces are competitive enough to sell higher value goods to China and to compete with Chinese goods in third country markets.

A second factor in determining success will be how well countries of the region manage basic macroeconomic and regulatory policy. Do they maintain sound monetary policy that avoids a buildup of inflationary pressures? Can they utilize fiscal policy in a way that combats occasional periods of export weakness, as the South Koreans have done so well during the recent global downturn, while avoiding chronic deficits by running surpluses when fiscal stimulus is not needed? Can they reduce the stock of nonperforming loans in an orderly and purposeful way, thereby enabling the banks to be in a position to lend more to newer and more profitable companies? South Korea, again, has demonstrated the benefits of effective bank reform. Many of its banks no longer are locked into loans to older export-oriented companies that are vulnerable to a global downturn and are now freer to lend to smaller domestic companies and to provide mortgages and other home loans; this broadens the base of South Korea's growth and reduces the country's overall vulnerability to foreign market swings.

This consideration raises the broader issue of bank and financial reform. Most nations of the region do not have highly developed debt markets, complicating the task of efficiently intermediating their large pools of domestic savings and better managing financial risk. In many of these countries, capital tends to flow to a relatively small number of large companies—usually ones dependent on sales abroad—or it goes to governments, or government monopolies, which are often the dominant borrower, thus crowding out private borrowers. Often risk spreads do not reflect the magnitude of the risk. Due in part to weak domestic financial markets and limits on the range and liquidity of investment products, surpluses are often invested in capital markets in North America, Europe, or Japan. Indeed much of the financing of the record U.S. account deficit comes from Asia. Improvements in the regulation, supervision, and range of financial products, as well as access of newer and smaller companies to equity and debt markets, could increase the efficiency, and reduce the vulnerability, of these economies.

The ASEAN region would also be in a stronger position if it could take advantage of the potential of its own regional market. The ASEAN Free Trade Area (AFTA) was designed to open up trade among the nations of Southeast Asia, thereby creating greater efficiencies and making the region more attractive to foreign investment, because of the large, unified regional market. The concept has not lived up to expectations, in part because countries often have claimed "temporary exceptions" and in part because intraregional trade has not been very active in the many similar products—such as electronics—produced in several countries in the area. Also, "sensitive" agricultural products are excluded. Making AFTA work better would also enhance the competitive strengths of the region vis-à-vis other areas.

Investor's Outlook

THE FUTURE INVESTMENT outlook in the Asian region will depend on the continued growth of China and on how businesses in other countries relate to it. For most companies in the Asian region, and in the United States as well, it will be virtually impossible to have a successful global business strategy without having a successful China business strategy. Virtually every CEO will have to make important strategic decisions on how his or her company can compete with Chinese products, participate in China's future growth, or market Chinese-produced goods abroad. So investors looking at companies that are projecting increased foreign sales or that depend on foreign sourcing should consider their ability to relate to China as a market or supplier; doing so effectively will be of considerable importance to their future success. Even companies that do business only in the United States will confront the competitive forces emanating from China, and investors will need to judge how well they respond to such forces.

As noted above, no country, not even China, can have a comparative advantage in everything. This point bears repeating time and time again. China's neighbors must be flexible enough and smart enough in the way they manage their economies, in their corporate governance, and in the quality of their financial systems to permit their private sectors the ability to fully develop their own competitive advantages. Those that can do so will present profitable investment opportunities, by selling more in their home markets and in China, North America, and Western Europe.

In addition, for most of this decade a large portion of the economic activity in the Asian region will still be directly or indirectly related to sales to, investments from, partnerships with, or financing by Japan, North America, and Western Europe. Only a modest portion of the growth of the region is "independent" of exports to the larger economies. China and South Korea, because of the size of their domestic economies and the robustness of nonexport-oriented sectors, have proved to be less vulnerable than their neighbors to downturns in exports. However, most still are very vulnerable. And even though China is growing rapidly, and thus is an important market for its Asian neighbors, it is still a relatively small economy by world standards. In 2000, for example, China accounted for only 3.5 percent of world imports; the six largest emerging economies in Asia outside of China accounted for 9.5 percent. Exports of most countries of East Asia to the large industrial markets will continue to be vital to their growth prospects and to the profitability of their companies. And how well the industrialized nations can sustain their own healthy growth will have an enormous impact on the emerging economies of Asia— particularly in the electronics, IT, and manufacturing sectors.

Finally, American portfolio investors tend to be skittish about investing abroad, particularly in emerging markets, when they feel insecure about their home stock markets. If the stock markets in the United States do well, they feel more confident about investing abroad. Much of the success of Asian markets, therefore, will be linked to the robustness of the American market. The broader fact is that recently foreign stocks as an asset class have not served as an effective way for U.S. equity investors to reduce the volatility and increase the profitability of their investments. This has been true for a variety of reasons: increased dependence of American companies on sales to foreign markets; even greater increases in the dependence of foreign companies on sales to the United States, particularly in areas of high technology; and closely linked cross-border supplier/ purchaser/processing/assembly networks. Trade in general has become far more open, and capital markets around the world have become more closely integrated. Nonetheless, if emerging Asian economies can establish sustained areas of comparative advantage and profitability, and demonstrate their ability to achieve greater "independent growth" (that is, growth less dependent on sales to the United States or the EU)—while exhibiting continued improvements in economic and corporate governance—they can offer an increasingly compelling way for American, Japanese, and European investors to diversify their risks and achieve superior returns.

Tools of the Trade for Today's Investor

C h a p t e r **16** *S i x t e e n*

Equity Research and the Investor's Right to Know

HENDRIK KRANENBURG
Executive Vice President, Standard & Poor's

SAM STOVALL
Chief Investment Strategist, Standard & Poor's

INVESTORS AND THEIR ADVISERS are demanding more and more sophisticated, independently derived information to guide them through the ups and downs of market volatility. In part, this demand is driven by industry consolidation and cost pressures leading customers to insist on a wider range of services from fewer providers. But other factors influencing change include the voluminous amount of information available to all market participants; the increasing responsibility of individual investors over their entire retirement portfolios, driving demand for a wider range of investment vehicles; and, not least, a widening mistrust of sell-side research among investors, which affects the reputations of advisers. According to a September 2002 Standard & Poor's/*BusinessWeek* survey, fully 78 percent of investors have less trust in investment analysts' stock recommendations because of recent events, and 65 percent are concerned about the objectivity of investment advisers' recommendations.

Investors, securities firms, regulators, and independent research organizations face a unique opportunity in the current market to rethink the way equity research is conducted and used. All undoubtedly agree that an open and transparent marketplace for investment analysis is the best way to ensure an effective market for the allocation and formation of capital. At issue is the extent to which that research comes from an independent provider versus the research unit of a securities firm.

For more than 140 years, Standard & Poor's has been recognized as a leader in providing independent and widely recognized financial data, analytical research, and investment and credit opinions to the world's financial markets. While also known for its credit ratings and global indexes (including the S&P 500), Standard & Poor's, a division of The McGraw-Hill Companies, Inc., has the broadest range of equity coverage in the United States among research firms that are not affiliated with a Wall Street investment bank. Its quantitative models cover some 7,000 stocks and its 75 equity analysts provide qualitative recommendations on nearly 1,300 stocks in the United States, 150 stocks in Europe, and 100 stocks in Asia.

Standard & Poor's traces its roots to 1860 and the publication by Henry Varnum Poor of the *History of the Railroads and the Canals of the United States*, the grandfather of all investment publications. Sketching the development of 120 public companies, including the Erie and the Baltimore and Ohio Railroads, the *History* was the first major attempt to record the past and present operations of an industry based upon a novel idea at the time, something Poor called "the investor's right to know." The publication was an immediate success that grew into Poor's Railroad Manual Company, expanded into Poor's Publishing Company, then merged, in 1941, with the Standard Statistics Co. to form Standard & Poor's (which The McGraw-Hill Companies acquired in 1966). Henry Poor's early commitment to the investor's right to know remains the watchword that informs and guides the work of Standard & Poor's today.

Underlying Analytic Model

PRODUCED BY THE firm's Investment Services unit, Standard & Poor's equity research and stock recommendations revolve around a four-point model that emphasizes analyst independence, breadth of company coverage, depth of analysis, and company performance. It is also guided by an understanding that today's investors want to be able to track independent research recommendations over time and through market cycles and can, thereby, appreciate the transparency that Standard & Poor's provides them through its qualitative Standard & Poor's STARS recommendations, and through its quantitative stock analyses.

Standard & Poor's qualitative equity research and recommendations are based on the goal of "Growth At A Reasonable Price" (GARP). This qualitative analysis begins with a top-down overlay, which puts an emphasis on economic sectors that are identified as relative outperformers by the firm's senior investment strategists. These forecasts rely on collective economic and market projections by the Standard & Poor's Investment Policy Committee, which meets on a weekly basis and is comprised of Standard & Poor's senior analysts in the fields of economics, equities, fixed-income investments, technical market analysis, and mutual funds. From this starting point, Standard & Poor's analysts conduct a fundamental securities analysis, which includes:

➤ An intrinsic value analysis, determining "fair value" based principally on discounted cash flow (DCF) analysis

➤ Relative valuation, assessing a security's relative value by comparing appropriate financial ratios of the security's closest peers

➤ "Sum-of-parts," determining "fair value" of a stock by determining market values for identifiable, separate units

➤ Technical analysis, which favors stocks with positive Relative Strength (momentum), generally according to 200-day moving averages

Standard & Poor's qualitative analysis is the basis for its Stock Appreciation Ranking System (STARS), which was first introduced on December 31, 1986, and which reflects the opinions of Standard & Poor's equity analysts on the price appreciation potential of nearly 1,300 U.S. stocks for the next six- to twelve-month period. Rankings range from 5-STARS (strong buy) to 1-STARS (sell).

Standard & Poor's 5-STARS Stock Selections* increased in value by 885 percent from STARS' inception on December 31, 1986 through December 31, 2002, compared with growth of 263 percent

---

* It should not be assumed that recommendations made in the future will be profitable or will equal past performance. The above performance of STARS does not take into account reinvestment of dividends, capital gains taxes, or brokers' commissions and fees. A complete list of STARS recommendations made during the past year is available from Standard & Poor's upon request. STARS are published by Standard & Poor's Equity Research Department, which operates independently from, and has no access to, information obtained by Standard & Poor's Ratings Services, which may in the course of its operations obtain access to confidential information.

for the S&P 500 during the same period, excluding dividends. In addition, stocks ranked as 4- and 5-STARS have, as a group, outperformed the S&P 500 Index during the past one-, three-, five-, ten-, and fifteen-year periods. On an annual basis, STARS have outperformed the S&P 500 Index eleven times, underperformed three times, and tied once. Stocks ranked as 1-STAR and 2-STAR have, as a group, significantly underperformed the S&P 500 over the past ten and fifteen years. Standard & Poor's is proud that it has been a leader in issuing "sell" recommendations on stocks, accounting in some years for more than 20 percent of all sell recommendations on Wall Street.

In addition to the STARS qualitative research, Standard & Poor's also provides several quantitative analytical models to use when analyzing particular companies and their stocks. These include its Quality Ranking System, Fair Value Model, Neural Fair Value Model, and the Investability Quotient.

Since 1956, Standard & Poor's has appraised the growth and stability of earnings and dividends on individual companies using the Standard & Poor's Quality Ranking system, which ranks them on a scale of A+ (highest) to D (in reorganization). Two of Standard & Poor's analysts recently completed a study showing that a portfolio of U.S. stocks with high Quality Rankings has outperformed the S&P 500 Index over the study period of seventeen years. The portfolio also provides a cushion in times of earnings deceleration and increased credit risk, significantly outperforming portfolios of stocks with lower Quality Rankings. The analysts also found that companies with high Quality Rankings have historically reported lower nonrecurring, special, and extraordinary items than lower-ranked companies. As a result, there is an association between a Quality Ranking and the difference between reported earnings and Standard & Poor's Core Earnings of a company.

The Standard & Poor's Fair Value Model, introduced in 1995, is a quantitative model that is influenced by profitability, relative value, and changes in future earnings estimates. This model is fundamentally driven by consensus earnings and growth forecasts, does not use discounting methods but rather relational current value analyses, and ranks about 3,000 U.S. stocks by degrees of attractiveness. Standard & Poor's Neural Fair Value Model uses the Fair Value

Model and adds a neural (i.e., a computer-generated, mathematic) classifier screen to make it more sensitive to market conditions during the next six months.

The Standard & Poor's Investability Quotient (IQ) is an evaluation score assessing how attractive a particular stock is for further consideration as an investment. The IQ model is a combination of four different submodels: a proprietary model that includes STARS, Credit Ratings, Quality Rankings, and S&P Indices; a multifactor model that includes valuation, profitability, risk, and price and earnings momentum factors; a technical model based on relative strength; and a liquidity and volatility model that measures liquidity and downside risk.

Research Investors Can Act On

KEY TO Standard & Poor's success as an independent equity research house is its focus on research that investors can act on and that can be tailored to private clients. In addition to developing a number of successful model portfolios driven by in-house research, the firm publishes concise reports with key fundamental and technical information that, over various Web-based operating platforms, has been licensed for use by more than 120,000 financial advisers. The result is comprehensive equity research, emphasizing both quantitative and qualitative information.

Through licensing arrangements with such firms as Charles Schwab, E*Trade, Fidelity, Merrill Lynch, TD Waterhouse, and others, Standard & Poor's stock research information and recommendations reaches more than 20 million investors. Investors can read *Standard & Poor's Analytical Stock Reports* (including STARS qualitative analysis), *Corporate Profiles, Industry Surveys,* articles from *Fund Advisor,* and more just by asking their broker.

Nearly all of this information is available over Advisor Insight, Standard & Poor's Web-delivered platform that integrates Standard & Poor's equity, fund, and variable annuity investment research targeted to professional advisers. Advisor Insight also offers up-to-the-minute news and information on stocks and funds and provides users with access to Standard & Poor's extensive databases and variable annuity information to search and screen potential investments. In addition, it contains comprehensive NASD-approved reports on over 6,000 stocks, 10,000 funds, and 500 variable annuities and 10,000 subaccounts.

Standard & Poor's MarketScope, available independently or through Advisor Insight, contains actionable, real-time information for brokers and advisers and includes suites of model portfolios; real-time news and market commentary; forecasts; news and technical market analysis; stock quotes; and explanations and interpretations on what is happening in the markets, with updated features like Marketmovers, Market Commentary, and Views and News.

Among Standard & Poor's model portfolio offerings are the Top 10 Portfolio, consisting of the strongest STARS recommendations; the Platinum Portfolio, combining the top-rated stocks from STARS and its proprietary Fair Value quantitative ranking system; the Neural Fair Value Portfolio, which overweights fair value factors that have worked best during the past six months; Master Lists of stocks for the long term; and Power Picks, what Standard & Poor's refers to as the single best idea by forty of its equity analysts for the coming year.

In addition to its work in equities, Standard & Poor's Investment Services is also a global leader in mutual fund data and research. With one of the world's largest fund databases, Standard & Poor's tracks performance and holdings data on nearly 80,000 equity, bond, and money market mutual funds globally. Through a team of seventy fund analysts in the United States, Europe, and Asia, Standard & Poor's conducts fundamental analysis of manager quality on over 1,100 funds and provides fund STARS rankings on 14,000 U.S. mutual funds. It also covers 500 variable annuity policies and 10,000 sub-accounts. Its Web-based Fund Advisor tool for investment advisers can be accessed through Advisor Insight. Funds-sp.com contains fund information for retail investors and is free of charge.

While much of this information is produced for large, institutional clients, a consumer version of it is published every week in the form of Standard & Poor's *The Outlook,* an investment advisory newsletter that has been informing personal investment decisions since 1922. *The Outlook* offers objective market commentary and perspective by the same team of equity analysts, economists, and investment strategists behind Advisor Insight. A subscription to *Outlook Online* provides a full year of back issues of *The Outlook's* research; the latest changes to the STARS recommendations; a complete list of all the stocks in each of the STARS categories, Standard & Poor's Platinum, Fair Value, and Small Cap/IPO portfolios, and monthly stock and fund reports; as well as the latest articles by Standard & Poor's chief investment strategist and chief technical analyst.

Ongoing Innovation

STANDARD & POOR'S recognizes that the fee-based business model for brokerage firms is growing at a very rapid pace. By leveraging its existing capabilities, Standard & Poor's is looking to serve the needs of investment advisers by positioning its Investment Services unit as an asset-gathering partner for alternative channels, regional brokers, and nationwide intermediaries.

Standard & Poor's has had highly successful entries into the alternative investment arena with the use of its STARS as the basis for a new long/short hedge fund and the launch of a hedge fund index. The S&P Hedge Fund Index is designed to be investable and representative of the broad-based investment experience of the hedge fund marketplace. Its calculation of daily values for the index and sub-indices provides a new level of transparency in hedge fund investing.

Standard & Poor's Investment Services continues to strengthen its core activities in equity research and fund research outside the United States as well. Global initiatives include the build-out of data and analysis covering equities and funds in Europe and Asia.

Fundamental to Standard & Poor's commitment to the investor is an emphasis on innovation and thought leadership, demonstrated most recently by the launch of two projects aimed at helping investors compare investments and discern corporate earnings. In August 1999, Standard & Poor's, with MSCI, unveiled the Global Industry Classification System (GICS), a system of numeric codes for identifying companies by economic sector, industry group, industry, and subindustry. GICS currently covers more than 25,000 companies globally and is expanding every year.

In May 2002, Standard & Poor's quantitative analysts announced a new system to calculate a company's after-tax earnings generated from its principal businesses, removing items such as option costs and pension gains so as to be able to deduct them and arrive at a "core earnings" number. Heralded by the *New York Times* as one of the best new ideas of 2002, Standard & Poor's Core Earnings also strips out company one-time gains or losses to determine a figure that reflects the true performance of a company's ongoing operations. Although few companies, as yet, have adopted the measurement when issuing their earnings reports (2001 Core Earnings calculations shaved an average of 31 percent off companies' reported earnings), many are nonetheless adopting some of the ideas central to the concept, and Standard & Poor's equity analysts will use Core Earnings in forming their investment recommendations on the companies they cover. Since May 2002, more than 100 companies have announced plans to deduct the cost of stock options as an expense, and the accounting standards board is considering making that deduction mandatory.

For nearly a century and a half, Standard & Poor's has excelled at analyzing, understanding, and navigating the world's financial markets. The firm's products, services, and independent benchmarks shed light on an increasingly complex global market. More than ever before, the world financial community seeks out Standard & Poor's for information, analysis, insight, valuation, and innovative solutions. Building on Henry Varnum Poor's commitment to protecting and ensuring the investor's right to know, Standard & Poor's is shaping the future of financial services.

Chapter Seventeen

The Promise and Peril
of Fund Investing

BRIAN PORTNOY
Senior Mutual Fund Analyst, Morningstar

M UTUAL FUNDS ARE the investment vehicle of choice for millions of Americans—and for good reason. Without poring over
cryptic financial statements to understand individual equities or hard-
to-buy fixed income securities, investors can easily buy a basket of
stocks or bonds that immediately delivers diversified exposure to different corners of the market. Assembling and monitoring those bas-
kets are professional money managers, whom investors essentially
hire—sometimes at very reasonable cost.

Then again, it's hard for many fund investors to avoid having a sour
taste in their mouths these days. Obviously, fund shareholders have
endured steep losses during the course of the bear market. From the
market peak in March 2000 through the end of September 2002, the
average diversified U.S. equity fund posted a cumulative loss of 36.3
percent, marginally better than that of the S&P 500.

More general problems plague fund investing as well. For starters,
trying to pick a "good" fund can frequently feel like navigating an
impossibly difficult maze. One reason for feeling perplexed is the
shear breadth of choices available. Once a sleepy industry that
touched relatively few lives, the fund business exploded during the
nearly twenty-year bull market that began in the early 1980s. There
are now approximately 6,000 distinct funds to choose from—about
the same as the number of publicly traded companies. Mutual fund

sales pitches rarely clarify the matter. Funds are now sold like other consumer products such as toothpaste or automobiles, so investors can be overwhelmed by glossy ads, not to mention confusing prospectuses and an overabundance of hard-to-interpret data.

Thus, how to whittle down the choices to find a good fund can be an extremely frustrating experience. Investors are sometimes constrained to the handful of choices provided through their tax-privileged retirement accounts, such as an employee-provided 401(k) plan, but even in that situation, pulling the trigger on one fund versus another can amount to guesswork.

Independent Thinking on Mutual Funds

MORNINGSTAR HAS BECOME an important voice in steering investors through the mutual fund maze. Its mission, simply put, is to help investors make better decisions to reach their financial goals. Indeed, the company's abiding ethic is "Investors come first." Founded in Chicago in 1984 and now a global investment research firm with operations in eighteen countries, the firm has become a preferred destination for individual investors, financial planners, and institutions seeking investment information, data, and security analysis.

In an era racked by Enron-style malfeasance, Jack Grubman–style analyst conflicts, and steep market declines that have seriously damaged the quality of life for many investors, Morningstar's calling card is its independence and objectivity. It lacks any of the much-publicized conflicts found in some prominent financial institutions where research has been, for all intents and purposes, an extension of investment banking and "buy" ratings have been basically rewards for firms that give those institutions lucrative underwriting deals. Morningstar analysts simply don't have those conflicts and can essentially play the role of consumer advocates.

With nearly twenty years of experience as an objective industry observer, Morningstar can point to two core lessons that should serve the typical investor well. Let's call these the dual pillars of smart fund investing: *diversification* and *minimizing expenses*. We can elaborate on each through the lens of what Morningstar research and tools have taught us over time.

Diversification

THERE'S NO SAYING where the market's going next. The airwaves are filled with pundits speculating on which stock, sector, or country will be the next "hot" place to invest—but no one really knows. As a result of such uncertainty, the simplest and most profound rule of investing is to diversify. Cover your bases with investments in different segments of the market because you just don't know which one will perform best next.

The idea is simple, but putting it into practice isn't always easy. Fund prospectuses can sometimes be less than illuminating, and fund names rarely tell you what you need to know. For example, Fidelity Growth & Income, Liberty Growth & Income, and One Group Growth & Income don't share the same investment style, even though their names suggest that they do. Meanwhile, more colorful names such as Fidelity Magellan and American Century Ultra don't provide any insight into what types of stocks their respective managers invest in.

The Morningstar Style Box™, which was invented in 1992 and significantly revised in 2002, allows investors to quickly gauge the investment positioning of a mutual fund. In the world of equities, the Style Box categorizes portfolios by both their investment style and market capitalization. A fund's style scores as growth, blend, or value-oriented. Morningstar evaluates each stock in a portfolio using ten variables— five "growth" factors such as long-term projected earnings growth and five "value" variables such as price-to-projected earnings. Examining portfolios on a stock-by-stock basis, some funds are tilted toward companies with fast earnings, cash flow, and sales growth, for which the market typically pays a premium. On the other hand, some funds prefer slower growing or temporarily troubled firms that are cheaper on price-to-earnings, price-to-cash flow, and price-to-sales bases. Funds that mix both growth and value stocks, or invest in what are commonly referred to as "core" stocks, fall into the "blend" style. Market cap methodology defines large-cap stocks as the top 72 percent of the capitalization of Morningstar domestic stock; midcap stocks represent the next 18 percent; and small-cap stocks represent the balance.

Morningstar goes through all that work for a reason. The Style Box forms the basis for investment categories—such as "large-growth," "mid-blend," and "small-value"—which facilitates apples to apples comparisons among funds. These categories make it easier for investors to build diversified portfolios. Of course, there's no need to buy one fund from every category, but there are some generic combinations that will allow most investors to cover their bases. One sensible possibility is to anchor one's portfolio with a "core" large-blend offering and then supplement it with a small-cap, foreign stock, and high-quality bond fund. Specialty funds—those that invest in just one sector or quirky securities such as "bear market funds" that short-sell the market—should be used sparingly.

An important lesson from the past decade is that in the short term, different corners of the market will soar while others will swoon. Look, for example, at what might seem like a narrow part of the stocks universe—midcap stocks—to see how different investment styles come in and out of favor. Midcap growth stocks were a huge success in the late stages of the bull market. In 1999, the average midgrowth fund jumped a whopping 62.5 percent. Meanwhile, the typical mid-value offering, which specializes in banks, industrials, and utilities—a galaxy away from then white-hot Internet and semiconductor stocks—gained 7.3 percent that year. Many value funds were heavily redeemed in the late 1990s as investors sought out those categories with the highest returns.

What happened next should come as no surprise. Dot-coms and other tech-related stocks crashed and burned while "old economy" stocks became sexy once again. In 2000, midgrowth and mid-value funds reversed fates: The former lost 5.4 percent on average, while the latter gained 18.4 percent. Generally, the bull market's unloved—small-value and mid-value funds—have been just about the only saving grace for equity investors. The opposite corner of the market—large-growth and midgrowth funds—attracted the bulk of new investments in the late 1990s and 2000 and has been by far the hardest hit.

In sum, whenever the market swings wildly, as it certainly has in recent years, investors risk seeing their portfolios thrown out of whack. A once-balanced portfolio can be skewed (sometimes imperceptibly) toward the market's winners, which can leave the portfolio flat-footed when the market inevitably begins to prefer a different investment style. As a result, one of the most popular portfolio tools on Morningstar.com, the company's well-regarded website, is the

"X-Ray" feature. This tool allows an investor to quickly assess portfolio diversification by examining all of the funds' stock holdings and
determining the portfolio's investment style bias. The X-Ray tool also
tells investors about stock and sector overlap across their funds. It can
tell that investor if any particular stock, say AOL Time Warner, or
General Electric, makes up a large portion of the overall portfolio—
something that probably wouldn't be obvious by looking at each individual fund in isolation. It can also point out that a portfolio is heavily
tilted toward some sectors, say technology or telecom, and away from
others, such as financials or energy.

Costs

THE SECOND PILLAR of smart fund investing is even simpler but just
as powerful: Buy low-cost funds. Over the years, Morningstar has
conducted numerous studies that all echo the same point: Low-cost
funds outperform high-cost funds. Here the comparison between
mutual funds and other consumer products is misleading because, in
fact, buying a mutual fund is not like buying a television. With a television, more money buys you lots of good things: bigger screen,
sharper picture, more features, and so forth. With a mutual fund,
there is no reason to assume that the managers of higher-cost offerings are better than those who run low-cost funds. When you pay
more, the odds are that you will get less.

The argument is straightforward. Say an investor puts $10,000 in
two funds for the same period of time and both portfolios delivered the
exact same pre-expense performance: 7 percent per year for twenty-
five years. The only difference between the two funds is the expense:
One has an annual expense ratio of 0.5 percent while the other costs 1.5
percent annually. The difference in after-expense investment performance is striking: The lower-cost fund would have returned $48,277 over
the period while the higher-cost fund would have returned $38,134.
Considering what most investors need to save for retirement, that
roughly $10,000 difference in investment performance would be mul-
tiplied many times for most real-world portfolios.

The available evidence powerfully supports the argument. In a
March 2002 commentary in *Morningstar Mutual Funds,* a biweekly
investment report, senior analyst Scott Cooley ranked funds by their

1996 expense ratios and looked at their returns over the subsequent five-year period that ended in December 2001. He found that in eight of the nine domestic Morningstar style boxes, funds with the cheapest expense ratios significantly outpaced those sporting heftier price tags. Moreover, Cooley found that high-cost funds that had managed to post strong returns in the first half of the decade had a difficult time maintaining their edge.

For bond fund investors, fishing in the low-cost pond is perhaps even more important. Compared with equities, the dispersion of bond fund returns is quite narrow, so separating the winners from the losers can sometimes be a matter of only a few basis points. For example, the average intermediate-term bond fund sports an annual expense ratio of 0.96 percent. Nearly all of that category's top-rated funds have lower expenses, and many cost less than 60 basis points (or 0.6 percent) per year.

In another *Morningstar Mutual Funds* commentary, Cooley makes an interesting, less-obvious finding: High-cost bond funds often take on more risk than their low-cost rivals. That's because in order to more effectively compete, high-cost fund managers sometimes look to riskier investments to make up for the ground given up to lower-cost competitors. That translates into costly funds with extra portions of low-rated or nonrated debt. Such issues typically offer higher coupon payments than more highly rated debt. More high-yield paper, however, means more credit risk and a greater likelihood of defaults, especially in a sluggish economy.

Overall, as Morningstar research has shown, diversification and low costs will keep many investors in good stead over the long haul. Of course, a nondiversified portfolio—one tilted toward nothing but growth stocks—was the big winner of the late 1990s. But clearly investors with diversified portfolios have survived the past several years much better than those without. Also, costs didn't seem to matter much a few years ago. A shareholder who owned a fund with a 1 percent expense ratio that returned 25 percent in one year was forfeiting only 4 percent of her gains. But that 1 percent price tag will be tougher to swallow in a market where single-digit gains might be the norm. If that fund returns 5 percent in a year, then the investor is foregoing a staggering 20 percent of her gains to expenses. In short, investors should follow these simple but powerful lessons to achieve a much more rewarding mutual fund experience.

Rethinking the Risks of Investing

IT WASN'T THAT long ago that the risks of investing were thought of primarily in terms of missed opportunities. Not owning that "hot" stock or fund was perceived to be the downside to investing in the late 1990s. To put things in perspective, a small growth fund that went up "only" 50 percent in 1999 was a bottom-half performer that year!

Yet the fundamental nature of risk hasn't changed just because the market has gone down and scandals have proliferated—it's still about losing money and not meeting your investment goals. So how can investors, many of whom unfortunately got the wrong ideas a few years ago that equity investing is a largely risk-free exercise, refocus on the true risks of investing?

Many of Morningstar's analyses say that chasing performance is a sure way to get burned. Investors who bought those "hot" funds in the 1990s surely have gotten hurt the worst. Take technology funds, for example. Between 1998 and 2000, the fund industry launched more tech-focused funds than other type—259 to be precise, the most (160) in 2000. Billions of dollars flooded into these funds and, subsequently, most of those investors lost their shirts. From the market peak in March 2000 through the end of September 2002, the *average* tech fund shed 83 percent of its value. Some were much worse: Those who invested $10,000 in the Jacob Internet fund when it launched in January 2000 would have seen their investment dwindle to $495 by September 2002—a nauseating decline of 95.6 percent.

The point here is to beware of trendy funds. Going back to 1991, Morningstar looked at the timing and performance of the fund industry's most popular product introductions. Other favorites included financials-oriented funds in 1996, communications funds in 1998, and real estate funds in 1997. Each wave of new rollouts followed years of great performance in each sector. Real-estate funds shot the lights out in 1996 and 1997, for example. But in each case, the market sagged shortly after the peak of each group's popularity. Generally, sector-specific funds have been a minefield for investors. Morningstar has found that sector funds attract most of their inflows in "hot" markets that subsequently turn cold. Looking at performance of sector funds on a dollar-weighted basis, meaning taking into account when they were actually purchased, shareholders received much worse performance than they would have gotten with more diversified offerings.

Along the same lines, Morningstar has found that performance chasing has been at work at the fund family level, too—with predictable consequences for investors. The most popular fund complex during the bull market was Janus, which attracted a massive amount of new assets. Nearly all of their equity funds posted huge gains in 1998 and 1999, but that was largely because the shop was focused on growth stocks—which have tumbled since 2000. Many Janus shareholders bought in near the market peak, so the family's dollar-weighted performance has been poor. For example, Janus Mercury had less than $2 billion in assets at the end of 1997, when it had a so-so performance record. After it posted huge gains in 1998 and 1999, the fund's asset base grew to more than $13 billion by the end of 2000. But the fund lost 22.8 and 29.8 percent in 2000 and 2001, respectively, and has endured steep losses in 2002 so far. Meanwhile, fund families that offer broader, more diversified lineups have treated shareholders much better. The dollar-weighted returns for Fidelity, American Funds, and Vanguard have been competitive, for example, because when some of their funds have struggled, others in healthier corners of the market have picked up the slack.

One final element of performance chasing deserves its own red flag: paying any attention to mutual fund asset flow data. The media frequently makes a big deal of how many billions of dollars flow in and out of funds. Investors might interpret big inflow numbers as a "buy" signal (if everyone's buying, it must be time to get in, right?) and big outflow numbers as a signal that the market's going to fall further, so it's time to sell. That would be a mistake. For starters, the big numbers bandied about usually lack any context. Billions of dollars may sound like a lot of money, but there's roughly $7 trillion invested in mutual funds currently, about $4 trillion of which is parked in stock funds, the balance in fixed-income and money market vehicles. Most "huge" numbers actually aren't—$10 billion in flows represent less than 1 percent of assets, for example—so ignore them.

But more important, there's simply nothing meaningful investors can learn from watching fund flows, regardless of how big the numbers are. Some might think that they can game the system, dodging a falling market and then latching back on when flows and the market

rise again. That's not true: Using fund-flow data to drive one's investment decisions is an ironclad way to chase market returns because
fund flows don't drive long-term market returns. In 2000, the fund
industry set an all-time record for inflows but that year's market was
pretty lousy, and the subsequent years have been even worse.

Put simply, fund flows are a lagging indicator of market performance. For example, value-stock funds were outperforming growth
funds in March 2000, but it wasn't until nearly a year later that they
began to attract more assets. In 2002, bond funds saw better inflows
than stock funds because the former had recently posted better
returns. There's no guarantee that trend will continue in the future,
and with interest rates at multidecades lows, it's unlikely that bond
funds will perform as well in the future as they have over the past few
years. Blindly following the trends is a sure way to invest in yesterday's winners.

In sum, the fundamentals of investing haven't changed in this
post-Enron environment. In fact, the market doldrums and disturbing
scandals will augur, hopefully, a back-to-basics market where
investors stick to time-tested principles such as building and maintaining a well-diversified portfolio and avoiding high-cost investments. Also, as Morningstar has witnessed over the years, it's important to buy the securities that match your investment goals, time
horizons, and risk tolerance and avoid—if at all possible—trendy
products that look great today but have a high chance of turning
ugly tomorrow.

To end on one controversial thought, the bear market may have
actually *highlighted* the virtues of fund investing. Contrast it to stock
investing, where investors have virtually no safety net when things go
awry. Well-chosen funds can provide investors with a diversified basket of securities that actually do offer some protection because
there's an experienced manager at the helm separating the winners
from the losers. That's not to say that good funds in bad markets
won't lose money and, of course, there are always bad apples in the
barrel. But these days, the risk-return profile of owning funds is certainly more palatable to most investors than picking stocks on their
own. Moreover, most investors can't get diversified exposure to certain market segments without a mutual fund. Small-cap value funds
have been the bear market's best equity-focused performers, but few

individuals have the time, resources, and expertise to tread into that market. The same applies to the world of fixed income—this decade's true winner so far—where individual investors have little entrée outside the relatively transparent and accessible government bond market.

Finally, funds do provide some shelter to the scandals that have racked the markets if only because the true scandal stocks such as Enron and WorldCom are likely to be only a small portion of any individual fund portfolio, if they're present at all. The fund industry is relatively scandal-free compared with the world of equities and corporate bonds, and there's an abundance of information available on nearly all mutual fund products. In that regard, information is the individual investor's most powerful tool in today's market. There are certainly downsides to fund investing, as have been highlighted above, but with the help of Morningstar and other trusted advisers, investors can avoid some of the major pitfalls of market participation and earn a much more rewarding investment experience.

Chapter Eighteen

A Standard of Value

JEAN BERNHARD BUTTNER
Editor-in-Chief, The Value Line Investment Survey

VALUE LINE WAS FOUNDED by my father, Arnold Bernhard, in 1931. He was known as the "Dean of Wall Street" by many in the investment community because of his pioneering work and statistical methods, and the number of security analysts he trained. Since then, our family has built Value Line into the nation's largest independent research firm.

Ironically, a series of catastrophes turned out to be the most fortunate events of Dad's business life, and they taught his family that adversities—when they strike—should be looked at as opportunities. Here's how he and we, his family, learned that lesson.

Dad worked his way through Williams College and graduated in 1925. He and Mom enjoyed a colorful courtship during his first job as a theatre critic and reporter. Although he was poor, several times a week he would take her out to a dinner and a show—both free because he was reviewing the show and the restaurant for newspapers. Between seeing more shows in a few weeks than she had seen in her entire life, eating rich food, and having to get up at 6 A.M. to go to her high school teaching job, Mother became ill—and Dad decided it was time to change careers. He left the field of daily journalism (although never giving up his love of the theatre) and became a trainee at Moody's Investors Service.

He said, "In those days, the late 1920s, the business of America, it was proudly proclaimed, was business. The financiers of Wall Street were the Lords of Creation. It was prestigious just to be on Wall Street in almost any capacity. The country was about to enter a new era in which poverty would be abolished throughout the land once and for all. Stock prices were bid up and up in anticipation of the great new era."

Then came the crash of 1929. "It was a shock," my father recalled. "But 1929 was just the tip of the iceberg. The stock market lost about 40 percent of its value in the last quarter of 1929 alone. But it recovered about half of the loss in the early months of 1930. Then came the real deluge in 1931–32. When the market finally struck bottom in 1932, the Dow Jones Industrial Average had lost 90 percent of its 1929 peak value. Stocks, as measured by the Dow, sold for only 10 percent of what the market said they were worth only a few years earlier."

That experience forced Dad to conclude that a standard of value had to be discovered, a standard indicating when stocks were overvalued and when they were undervalued, a standard that was rational, not emotional. There was no such thing in existence at the time. Moody's had bond ratings, but there were no stock ratings. Indeed, even today theory holds that the market is efficient: that the price in the marketplace is the correct value. Efficient market theorists say that there can be no independent standard of value—that the market price itself is the only correct value. Dad disagreed and was determined to find a standard of normal value so that the investing public would not again suffer when there are extremes such as those in 1929 and 1932. That was how the idea of the *Value Line Ratings of Normal Value* was born.

"The Value Line Rating I designed," he said, "was a correlation between the monthly prices of a stock over a period of twenty years on the one hand, and the company's concurrent annual earnings and book values on the other. United States Steel, for example, might be described as having been worth one-third of its book value and six times earnings. When the price deviated markedly from the standard thus derived, as in 1929, it was determined that the deviation was a measure of overvaluation. When it declined below the standard, the deviation was a measure of undervaluation."

He worked out these equations for 120 individual stocks. Each was a separate equation. He charted the prices and earnings and calculated and drew in the corresponding Value Line Ratings. He bought a multilith press and printed 1,000 copies of his book of *Value Line Ratings of Normal Value*, which he thought of as a discipline that would control the market—and would sell for only $200 a book.

One of my vivid childhood memories was listening to Dad talking of his experiences selling his first publication door to door. In those days people would still open the door for salesmen who called. But the world wasn't very interested, and the unsold books took up an embarrassingly large percentage of his office space.

Just when Dad thought he would never sell his books, a very well-respected investment counselor of that era, Major L. L. B. Angus, said he might study it and, if impressed, would mention it in his influential bulletin.

"A couple of days later," my dad said, "he called to say that he found the stuff interesting and would comment favorably upon it in his forthcoming bulletin, which he did—sort of. He said in his bulletin that "This young fellow Bernhard has published a book of ratings which show when stocks are too high or too low. Everybody should own one. Write to Bernhard at 347 Madison Avenue, New York City—the price of the book is $55."

You can imagine my father's dismay at seeing his inventory of $200,000 in books written down to $55,000 almost overnight. He was still more dismayed when he received a bill for $800 from the Major to cover the expense of printing the bulletin in which the endorsement appeared. Not only did his inventory shrink, but his current assets were at one stroke diminished by about 75 percent.

But again, catastrophe proved to be opportunity. A little while after this happened, some sixty $55 checks appeared on Dad's desk in response to the Major's recommendation. That was how Dad learned that services didn't have to be sold face to face.

Just when my father was thinking how difficult it would be to build up his customer base, a Mr. McQueen, selling ad space in *Barron's,* called.

"His advice turned out to be invaluable," said my father. "He persuaded me to advertise in *Barron's* for two weeks. Each ad would cost $35 for a total commitment of $70. The advertisements were designed to bring in leads of $5 each—that is to say, the reader of the ad would send me $5, and I would send him a sample of the *Value Line Ratings of Normal Value.*"

Today we still sell our publications by selling discounted trial sub-scriptions and offering potential subscribers a thirty-day, money-back guarantee if they subscribe to Value Line's services. Over the past seven decades, *Value Line Ratings and Advisory Reports* have meta-morphosed into many additional investment products. The ranking system has changed from time series to cross-sectional correlation using multiple regression analyses and other statistical techniques.

We constantly strive to improve the ranking system, which has shown statistical success that could not be due to chance. The format of *The Value Line Investment Survey* page is equally famous. Nowhere else can an investor find so much financial information on a company on one 8½″ x 11″ sheet of paper.

Sometimes the worst crises have happy endings. As my father's family has learned, it's important to look at catastrophe as opportunity and to work hard at pursuing your dreams. Although Dad's business was beset by many catastrophes, his vision of a rational, disciplined approach to stock analysis and his persistence and hard work, along with a little luck, resulted in his becoming a Wall Street legend.

Value Line's traditions of independence and accuracy have been faithfully maintained through two generations of Bernhard family leadership. In addition, while other financial services companies were diversifying into investment banking and retail brokerage, Value Line's dedication to independence and unbiased research for all investors, both large and small, kept the company from straying from its roots. The concept of competing business interests under the same corporate umbrella can lead to conflicts of interest and misleading research, and may ultimately be harmful to the investing public. Recent investigations by the New York State Attorney General's office have revealed just how dangerous these conflicts can be as facts come to light revealing how investment research has been used to benefit a few at the expense of many.

Value Line's Stock Ranking System

IN APRIL 1965, after considerable experimentation and testing, Value Line adopted a "cross-sectional" approach in its search for successful stock discrimination. In simplest terms, a cross-sectional approach examines data *at a point in time rather than over time*. A multiple regression analysis of earnings and price data for thousands of stocks yielded one formula that can now be applied across all stocks, providing a common yardstick. The Value Line Timeliness Ranking System ranks the approximately 1,700 stocks in *The Value Line Investment Survey* from 1 to 5, as follows:

RANKS	NUMBER OF STOCKS
1 (Highest)	100
2 (Above Average)	300
3 (Average)	900
4 (Below Average)	300
5 (Lowest)	100

Stocks ranked 1 and 2 are likely to outperform the market in the coming six to twelve months. Stocks ranked 3 are likely to be average performers. Stocks ranked 4 and 5 are likely to underperform the market.

The record of the stock Ranking System over the more than thirty-seven years since it was introduced has been truly outstanding. The results, which are published every six months, are shown in Figure 18-1. From the chart, you can see that a portfolio of 1-ranked stocks, updated weekly, would have increased in value by 34,064 percent from 1965 through December 2002. That percentage figure equates to an annual compound gain of 16.7 percent. That compares with gains of 6.3 percent for the Standard & Poor's 500 Stock Index and 6.0 percent for the Dow Jones Industrial Average over the same period of time. That's quite a significant difference. You might also note that the stocks ranked 1 did better than those ranked 2, the stocks ranked 2 did better than those ranked 3, those ranked 3 did better than those ranked 4, and those ranked 4 did better than those ranked 5. The performance of each of the three indexes mentioned above was calculated without allowing for trading costs.

The Value Line Investment Survey

THE INVESTMENT SURVEY is often called the "Bible of Wall Street." A weekly service, it includes concise one-page reports on approximately 1,700 of the largest and most actively traded stocks and on more than ninety-five industries. Investors can subscribe to the

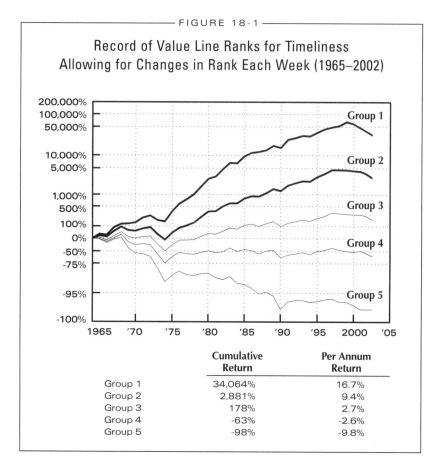

FIGURE 18-1

Record of Value Line Ranks for Timeliness
Allowing for Changes in Rank Each Week (1965–2002)

	Cumulative Return	Per Annum Return
Group 1	34,064%	16.7%
Group 2	2,881%	9.4%
Group 3	178%	2.7%
Group 4	-63%	-2.6%
Group 5	-98%	-9.8%

Survey in any of three versions: in print; on the Internet; or on a CD. Print or CD subscribers also get free access to the material on our website. Each company report contains a wide variety of information designed to help investors make stock selections. The material includes: the Value Line Timeliness, Safety, and Technical ranks; three- to five-year forecasts of stock prices; three- to five-year forecasts for a company's income statement and balance sheet; a stock price chart; up to seventeen years of historical financial data; analytical commentary written by a Value Line analyst; a description of the company's business; and quarterly sales, earnings, and dividend data. Other items include Beta, Insider Purchases and Sales, Institutional Ownership, and historical and projected growth rates. In short, you can find almost anything you want to help guide you in making investment decisions.

Each week's *Investment Survey* comes in three parts. Part 1 is the *Summary & Index*, which contains a list of all companies in the publication along with a page number to guide the user in finding a particular report. It also contains many up-to-date financial statistics on the companies (the latest Value Line ranks, the latest Target Price Range, the Current P/E Ratio, the most recent quarterly earnings and dividends, and more) and a large variety of stock screens, including Timely (most attractive) stocks in Timely Industries, Highest Yielding Stocks, Best Performing Stocks, Stocks with the Highest Annual Total Returns (next three to five years), and Highest Growth Stocks.

Part 2 is *Selection & Opinion*, where we publish our current opinions about the economy and the stock market. Regular features include a Stock Highlight, where we analyze a stock currently ranked 1 for Timeliness, selected stock screens, information on the fixed income markets, and a wide variety of stock market statistics. This is also where we publish three very popular Model Portfolios, which are designed to give subscribers guidance in setting up portfolios with particular objectives. Each of the twenty-stock portfolios is managed by senior security analysts.

The portfolios have quite different objectives. Portfolio I contains stocks with above average year-ahead price potential. To qualify for purchase in this portfolio, a stock must have a Timeliness rank of 1 and a Financial Strength Rating of at least B+. If a stock's Timeliness rank falls below 2, it is automatically removed. Portfolio II contains stocks for income and potential price appreciation. To qualify for purchase here, a stock must have a yield that is in the top half of the Value Line universe, a Timeliness rank of at least 3, and a Safety rank of 3 or better. If a stock's Timeliness rank falls below 3, a stock will automatically be removed. Portfolio III contains stocks with long-term price growth potential. To qualify for purchase here, a stock must have worthwhile and well-defined appreciation potential. Among the factors considered for selection are a stock's Timeliness and Safety ranks and its three- to five-year appreciation potential. These portfolios have all outperformed the broad stock market, as measured by the Dow or the S&P 500, since we introduced them in 1995. We publish results in *Selection & Opinion* each quarter.

Part 3, *Ratings & Reports*, presents reports on about 1,700 companies and more than 95 industries. It also contains supplementary reports, providing updated information and opinions on companies and stocks for which there have been important recent developments.

The Value Line Investment Survey **online.** By going to the Value Line website, www.valueline.com, an investor may get recent stock prices (normally with a twenty-minute delay), stock price charts, or company news on almost any public company. He or she may also set up and monitor portfolios and read our extensive educational material. Online subscribers have access to much more information and can manipulate the numbers to come up with almost any ratio they want. The website contains an archive of all issues published in the past thirteen weeks. Other features include a stock screening section, supplementary reports on important developments, and reports that the investor may customize.

The Value Line Investment Survey **for Windows.**® This powerful software service provides unprecedented stock analysis on CD. Capabilities include powerful sorting, screening, graphing, and reporting on individual common stocks, industry groups, or portfolios. The service includes full-page reports and analyst commentaries, as well as Timeliness and Safety ranks on the 1,700 stocks covered by *The Value Line Investment Survey,* with an expanded version providing information on more than 7,000 stocks. The software includes over 300 data items for screening groups of stocks. Data is updated monthly on disk and weekly via Value Line's website (www.valueline.com). Stock prices can be updated throughout each day.

The Value Line Investment Survey—Small- and Mid-Cap Edition. Complementing *The Value Line Investment Survey,* this weekly publication covers approximately 1,800 additional, mostly small-capitalization, issues. It features, among other things, a business description of each company, including recent corporate developments; consensus earnings estimates, when available; Value Line's Performance, Technical, and Safety ranks; and considerable historical financial data. This publication's Performance Ranking System has continued to outperform the Russell 2000 Index, the key benchmark for this equity category. Stocks ranked 1 and 2 for performance, as a group, outperformed the Russell 2000 by a margin of more than 10 to 1 from March 1995 (the inception of this publication) through December 2002.

The Value Line 600. This monthly service contains full-page reports on more than 600 stocks. Its reports provide information about many actively traded larger capitalization issues as well as some smaller capitalization stocks. Since introduced in 1996, it has proven to be very popular among investors who want the same type of analysis provided in *The Value Line Investment Survey*, but who don't want or need coverage of the 1,700 companies contained in that publication. All of the reports included in *The Value Line 600* are reprinted from the weekly *Value Line Investment Survey* and include our estimates and forecasts. Readers also receive supplemental reports as well as a monthly index, which includes updated statistics.

Value Line Select. This report service recommends one stock per month for inclusion in subscribers' investment portfolios. The stocks chosen have favorable risk/reward ratios, as determined by Value Line's senior research staff, although the level of risk is sometimes greater than average. Each initial report devotes as much space as necessary to analyzing the company, its competitive position, future prospects, and risks related to the business and the stock, as a basis for the recommendation. Supplementary reports are issued as needed to keep subscribers immediately abreast of the companies' performances and of any other developments that may alter the investment merits of the shares. These reports include specific recommendations, in the form of Buy, Hold, and Sell pronouncements.

The Value Line Mutual Fund Survey. Launched in 1993, this service has become one of the premier and most complete sources of analysis on mutual funds. It provides full-page profiles of more than 650 leading equity mutual funds. Annual subscribers receive condensed coverage of an additional 630 bond funds plus unique profiles and analyses on approximately 100 of the nation's leading fund families. Every three weeks, subscribers receive an updated issue containing about 200 fund reports plus a "Performance & Index" section that provides current rankings and performance figures for a universe of more than 2,000 funds as well as articles that analyze important investment trends and matters of concern to mutual fund investors.

The Value Line Special Situations Service. This service opens the world of emerging companies with bright futures to the more aggressive investor. Our analysts are constantly on the lookout for lesser-known stocks where unusual developments may pave the way for extraordinary rewards. Stocks covered in this publication may well include another Wal-Mart or Microsoft—stocks for more experienced investors who can take substantial risk while seeking exceptional appreciation potential. The service, published twice each month, provides subscribers with twelve new recommendations each year, follow-up reports on recommended companies, and in every issue, a summary of advice on all stocks under review.

The Value Line Options Survey and The Value Line Convertibles Survey. Options and convertibles are of primary interest to the most sophisticated investors—especially those looking for maximum profit but willing to take risk. These two services are designed to pinpoint the issues and investment strategies best suited to accomplishing these goals. Two decades ago, Value Line extended its common-stock Timeliness Ranking System to cover convertible debentures, convertible preferreds, and warrants. Subsequently, the system was expanded further to include 80,000 stock and stock-index options.

VALUE LINE HAS LONG BEEN RECOGNIZED as a truly independent source of research, and I hope that never changes. We are not stock-brokers or investment bankers, and we don't receive commissions from customers. We have never charged companies to be included in our publications, and we have never accepted advertising. Our revenues come from the subscription fees paid by our subscribers. Our sole interest is in providing those subscribers with the best information possible.

To ensure that our security analysts are also independent, we prohibit them from owning stock in any company they cover. When our analysts recommend the purchase or sale of a stock, our readers can be certain that the analysts will not benefit personally if the stock goes up or down. We are also eager to improve our products any way we can and welcome suggestions from our many hundreds of thousands of readers.

Chapter Nineteen

A Sounding Board for Business

RANDALL POE

Executive Director of Communications, The Conference Board

THE U.S. AND WORLD ECONOMY is in a slump. So is investor and public confidence in companies, the capital markets, and economic and business intelligence.

It has never been easy finding credible sources of economic and financial information. But in an economy darkened by discredited financial analysts, tainted research, and overcooked corporate books, honest information is at a premium. Despite firings and calls for reform, the marketplace is still being flooded by dubious data from conflicted sources, outright hype, and old-fashioned gossip. It's not surprising that investors and even people in high places don't know whom, or what, to trust.

·Since 1916, The Conference Board, a nonprofit economic research group based in New York, has been delivering objective, reliable data and analysis on virtually all aspects of the economy and on fast-changing management practices as well. The Conference Board has a track record for both innovation and objectivity. In 1919, The Conference Board created the first continuous measure of the cost of living in the United States, which was later turned over to the U.S. government. It is only one of many economic series (that is, measures) The Conference Board has created.

Supported today by more than two thousand companies in sixty-six nations, The Conference Board's economic analyses and management reports are widely watched by the financial markets, by management, and by the White House and the Federal Reserve. While hardly infallible, The Conference Board has become a trusty guide to the inner workings of the economy and a sounding board for business.

The Conference Board's economic analyses unit is headed by Gail Fosler, its chief economist, who has twice won the *Wall Street Journal's* award as America's most accurate forecaster. Its widely quoted experts also include Victor Zarnowitz, a world-class economist who is one of six business cycle experts who officially decide whether the United States has entered or moved out of recession; Dr. Dale Jorgensen, the respected Harvard University economist who is a senior fellow of The Conference Board; Robert McGuckin, a leading expert on productivity and economic growth; and Delos Smith, its oft-quoted senior business analyst.

> *The Conference Board has been an important institution in my life. It was here I started as an economist. It was here I came into contact with a business world I had never known before. What I learned during my five years at The Conference Board proved invaluable in my later life.*
> —ALAN GREENSPAN

The Conference Board also has been a leader in the drive to restore confidence in the financial markets through its blue-ribbon Commission on Public Trust and Private Enterprise. This twelve-member Commission, in a series of reports, has called for wide-ranging reforms to strengthen and improve corporate governance practices, make executive compensation more equitable, and improve auditing and accounting practices throughout business. Members of the Commission include Paul Volcker, former chairman of the Federal Reserve; Arthur Levitt, former SEC chairman; current Secretary of the Treasury John Snow; and Intel chairman Andy Grove. The group also includes former Senator Warren Rudman; John Biggs, former chairman, president, and CEO of TIAA-CREF; John C. Bogle, founder and former chairman, Vanguard Group; Peter M. Gilbert, chief investment officer, State Employees' Retirement System, Commonwealth of Pennsylvania; and Lynn Sharp Paine, Harvard University ethics expert.

Cochair of the Commission, along with Snow, is Peter G.

Peterson, the former Secretary of Commerce and now chairman of the New York Federal Reserve Bank and chairman of the Blackstone Group. The Commission was formed in response to widespread business scandals and a decline in business ethics that Peterson described as "a moral cancer." One of its basic objectives is to compel companies to focus on long-term strategies, not short-term fixes.

Many corporate leaders have endorsed the Commission's calls for action, including Warren Buffett, CEO of Berkshire Hathaway, who joined forces with the Commission in its controversial call for the expensing of stock options and appointing more independent boards of directors. As Buffett told a Commission press conference in New York: "There has been a tendency to put cocker spaniels on the compensation committee, not Dobermans."

> *We need to restore a constitutional democracy in our corporations, in place of the fiefdoms many have become.*
> —ANDY GROVE, CHAIRMAN, INTEL

To help companies improve the quality, independence, and effectiveness of their directors, The Conference Board has created The Directors' Institute. It has become a kind of university for directors, providing education and training on everything from legal compliance and codes of conduct to auditing practices, liability, and compensation. The institute's faculty includes leading authorities on corporate governance and the structuring of boards of directors. Founding sponsors of the institute are The Chubb Group of Insurance Companies, executive search firm Heidrick & Struggles, law firm Jones Day, and management consultants McKinsey & Company. The program is headed by Dr. Carolyn Brancato, an authority on corporate governance.

But even The Conference Board is being forced to work overtime to make sense out of the U.S. economy, which is suffering almost nonstop stress and a meltdown in public trust. The longest expansion in the 200-year history of the U.S. business cycle has given way to the longest and one of the most brutal bear markets ever. A throttled stock market has been accompanied by a sharp fall in corporate profits.

Growth continues to be sluggish and stop-and-go. Business investment, which powered growth in the late 1990s, has declined sharply in the past few years. Numerous industries continue to have more capacity than they can use and are bearing rising labor costs. That has depressed both profits and employment.

To compound problems, the slowdown has gone global. The recession of 2001 has given way to spotty growth that has weakened demand, stifled profits, and reduced investment virtually around the globe.

Says economist Zarnowitz: "The big problem is separating all the random noise from significant economic signals that can help us understand the present and where we are heading."

The Conference Board's Economic Indicators

TO HELP TIME-STRAPPED EXECUTIVES stay out in front of economic twists and turns, The Conference Board provides more than a dozen major economic barometers that chart the health of key sectors of the economy. Here are summaries of the most widely watched indexes.

The Conference Board's Consumer Confidence Index is a running monthly record of consumers' views of the economy. Since its creation in 1967, this index has been widely used as a guide to consumers' attitudes about the economy, jobs, and incomes. Because the index is a proven mover of financial markets, its release is tightly controlled. The press release is embargoed for release at precisely 10 A.M. the last Tuesday of every month. It is the largest consumer attitudes survey in the United States, covering 5,000 families throughout the country, showing how people in different parts of the country feel about the state of the economy.

The Consumer Internet Barometer, launched in 2002, is a quarterly report on who's doing what on the Internet. It focuses on consumers' trust and satisfaction in their Internet experience, including who is buying what and how consumers are using the Internet on a daily basis. It surveys 5,000 male and 5,000 female heads of household. The Conference Board's two partners in producing the barometer are the NFO WorldGroup, a leading survey organization, and Forrester Research, widely known for its Internet research.

The Help-Wanted Advertising Index measures job openings across America, based on the volume of classified job advertising appearing in fifty-one major daily newspapers. Because the volume of advertising is very sensitive to labor market conditions, this index is widely used to measure changes in the local, regional, and national supply of jobs. Among the newspapers included in this index are the *New York Times*, the *Boston Globe*, the *Washington Post*, the *Atlanta Constitution*, the *Chicago Tribune*, the *Miami Herald*, the *Nashville Banner*, the *San Diego Times-Union*, the *Seattle Post-Intelligencer*, the *Dallas Morning News*, the *St. Louis Post Dispatch*, the *Rocky Mountain News*, the *Salt Lake City Desert News*, the *Sacramento Bee*, the *Los Angeles Times*, and the *San Francisco Chronicle*.

The Leading Economic Indicators. In 1995, The Conference Board became the first private organization to assume responsibility for a major U.S. government economic series. The U.S. Department of Commerce selected The Conference Board to produce the Business Cycle Indicators, which include the Leading Economic Indexes. Since then, The Conference Board has created databases covering over 250 economic series. They include the Leading, Coincident, and Lagging Indicators. These indexes include latest official data on new orders for materials and consumer goods, new orders for capital goods, housing starts and permits, contracts for commercial and industrial plant construction, and new capital appropriations. Changes in this data can signal important shifts in the economy. Also included: changes in the U.S. labor market (such as two widely followed series—average workweek and unemployment insurance claims), which tend to move ahead of changes in overall employment and unemployment. Today The Conference Board produces not only the U.S. Leading Economic Index but leading indexes for Germany, the United Kingdom, Japan, Korea, France, Mexico, Australia, and Spain.

Although many of these numbers can glaze the eyes, they are carefully followed not just by stock market wonks and trading desks. That's because since 1948, The Conference Board's U.S. Leading Index turned down before each of the ten U.S. business cycle peaks, while it turned up before each of the business cycle troughs.

Some insiders think the best monthly barometer of total economic growth in the United States is The Conference Board's Coincident Index, which provides a sweeping picture of current economic conditions. It combines the latest data on real personal income, manufacturing, retail and wholesale trade sales, employment, and industrial production. These are vital statistics about current economic activity used by both business and government to gauge overall economic health. The Coincident Index is more timely, appears more often, and is more diversified than the widely reported figures for gross domestic product (GDP), the quarterly record of national output.

The Conference Board's Ongoing Focus

THE CONFERENCE BOARD'S not-for-profit structure and its focus on objective research have been hallmarks of the organization since its founding in 1916. The Conference Board was born during a period of prolonged economic and social turmoil. The rapid growth of labor unions, a wave of new government laws aimed at regulating business, and abuses by many companies that led to negative media coverage triggered discord among labor unions and corporations, resulting in bombings, deaths, and violence of all kinds.

Disturbed, a group of business leaders met in upstate New York to discuss America's volatile economic climate and the widespread public ignorance about free enterprise and the capital markets. The group was led by a prominent engineer from General Electric named Magnus Alexander. It was quickly decided that what the nation needed was not another "propaganda machine," in the words of Alexander, but an organization that would produce sound economic and management research and share that research with the public. Alexander would later become The Conference Board's first president.

The Conference Board, from its inception, represented a new direction for American industry, a body dedicated to discovering and spreading accurate and objective information about business and the economy.
—THE LATE DR. LEONARD SILK, MEMBER OF THE EDITORIAL BOARD, *NEW YORK TIMES*

From its inception, The Conference Board focused on unbiased fact-finding and has made its research results available to the public and the media. It also created what today is a formidable meeting network, bringing together more than 15,000 executives each year to share knowledge and insights with each other.

Under the leadership of its current president and CEO, Richard E. Cavanagh, The Conference Board has globalized both its membership and reach. Among its high-powered Board of Trustees, about one-third are chief executives based outside the United States. Virtually all of its economic and management intelligence includes business experiences not just from the United States but also from throughout the world.

The Board's overall mission continues to be simple: to create and disseminate knowledge about the economy and management and to help business strengthen its performance and better serve society.

The Conference Board's mission, and its work, have never been more important. Bombarded by questionable, self-serving data and analysis, and confusing economic signals of all kinds, the integrity of The Conference Board's work makes it a rare commodity indeed.

C h a p t e r 20 *T w e n t y*

Sarbanes-Oxley Act
and Securities Fraud

L E W I S   D .   L O W E N F E L S
Partner, Tolins & Lowenfels

J O H N   D .   T O R T O R E L L A
Associate, Paul, Weiss, Rifkind, Wharton & Garrison LLP

A MONG THE CHANGES wrought by the Sarbanes-Oxley Act of 2002 (the Act), perhaps the least remarked upon, although one of the most remarkable for investors, is the new statute of limitations provision (section 804 of the Act, which is reprinted at the end of this chapter). On first reading, it may appear that the Act does nothing more than extend the statute of limitations for private lawsuits filed under the general antifraud provision of the Securities Exchange Act of 1934 (the 1934 Act), section 10(b) and Rule 10b-5. A closer examination of the statutory language, however, reveals a far more sweeping change, which is likely to have a significant impact upon and introduce significant uncertainties for both the business community and the courts.

Whether through design or inadvertence, the Act increases the limitations period not only for private rights of action under section 10(b) and Rule 10b-5, but for every other private right of action involving a claim of fraud, deceit, manipulation, or contrivance under the securities laws. Moreover, when an investor cries fraud, the investor's cause of action will not accrue until he discovers the fraud, even if he could have discovered it years earlier by exercising reasonable diligence. With the passage of Sarbanes-Oxley, a claim of fraud in connection with an alleged securities violation will entitle a plaintiff to a significantly longer limitations period and will deprive defendants of the defense that the suit is untimely because the alleged fraud could have been discovered earlier through the exercise of reasonable diligence.

Since 1991, when the U.S. Supreme Court delivered its watershed decision in *Lampf, Pleva, Lipkind, Prupis & Petigrow v. Gilbertson,* the governing law has been that an investor wishing to sue for securities fraud must file a lawsuit within one year after the discovery of the alleged fraud, deceit, manipulation, or contrivance, but in no case more than three years after the date of the violation. Lower courts applying *Lampf* have found that the one-year period—the statute of limitations—begins to run either from the date on which the plaintiff discovered the facts giving rise to the claim of fraud ("actual knowledge") or from the date on which the plaintiff could have discovered the facts through the exercise of reasonable diligence ("constructive notice"). Courts have consistently treated the three-year cut-off—often referred to as a statute of repose—as immutable.

During its argument before the U.S. Supreme Court in *Lampf,* the Securities and Exchange Commission urged the Court to apply a five-year statute of limitations to the implied private right of action under section 10(b) and Rule 10b-5. On a number of occasions since *Lampf,* Congress has considered extending the statute of limitations to two years and the statute of repose to five years. The movement for longer statutes of limitations and repose has invariably rested on the argument that by the time a complex securities fraud comes to light, many lawsuits or other meritorious actions will be barred due to the time limits. In testimony before Congress during its consideration of the Private Securities Litigation Reform Act in 1995, then SEC Chairman Arthur Levitt stated: "Extending the statute of limitations is warranted because many securities frauds are inherently complex, and the law should not reward the perpetrator of a fraud, who successfully conceals its existence for more than three years."

When the Enron debacle came to light, Chairman Levitt's comments were used to support a new initiative to extend the limitations periods. Congress heard testimony from state attorneys general, who complained that some state pension funds were unable to bring cases against Enron because their actions were time-barred by the three-year statute of repose. In response to this problem, Senator Patrick Leahy (D-VT) introduced the Leahy Amendment, to permit actions involving fraud, deceit, manipulation, or contrivance to be brought within two years after the discovery of the violation, but no more than five years after the violation. The Leahy Amendment became Title VIII of the Sarbanes-Oxley Act. In his analysis of section 804 of the Sarbanes-Oxley Act, Senator Leahy remarked to Congress:

> This provision is intended to lengthen any statute of limitations under federal securities law, and to shorten none .... It would set the statute of limitations in the private securities fraud cases to the earlier of five years after the date of the fraud or two years after the fraud is discovered. The current statute of limitation for most such fraud cases is three years after the date of the fraud or one year after discovery, which can unfairly limit recovery for defrauded investors in some cases. It applies to all private securities fraud actions for which private causes of action are permitted.

Investors Need Not Exercise
Reasonable Diligence to Uncover Fraud

A FEW COMMENTS about the plain language of section 804 and Senator Leahy's analysis of this section are in order. First, there is no mention that the two-year statute of limitations is triggered by anything other than actual knowledge of the fraud. This is a departure from the "constructive notice" (meaning the date on which a plaintiff could have discovered the fraud through reasonable diligence) standard that has been applied to actions under section 10(b) and Rule 10b-5 for more than ten years. Second, section 804 applies to more than only the traditional 10b-5 cases. Based on its plain language as well as Senator Leahy's remarks, the new provision applies to *all* private rights of action alleging fraud under the securities laws. If courts honor the plain language of the statute, the Act changes the securities litigation landscape dramatically.

This is not the first time that Congress has considered a two-year/five-year limitations period. During debate over the Private Securities Litigation Reform Act of 1995, Congress considered an amendment that would have created a two-year/five-year framework. Although the amendment was eventually tabled, the debate over the amendment shows that Congress was well aware of the difference between actual and constructive notice.

The Supreme Court in *Lampf*, when called upon to choose a statute of limitations applicable to the private right of action implied by the courts from the words of section 10(b) and Rule 10b-5, chose to apply language from section 9(e) of the Securities Exchange Act of 1934, rather than language from section 13 of the Securities Act of 1933. Both provisions state that a suit may be brought within a year of the discovery but no later than three years after the violation. Section 13 of the Securities Act, however, starts the clock running once there is constructive notice. The Supreme Court in *Lampf* noted the difference in the language between section 9(e) and section 13, acknowledged the potential significance of the difference, and then determined that the limitations period should not start to run until the plaintiff had actual knowledge of the facts giving rise to the cause of action.

Despite the Supreme Court's decision in *Lampf* to apply the limitations period under section 9(e), which requires actual knowledge before the one-year statute of limitations begins to run, as opposed to the limitations period under section 13 of the 1933 Act, in which the one-year limitations period is triggered by constructive notice, the lower courts post-*Lampf* almost universally chose to permit constructive notice anyway. In a crucial opinion by Judge Posner in the Seventh Circuit, the court justified the application of constructive notice by reasoning that the Congress that had passed section 9(e) never dreamed that the courts would create an implied private right of action under section 10(b), let alone that the limitations period in section 9(e) would be read to limit such an implied right of action. Given that Congress had not given thought to whether constructive or actual notice should govern a statute of limitations applicable to a right of action it had not imagined, it was up to the court to judge whether constructive notice or actual knowledge should apply. Never mind that the U.S. Supreme Court in *Lampf* seemed pretty clearly to have decided the issue. (See *Tregenza v. Great American Communications Co.*, 12 F.3d 717, 721 [7th Cir. 1993]). The other circuit courts and federal district courts quickly fell in line in the interests of uniformity. (See, for example, *In re The Prudential Ins. Co. of Am. Sales Practice Litig.*, 975 F. Supp. 584, 599 [D.N.J. 1996].)

Section 804, read literally, requires actual knowledge to set the statute of limitations running. Under section 804, it will be much harder for the lower federal courts to engraft a constructive notice requirement into the statute. To do so, the lower courts would have to ignore that the plain language of the statute was put in place by a Congress with knowledge of the judicially implied private right of action under section 10(b) of the 1934 Act and by a Congress with an awareness of, if not an appreciation for, the distinction between actual knowledge and constructive notice. Thus, under the plain language of the statute, plaintiffs indeed are not required to exercise reasonable diligence to discover facts that would give rise to a suit.

The Limitations Period Is Extended for *Every* Securities Claim Involving Fraud

IT IS CURIOUS that Congress, in changing the statute of limitations applicable to lawsuits regarding securities fraud, did not do so by modifying the 1933 Act or 1934 Act themselves. After all, both of these acts contain statute of limitations provisions for the express rights of action within them. Instead, section 804 amends 28 U.S.C. § 1658, which is the statute of limitations applicable to causes of action for which Congress has not specified a statute of limitations elsewhere. Placing the new limitations provision here is appropriate, then, since the broad, general language of section 804 suggests that Congress did not consider exactly which causes of action expressly authorized by the specific words of the statute ("express actions") and which causes of action implied by the courts from the statutory language ("implied actions") the section would affect. Determining the precise scope of section 804 is likely to occupy the courts and frustrate defendants for years to come.

Congress clearly intended the statute of limitations provision of section 804 to apply to the implied private right of action under section 10(b) of the 1934 Act. Parroting the language of section 10(b), 804 applies to actions "that [involve] a claim of fraud, deceit, manipulation, or contrivance." In addition, however, the new two-year/five-year limitations period would seem to apply in certain cases to other express and implied private actions under the 1934 Act, e.g., sections 14(a), 14(e), 18(c) and 29(b) and Rules 10b-6 and 14a-9. Arguably, the new limitations period also applies to a trader's express action for insider trading under section 20A of the 1934 Act. Paradoxically, this is the one provision where the statute of limitations period may actually be shortened by operation of section 804: whereas the section was previously subject to a flat five-year statute of limitations, that period may now be shortened to two years after the plaintiff had actual knowledge of the violation. It is worth noting that such a result would be at odds with Senator Leahy's comment that section 804 "is intended to lengthen any statute of limitations under federal securities law, and to shorten none."

Beyond the 1934 Act and its express and implied rights of action, the Sarbanes-Oxley limitations period will apply to the express causes of action under the 1933 Act, at least insofar as they involve a claim of "fraud, deceit, manipulation or contrivance." But here is the complication—not all claims under sections 11 and 12(a)(2) of the 1933 Act involve fraud. Where they do involve fraud, however, those claims will be subject to the new time limits under 28 U.S.C. § 1658(b).

The Sarbanes-Oxley Act appears to set up a two-tier limitations system for the express private rights of action under the 1933 Act. Where a plaintiff does not allege fraud, claims would be governed by the one-year/three-year statute with the cause of action accruing once the plaintiff should have discovered the transgression through the exercise of reasonable diligence. On the other hand, a plaintiff alleging that the transgression involved fraud might argue that 28 U.S.C. § 1658(b) takes the claim out of the limitations period defined in section 13 of the 1933 Act and is properly governed by the two-year/five-year regime. No doubt, plaintiffs will attempt to take full advantage of these two-tier possibilities by pleading in the alternative that a violation was negligent or fraudulent.

Moreover, the possibility of two statutes of limitations provisions applying to a single claim will apply to any express or implied right of action under the securities laws that might involve fraud, deceit, manipulation, or contrivance. And the Act defines securities laws to include not only the 1933 and 1934 Acts, but also the Public Utility Holding Company Act of 1935, the Trust Indenture Act of 1939, the

Sarbanes-Oxley Act of 2002 Statute of Limitations Provision

Section 804(a) of the Sarbanes-Oxley Act of 2002 (Pub. L. No. 107-204, 116 Stat. 745, § 804 [2002]) amends 28 U.S.C. § 1658, which now reads in full:

"Section 1658—TIME LIMITATIONS ON THE COMMENCEMENT OF CIVIL ACTIONS ARISING UNDER ACTS OF CONGRESS:

(a) Except as otherwise provided by law, a civil action arising under an Act of Congress enacted after the date of the enactment of this section may not be commenced later than 4 years after the cause of action accrues;

(b) Notwithstanding subsection (a), a private right of action that involves a claim of fraud, deceit, manipulation, or contrivance in contravention of a regulatory requirement concerning the securities laws, as defined in section 3(a)(47) of the Securities Exchange Act of 1934 (15 U.S.C. 78c(a)(47)), may be brought not later than the earlier of—

(1) 2 years after the discovery of the facts constituting the violation; or

(2) 5 years after such violation."

In addition to amending 28 U.S.C. § 1658, section 804 further provides:

(b) EFFECTIVE DATE—The limitations period provided by section 1658(b) of title 28, United States Code, as added by this section, shall apply to all proceedings addressed by this section that are commenced on or after the date of enactment of this Act.

(c) NO CREATION OF ACTIONS—Nothing in this section shall create a new, private right of action.

Investment Company Act of 1940, the Investment Advisers Act of 1940, the Securities Investor Protection Act of 1970, as well as the Sarbanes-Oxley Act itself.

A final note: Section 804 specifically provides that "nothing in this section shall create a new, private right of action," but that is precisely the practical effect it may have. For example, a lawsuit under section 11 of the 1933 Act alleging negligence in connection with a material misstatement or omission that was previously time-barred by the three-year statute of repose before section 804 was enacted, may now, with the extended five-year cut-off, be recast as a timely action alleging fraud in connection with the same misstatement or omission. Whether the courts ultimately permit such actions, answering the question will undoubtedly cost businesses and the courts considerable resources.

It appears that the SEC's (and, of course, investors') wishes may finally have been answered—and then some. Not only will corporations and their officers and directors be subject to an effective five-year statute of limitations for alleged violations of section 10(b) and Rule 10b-5, but the same extended statute may well apply to any lawsuit arising under the federal securities laws, so long as there is an allegation of fraud, deceit, manipulation, or contrivance. By its plain language the Sarbanes-Oxley Act establishes a uniform statute of limitations regime for all private securities claims involving fraud that dramatically increases the period of time during which corporations, officers, directors, underwriters, and sellers may be subject to suit. Moreover, it appears that defendants may no longer claim that an action is time-barred because a plaintiff "should have known, through the exercise of reasonable diligence" that his cause of action had accrued—only actual knowledge will suffice.

The impact for investors under Sarbane-Oxley's new and extended limitations period is both simple and far-reaching—the change increases the period of time during which to commence actions for damages resulting from violations of the federal securities laws involving fraud. The results will be more lawsuits, probably more recoveries for plaintiffs, and undoubtedly more meticulous care and due diligence on the part of the potential defendants—corporations, directors, underwriters, and sellers of securities.

Part Four

Corporate Models of Excellence in Challenging Times

Toyota's Responsibility to People, Process, and Environment

TOSHIAKI TAGUCHI
President and CEO, Toyota Motor North America

A COMBINATION OF transportation necessity and love of the automobile has propelled the auto industry into dramatic growth over the past half century. In 1950, there were about 2.5 billion people on the planet. Today there are 6 billion. By 2050 world population is projected to rise to 9.4 billion. That is very fast growth, but it pales in comparison to the growth of the worldwide vehicle population during that same period.

In 1950, there were about 69 million cars and trucks worldwide. Today, there are more than ten times as many. What is even more phenomenal is that each day another 150,000 vehicles are added by new production. Projections indicate that by 2050, the world's vehicle population will climb to 1.1 billion. Few other industries can chart such astounding growth.

For automobile manufacturers, these projections bring tremendous opportunity, but also obligation. Each time one vehicle burns one gallon of gas, it will emit twenty pounds of carbon dioxide (CO_2)—the primary suspect in global warming. So it is with great opportunity and social obligation that automakers should take substantial and aggressive action to develop technologies that will protect the earth.

Key areas Toyota Motor Corporation and its industry need to focus on when considering the motorized society of this century are environment, safety, information technology (IT), and globalization. In the twenty-first century, automobiles must incorporate a new range of value-added qualities, taking into account the needs of the individual, society, and the earth. Toyota is convinced that a harmonious relationship with the environment, the global economy, local communities, and its stakeholders is the key to the realization of long-term, stable growth. The company is investing aggressively in environmental technologies because it believes the area of environmental responsibility poses the most urgent challenge.

Cleaner Cars

CARS TODAY RUN much cleaner than they did in years past. Nonetheless, the huge car population of 2050 still will place a terrible burden on the planet unless automakers, energy providers, governments, and suppliers join hands to fund the massive investments necessary to develop quickly even greener drivetrains, fuels, and fueling networks.

The need to do these things quickly and the incredible costs involved are driving the auto industry's rapid consolidation. No single automaker will be able to go it alone. That is why Toyota has formed partnerships on green technology research and development with General Motors, Volkswagen, and Nissan. In fact, Toyota will supply hybrid system components to Nissan for vehicles it plans to sell in the United States by 2006.

Solutions to worldwide problems like climate change will not only require big companies to form cooperative relationships with governments and environmental groups; they also will require deep commitment and a willingness to take risks. When global warming began to attract scientific attention and develop political traction several years ago, Toyota established a corporate position, which says, "Although global warming may still be the subject of some debate in the scientific community, we believe it is prudent to continue to reduce all emissions from our plants, products, and processes—including CO_2."

Toyota has long been viewed as a very conservative company that avoids risk. However, the company took a big one in 1997 when it decided to deliver to the market a vehicle that would be a concrete example of its position on global warming. This is Toyota's high-mileage gas/electric hybrid, the Prius. This five-passenger vehicle achieves 80 percent better fuel economy and puts out 90 percent fewer emissions than a comparable internal combustion vehicle. The company placed its confidence in the breakthrough technology in Prius because it was convinced that hybrid technology would benefit the earth.

So far, Toyota's calculated risk seems to be paying off. Prius has won worldwide awards and widespread praise from environmental groups. In the United States, Toyota is selling every one it produces. It also has achieved status as a "politically correct" car, with many celebrities, prominent environmentalists, and some members of the U.S. Congress driving one. In the United States, the Prius has a sticker price of about $20,000, and buyers are currently eligible for a $2,000 federal income tax deduction. Worldwide, Toyota has sold more than 100,000 Prius vehicles, 90 percent of global hybrid sales.

Hybrids offer an immediate means of increasing fuel economy and lowering emissions. Given the success of the Prius, Toyota has introduced two additional hybrid vehicles in the Japanese market and is now accelerating the development of its next generation of hybrid technology for more products in the North American market. Most recently, Toyota announced it would offer the popular Lexus RX330 in hybrid form. Its V6 system performs with the power of a V8 and the fuel efficiency of a four cylinder, with greatly reduced emissions. The industry has taken notice. Honda has now introduced the Civic Hybrid in addition to the Insight, and other major automakers are also developing hybrids.

To date, at least, pure battery-electric vehicles don't sell, and practical, affordable fuel-cell vehicles are still at least a decade or more away. Nevertheless, Toyota continues to develop this technology and has begun limited marketing in the United States of vehicles like the Highlander Fuel Cell, dubbed the FCHV-4. In December 2002, Toyota delivered the first of these vehicles to the University of California, Irvine and the University of California, Davis. Both of these institutions are at the forefront of hydrogen fuel-cell vehicle and infrastructure research, development, and implementation.

Will the Consumer Buy It?

COMPETITION ALWAYS BRINGS out the best performance in companies. The race to be a leader in clean, fuel-efficient vehicles is a case in point. However, the biggest challenge for hybrids is not manufacturing; it is marketing.

Toyota has learned that to gain wide acceptance and to sell in volume, new-technology vehicles must be three things: user friendly, able to use readily available fuel, and affordably priced. Hybrids already meet two of these factors—convenience and access to fuel. That leaves price. As noted above in connection with the Prius, tax incentives in the United States are already helping automakers leap the third hurdle and jump-start high volume consumer demand for this useful technology.

The typical Prius buyer is very different from the typical subcompact buyer, which is the conventional vehicle segment where consumers rank fuel economy the highest priority. Current hybrid owners are willing to take a risk and believe that the selling price is good value for obtaining the latest technology. In contrast, subcompact buyers tend to be risk averse and shop on price. These differences are crucial because the subcompact segment is an obvious high-volume target for hybrids.

Manufacturers will continue to try to reduce costs, and Toyota expects to achieve some savings if higher levels of mass production are reached. However, government incentives will be necessary to get automakers past the early production years with their lower volumes.

Clean Manufacturing

A CARMAKER'S ENVIRONMENTAL efforts should go beyond product design and development. Its environmental commitment should apply to all aspects of the so-called life cycle of a vehicle. Carmakers should combine their enthusiasm for lean manufacturing with a passion for clean manufacturing. Toyota, historically known as an innovator and leader in lean manufacturing, now is working to set the clean manufacturing standard in the industry. Key to this undertaking is making improvements in the way Toyota manufactures vehicles throughout the world. In 2000, for example, Toyota's North American manufacturing operations set forth a five-year environmental action plan, which established specific goals to minimize the most significant impacts of energy use/emissions of greenhouse gases, volatile organic compounds, toxic chemicals, hazardous waste disposed at landfills, and water consumption. Currently, Toyota's North American plants are on track to meet these goals.

One such goal has already been achieved, which is ISO 14001 certification for all of Toyota's plants. The ISO certification verifies that each of the plants has a formal environmental policy, a system designed to track the plant's environmental performance and established mechanisms for continuous improvement.

Additionally, the North American operations are well on their way to achieving energy reduction of 15 percent, which corresponds to a 15 percent reduction in CO_2 emissions, by 2005. This is being achieved even during the challenging times posed by Toyota's rapid growth in production volume in North America.

Toyota views its responsibility as a leader as an opportunity to pass along high standards and processes to its suppliers. This responsibility was the motivation for setting environmental standards for Toyota's North American suppliers, and in 2000, the company issued Green Supplier Guidelines for them to follow.

The Toyota Way

TOYOTA'S COMMITMENT TO environmental responsibility applies to its companies worldwide. Toyota's more than 245,000 employees throughout the globe are integral players in carrying out this commitment. So, how does this large company achieve its vision? The answer is through the company's core operating philosophy, what is called the Toyota Way. It is an ideal, a standard, and a guiding beacon for Toyota employees all over the world—a philosophy at the heart and soul of the company.

The Toyota Way has two pillars. The first is continuous improvement. The second is respect for people. It defines how the people of Toyota perform and behave in order to deliver these values to customers, shareholders, associates, business partners, and the global community. It is how the company has been able to grow throughout the world. In spite of the fact that languages and cultures differ in the twenty-seven countries where the company builds vehicles and the 160 countries where it sells products, the Toyota Way is taught and understood universally within all operations.

It is Toyota's belief that it should build products where they are sold. It is the way the company carries out its conviction to think globally, and to act locally. In this way, continuous improvement and respect for people guide the company within each one of its communities.

Continuous Improvement

In every aspect of its commitment to making things, Toyota's culture is dedicated to continuous improvement: continuous improvement in quality, continuous improvement in technology.

To do this, the company is never satisfied with the current status, thereby improving its business by putting forth the best ideas and efforts. Continuous improvement is achieved through three main components: challenge, *kaizen* (which literally translates as "continuous improvements"), and what is called *genchi genbutsu*—or "go and see."

The *challenge* is in developing a long-term vision and the means to achieve it.

Through *kaizen*, Toyota improves its business operation continuously and always drives for innovation and evolution.

Genchi genbutsu means to go to the source to find the facts and make the correct decisions, build consensus, and take action.

The significance of these three elements of continuous improvement was best summarized by the late Taiichi Ohno, who is known as the father of the Toyota Production System. He said, "Observe the production floor without preconceptions and with a blank mind. Repeat 'why' five times to every matter. Seek out root cause rather than source. Root cause lies hidden beyond the source."

In other words, by seeing the process firsthand, the real problems can be identified. In doing so, real solutions can be offered, rather than a "Band-Aid" fix.

Respect for People, Customer First

The second pillar of the Toyota Way is respect for people. Only people can make things, so our culture of "making things" must be supported by a culture of respect for people. This means showing respect for the values of others, seeking mutual understanding with sincerity, asking for their ideas, and placing importance on teamwork as the consolidated strength of each individual.

To expand on this point further, the Toyota Way makes up the core of the Toyota Production System—or TPS. TPS is often described by observers with such terms as "just-in-time" and "automation" as the ways to achieve the goal of eliminating waste. However, the real connection in describing TPS most accurately is to use the term "people."

Simply put, the fundamental concept in TPS is to place the customer first in all aspects, offering quality products at lower prices and on a timely basis. In order to do this, the "people" who create the products must have a sense of responsibility in order to build quality into them and a determination to pursue their goals to the end, without compromise. TPS has been described as the "machine that changed the world." However, it is people who breathe the soul into machines and systems.

Employees are important human resources. Each one on the shop floor must have a sense of awareness for potential problems and a willingness to question whether what is being done is appropriate. Through such activities, creativity emerges and each person is able to upgrade his or her skills. For example, Toyota team members have the authority and responsibility to stop the production line if there is a question or problem. The idea behind this is to address the problem immediately instead of passing that problem to the next team member down the line. In essence, the next team member is the customer.

TPS is not a skill, but rather has been developed into a culture. It has been handed down to younger or newer workers as the essence of creative thinking accompanied with the enthusiasm of Toyota workers of prior years. Through TPS and the Toyota Way, the company has been able to transcend differences in language and culture. In doing so, Toyota is able to carry out its vision.

Indeed, the next half century for the automobile industry is certain to be every bit as exciting as the past fifty years. Toyota welcomes the opportunity and accepts its obligation of contributing to society through automobile manufacturing, marketing, and serving consumers all over the world.

Chapter Twenty-Two

Middle-Market Mortgages ...Then More

KERRY KILLINGER
Chief Executive Officer, Washington Mutual

OLD-ECONOMY DINOSAURS.

That's how banks were described a few years ago during the dot-com rage. Banks, it was said, would soon gather dust on the shelf next to the T-Rex and stegosaurus as financial services dot-coms showed how banking should be done. They would put every financial service consumers could dream of at their fingertips. No fuss, no bother—roll out of bed in the morning and get a home loan without changing out of your pajamas.

It was a wondrous vision, which one day might blossom into full reality. But for now it's still a seedling. As for those old-economy dinosaurs, some banks really were relics of the past and did vanish. The winners were those that continued to evolve as they had previously, realizing that competition for customers was going to be fiercer than ever. They recognized that customers now have convenient alternatives to "old school" banking. To remain in the race these traditional banks not only need a true understanding of who those people filling their lobbies are and what they want, but they also must give consumers rock-solid reasons why they should abandon their keyboards, change out of their pajamas, and come in to bank lobbies.

At the dawning of the dot-com boom, Washington Mutual saw the writing on the wall, and as a result was able to change by turning what had been a $44 billion regional company in 1996 into a $260 billion national enterprise by 2002, while remaining true to its strengths as a middle market player in the financial services industry. It's an enterprise in which a $10,000 investment in the company's common stock at the time Washington Mutual went public in 1983 would have grown to $486,335 by year-end 2002, assuming all dividends were reinvested. This compares with a total of only $99,365 had the same $10,000 investment been made in the Standard and Poor's 500 Index.

Roots in Community Banking

FOR MOST OF ITS one hundred years, Washington Mutual was a stay-at-home savings bank, seldom venturing far from the shadow of Mt. Rainier. It had taken a few tentative pecks at breaking out of that shell over the years, becoming the first bank in the nation to acquire a full-service securities brokerage firm in 1982 and entering the commercial banking arena in the 1990s with another acquisition. But it had stuck mostly to what it had always done—taking deposits in and lending money out—with a heavy emphasis on efficient, friendly service and community involvement.

That had been Washington Mutual's focus practically from the day it was founded in Seattle on September 21, 1889. That year was a rough time in the city's history. Three months earlier, a glue pot in a wood shop boiled over, touching off a fire that wiped out twenty-five city blocks. Commercial banks were reluctant to lend money for the rebuilding of homes that had been destroyed, so the mayor met with a group of local businessmen to discuss the formation of an alternate type of institution to meet that need. Out of that meeting emerged the Washington National Building Loan and Investment Association, which eventually became Washington Mutual. Just five months later, the association made history with the first monthly installment home loan on the Pacific Coast. The borrower was a Norwegian-born seaman who used the $700 loan to build a new house. Its image as a "no red tape" business where your money was safe hit home with people, and Washington Mutual became the dominant maker of home loans in Seattle.

Washington Mutual also became a presence in the local education community when it introduced a program called School Savings to Seattle in 1923 to teach students the value of saving. Eighty years later, it's still going strong, now a nationwide program that's the largest and longest running student savings program in the country.

But not long after that, Washington Mutual's image as a safe place for everyone to save was on the ropes as the stock market collapse of 1929 led to the Great Depression. Early in 1931—in the days before deposit insurance and as financial institutions collapsed around the country—most Seattle savings banks, fearing a run on their deposits, announced they would require waiting periods of one or two months before permitting withdrawals. This made perfectly good sense from a business standpoint, but Washington Mutual looked at it from the customer's standpoint and decided against a waiting period.

On the morning of February 9, 1931, nervous customers flooded the bank's lobby anyway. Holding true to its image as a safe place where wage earners could put their money, tellers were told to be "unhesitating in requests for withdrawals" and—despite any tumult that ensued—to continue smiling and calling every customer by name.

Hundreds waited on the sidewalk throughout the day and more continued to come for the next three days. At its peak, depositors were withdrawing $400,000 an hour, but every withdrawal request was met.

The scene repeated two years later when the governor of Michigan declared a bank holiday during which all financial institutions in the state would remain inactive. The reverberations were felt nationwide, and bank runs became endemic.

Washington Mutual faced a run on its deposits in March 1933, but once again tellers were told to make payments with a smile and a "See you again." The bank's doors remained open until 9 P.M. as panicky customers withdrew nearly $2.5 million in cash. The next day, a proclamation by the governor closed Washington banks for two weeks until the inauguration of Franklin D. Roosevelt. When Washington Mutual reopened its doors, only a few people were waiting to get in.

That emphasis on efficient, friendly service for all customers—regardless of their income level—and a commitment to the community proved popular, and the people of the Northwest continued putting their trust in Washington Mutual for the next forty years.

Growth Without Sacrificing the Culture

WHEN THE "grow or be acquired" dilemma of the 1990s hit, Washington Mutual was still a relatively small company anchored in the Northwest. Earlier in the decade, it had expanded into Oregon, Idaho, and Utah through acquisitions, but it was still a guppy-sized target for larger banks wanting to move into the area.

Washington Mutual's board of directors decided to fight to remain independent, feeling that the company offered something of value to consumers, shareholders, and communities alike. What it offered was a commitment to community service and banking for those wage earners it left its doors open for during the Depression—the ones in the vast middle market historically ignored or unappreciated by most large banks.

When growth became the mandate, California was the logical place to expand, but there was hesitation. Washington Mutual's style of casual "family friendly" banking with a commitment to the community was a hit in the Northwest, but how well would it play elsewhere, and how badly would its corporate culture be diluted the farther it moved from Seattle?

That culture had existed from Washington Mutual's birth, but wasn't put into words until nearly one hundred years later when 220 employees got together to formalize its corporate values. They were fine-tuned nine years later, and those values of "ethics, respect, teamwork, innovation, and excellence" guide the company today. It's a culture linked hand-in-hand with the company's efficient, friendly approach to financial services, where its responsibilities are taken seriously, but with a sometimes unconventional spin. It's a culture that gave birth to the Washington Mutual Action Teller Doll and where employees can nominate each other for recognition through baseball-style trading cards. (The cards, which employees collect and trade among themselves, recognize those who go out of their way to live up to Washington Mutual's brand promise: great value with friendly service for everyone.)

But it wasn't simply concern for how well employees outside the Northwest would buy into corporate values and Washington Mutual's style of banking that caused hesitation. It was also a question of how well they would understand the value of community involvement as a way not only to help those around them, but also as a way of ensuring they never lose touch with the people they serve.

Washington Mutual encourages "hands on" community involvement by employees and a commitment to help make their communities better places in which to live, learn, and work. Over the years, the company's emphasis on community involvement has grown into a nationally recognized effort for which Washington Mutual was awarded the 2002 Points of Light Award for Excellence in Corporate Community Service, one of the highest community service awards in the country.

That "hands on" involvement is supported by the four hours of paid time off each month given to employees working at least twenty hours per week so they can do volunteer work. And if they're not sure what they can do to help, the Committed Active Neighbors (CAN!) program allows employees to solicit help from coworkers for community projects they're working on. In 2002, employees volunteered nearly 200,000 hours to help their communities.

Despite concerns about what might come with expansion into California, when the opportunity to acquire a savings institution there came along in 1996, management decided the company couldn't pass it up. It proved to be the first of three major acquisitions in California that would more than quadruple the bank in size—and it provided a valuable lesson.

Management learned that Washington Mutual's corporate culture was stronger than imagined—strong enough to sustain it through any future management chose to pursue and strong enough to permit growth without losing touch with the company's image.

Thirty acquisitions and mergers over nine years, stretching coast to coast, proved that point as employees across the country demonstrated that when given a set of corporate values truly reflecting what the company stands for and an unwavering corporate focus, they'll wholeheartedly embrace them.

Personal Service in the Age of Automation

IN 1998 WASHINGTON Mutual noticed how other large banks were driving customers out of their lobbies toward automated forms of customer service, having concluded that personal service was too costly. Washington Mutual recognized that it was the perfect time to separate itself from the pack by reinforcing its brand image of personal service.

Although the company had helped pioneer the first shared ATM network, "The Exchange," it viewed ATMs as a customer, not a company, convenience. ATMs were also one more way to interact with consumers in the company's unique brand voice. Instead of a message simply saying, "Please insert your card," Washington Mutual ATMs welcome customers with "How can I help you?" And when the customer is finished they say, "We're all done. Can I help you with anything else?"

But rather than follow the usual path of a tweak here and a tweak there, to emphasize that the squeezed-out middle market—and all other customers—were still welcomed at Washington Mutual, the bank blazed a new trail. Seeing where the banking world was heading, and the need to give consumers a reason to visit, Washington Mutual decided to completely change people's banking experience.

Every process customers go through, every aspect of how they conduct business, the look and feel of branches, how staff is hired—everything from top to bottom was looked at from the customer's standpoint, the same perspective the bank took during the Depression. The result was "Occasio," Latin for "favorable opportunity," a prototype for Washington Mutual's new stores that gave branches a contemporary retail look and feel to create an inviting experience from the moment a customer or prospective customer walks through the door.

The first new stores were tested in Las Vegas in April 2000. Gone were the high counters and teller windows greeting customers in most banks. Instead, a casually dressed "concierge" greeted customers, directing them to the right service area. There were touch-screen computers for anyone wanting to learn more about bank products independently. And to keep children busy while their parents "shopped" for bank services, many stores came with a well-equipped play area. Customers said they wanted the sort of interaction with employees that they experienced in retail stores, so instead of the customary teller windows there were teller "towers" automatically dispensing cash, allowing easier interaction between customers and service representatives.

These new stores—which reached break-even profitability within eighteen months—are part of a strategy driven by the belief that there aren't enough of the wealthy customers and big commercial loans pursued by large commercial banks to sustain every bank. The greatest profit potential, as shown by Wal-Mart and other retailers, rests with the middle market, those consumers most likely to regularly visit Washington Mutual "stores" and make additional "purchases." The "category killers" of various industries, the ranks of which Washington Mutual hopes to join, share an unyielding pursuit of that vast middle market. They, too, look at things from the customer's standpoint and have heard the broad middle market say it wants good products at attractive prices, delivered with efficient, friendly service.

The financial services industry faces a number of internal hurdles to delivering those goods. Financial services companies traditionally view themselves as a group of business lines working toward a common goal—acquiring and retaining customers. But that viewpoint often works counter to their goal, with business lines focusing on their individual success rather than the company's.

So Washington Mutual employees are trained to look at things from the customer's perspective. Customers don't care—or sometimes even know—if they're dealing with someone from the consumer banking side or the mortgage side of the company. All they want is for the employee to be able to deliver what they need, whether it's a product, service, or solution to a problem. It's just one company to them, so Washington Mutual employees serve them with that in mind. As a result, the distinction between business lines is being blurred as the company positions itself as the nation's leading retailer of financial services for the broad middle market.

The Cross-Sell Strategy

WASHINGTON MUTUAL TRIES to "seed" new markets by first introducing its mortgage products, then, once that identity is established, introducing its full array of retail, business banking, specialty finance, and investment products. The success of this "middle-market mortgages ... then more" strategy was illustrated in three of Washington Mutual's newer markets—Las Vegas, Phoenix, and Atlanta. Customers there who had no relationship with Washington Mutual other than their home loans were two to three times more likely than the general population to buy its retail banking products, such as checking accounts. Those two flagship products, home loans and checking accounts, have been key to Washington Mutual's success at not only acquiring new customers, but also beginning a relationship that allows the cross-selling of its full range of products targeting the middle market.

Eighty percent of new customers come to Washington Mutual through mortgage and checking products. On average, mortgage relationships brought in to Washington Mutual an additional $11,500 in other loan and account balances over a four-year period in its "signature markets"—those markets with the combination of its retail banking and home lending operations. Checking accounts brought in an average of more than $23,000 in additional loans and deposits. Cross-selling as many products and services to households as possible is what maintains a company's foothold in the middle market. Research shows that more than 97 percent of households with five or more services are likely to remain with Washington Mutual after one year. And in its signature markets, Washington Mutual averages more than five products and services per retail banking household.

Washington Mutual has learned what other masters of the middle market have: Delivering what customers value, becoming an efficient provider, and shooting for the sort of friendly service that builds long-lasting relationships and leads to satisfied customers—service high on courtesy, helpfulness, and efficiency—are what the middle market wants. And the broad middle market is where the greatest long-term profit potential lies.

Chapter Twenty-Three

Transforming Whole Beans
to "Coffee Experience"

ORIN C. SMITH

President and Chief Executive Officer, Starbucks Coffee Company

WALKING INTO A STARBUCKS coffeehouse is an experience. You immediately recognize the aroma of freshly roasted coffee, the sound of frothing milk, the *barista's* lively pace, and the sight of a delicious cappuccino brimming with foam. The true pleasure comes while sipping a rich cup of coffee made from the finest quality beans. For many coffee lovers, this is a daily ritual and one for which they are willing to pay a premium.

Every day, nearly 3 million customers enjoy a "Starbucks experience" similar to this in more than 6,000 locations around the world. These encounters contribute to revenues, which totaled $3.3 billion in fiscal 2002. Consistently delivering a satisfying customer experience has generated a loyal following and made Starbucks one of the top 100 brands in the world, according to the August 5, 2002 *BusinessWeek*.

This is remarkable considering Starbucks' short thirty-one-year history, and more incredible given that Starbucks' growth and expansion really began in 1987 when the company refined its concept from a whole-bean retailer to offering a "coffee experience." We at Starbucks no longer ask ourselves how this happened. Starbucks' concept has proved to be successful, and we are convinced we got there by maintaining an unwavering commitment to our mission and guiding principles.

In 1990, several of the company leaders set out to define the type of company Starbucks was to become. We carefully crafted every word of our mission statement to emphasize the quality of our product and used our principles to characterize the quality of our company. What mattered most was that Starbucks put people first—before profits.

Since then, Starbucks has evolved and expanded, but its values have not changed. Fortunately, the original architects continue to be engaged, helping to guide the company in new endeavors while promoting the basic tenets on which the company was established. Starbucks' responsibility is to its stakeholders—its partners (employees), customers, shareholders, suppliers, community members, and others.

Core to our beliefs is that our partners are Starbucks' most vital asset. By investing in them, we hope they feel appreciated, valued, and respected by their company. In turn, we believe our partners are more inclined to create a satisfying customer experience that engenders long-term loyalty and results in bottom-line benefits. Years ago Starbucks led the industry by offering benefits to all eligible full-time and, in particular, part-time partners that include health, dental, and vision insurance, as well as stock options. Starbucks was also quick to recognize that when people know their opinions are considered, they feel valued. Several channels were established for our partners to share their concerns about the company and receive follow-up replies. These measures have contributed to high levels of satisfaction and some of the lowest turnover rates in the retail and restaurant businesses.

There are other visible signs that demonstrate Starbucks' commitment to its values. One of Starbucks' guiding principles is to contribute positively to its communities and its environment. Over the years, Starbucks has invested in its communities, often by linking the company's philanthropy to the causes its partners care about most. When its partners volunteer in their neighborhoods or donate to charities, they apply for a Starbucks gift match to their designated organization. Starbucks' partners have appreciated this opportunity, and the program has inspired many of them to support local causes.

Environmental stewardship is a necessity and a responsibility all companies must accept. One of the most significant steps Starbucks has taken has been to assess the environmental footprint of our supply chain operations to determine the company's impacts and identify areas in which we can improve. We discovered that we are on the right track when it comes to recycling and energy conservation, measures that minimize our environmental impact and help reduce costs. Some of Starbucks' greatest opportunities for environmental stewardship center on coffee farming practices that promote conservation. We consider this a top priority when selecting coffee suppliers.

Our values underscore the importance of stakeholder engagement and the need to be responsive to stakeholders' concerns. As Starbucks locates in new markets or neighborhoods, there is an occasional uproar that is often fueled by locally owned businesses or independent coffeehouses concerned that our presence will negatively affect their livelihoods. Experience has taught us that open dialogue and outreach are effective tools to reduce tensions and promote cooperation. In cases when Starbucks has been the target of activist groups intent on getting the company to adopt specific measures, we have not closed our door. Although these situations can be uncomfortable, we view Starbucks engagement as part of the process and a defining statement about the quality of the company.

Starbucks' principles are reflected throughout its supply chain operations, beginning with its commitment to the farmers who produce Starbucks coffee. We've sought ways that Starbucks can help improve their lives and communities, as well as address some of the pressing issues farmers currently face due to a global coffee crisis. More detail on our efforts is presented in the following pages.

Starbucks' position in the marketplace comes with certain expectations that the company behave in a socially responsible manner. But it didn't take Starbucks brand prominence to convince the company's leadership of this. We have always strived to follow a path that is guided by our principles as we account for our actions and grow Starbucks' business.

The Coffee Industry

TODAY, COFFEE RANKS just behind petroleum as the second-most traded global commodity, and it is one of the most popular beverages in the world. Coffee is produced in more than seventy tropical countries, most of which are developing nations. By World Bank estimates, more than 25 million smallholder farmers living in these countries earn their incomes by growing coffee.

Total coffee exports during the 2000–2001 crop cycle were $5.6 billion, compared to $12.4 billion just four years before. The dramatic drop in the value of coffee exports is primarily a result of a global surplus of coffee caused by overproduction, leading green coffee prices to plummet. Consumption, on the other hand, has remained relatively static for twenty years. For many producing countries, coffee exports represent a significant contributor to foreign exchange earnings, tax income, and gross domestic product. Low coffee prices have affected the national economies of producing countries and placed more demand on government funds for health and education, forcing governments further into debt.

The coffee industry comprises two distinct markets—the commodity and specialty markets:

➤ Commodity-grade coffee, which consists of robusta and arabica beans, is traded in a highly competitive market as an undifferentiated product. Robusta beans, considered the lowest in quality, are traded on the London International Financial Futures and Options Exchange (LIFFE), while arabica beans are traded on the New York "C." During 2002, a 2 billion-pound global oversupply of coffee drove prices to thirty-year lows of $0.17 per pound for robusta and $0.43 per pound for arabica.

➤ The specialty coffee market, which currently represents 10 percent of total worldwide green coffee purchases, consists of high-quality arabica beans primarily grown on smallholder farms located in middle- to high-altitude tropical forests. Prices for specialty coffee are partially determined by the quality and flavor of the beans and are usually higher than the prevailing price for commodity-grade coffee.

Although coffee prices have been declining steadily since the 1950s, trade experts argue that the current oversupply stems back to 1989, when coffee-exporting states failed to agree on production quotas after years of controlling the supply and price of coffee in accordance with the International Coffee Agreement. The 1990s were marked by Vietnam's entry into the market and Brazil's move to increase its already substantial production. At the same time, coffee-producing countries released their coffee reserves, thus flooding the market. The effect of these events has been an excess of primarily low-grade robusta and arabica beans sold at extremely low prices on the commodity market.

The impact of low coffee prices on smallholder farmers, which produce the majority of the world coffee supply, has been profound. Commodity prices are simply too low to offset the costs on a farm that relies on traditional, low-tech methods of production. Farmers who depend on coffee for income to purchase food and other essentials are especially hard hit. Many are heavily in debt, and some have been forced to abandon their farms or switch to alternative crops.

One bright spot in the coffee crisis is the rise in consumer demand for gourmet specialty coffee. Since the early 1990s, this segment of the market has grown dramatically, driven in large part by Starbucks, which today is the leading retailer, roaster, and brand in the specialty coffee market. The Starbucks' commitment to buy and offer customers only the highest quality arabica beans has, over time, educated and persuaded consumers that quality comes with a price. Consumers' willingness to pay premium prices for quality has fueled the rapid expansion of specialty coffee and enabled companies like Starbucks to pay farmers better prices for their crops.

As a result, some smallholder coffee farmers are working to improve their techniques and to produce high-quality coffees that command better prices, which subsequently improves their livelihoods. Future demand for high-quality arabica coffee is promising, which is encouraging more farmers to follow suit.

While paying higher prices is essential to sustain smallholder coffee farmers, the specialty industry has explored other solutions to help farmers and ensure the long-term sustainability of coffee production. Some solutions include stabilizing prices paid to farmers, developing long-term and direct relationships with producers, establishing low-interest loan programs, making social investments that benefit farming communities, providing tools to farmers so they can improve the quality of their coffee, and minimizing the harmful environmental effects of farming. The specialty industry has also brought *sustainable* coffees to market, those that are certified by independent parties for meeting certain criteria. Organic, Fair Trade, and shade-grown coffees, which comprise the sustainable coffee category, appeal to socially minded consumers who want the assurance behind a certification seal.

These measures are necessary and achievable. However, the best long-term solution to improve the lives of coffee farmers is to pay them higher prices for quality. This works only when consumers demand and are willing to pay a premium for high-quality specialty coffee in the marketplace. Therefore, quality is fundamental to the specialty coffee industry and necessary to maintain the consumer base.

Starbucks' Sustainable Approach to Coffee

TO SUSTAIN AND GROW the Starbucks' business over the long run, we must secure a continuous supply of the world's finest coffees. To do this, we need to ensure the livelihoods of farmers who produce high-quality coffee. Cashing in on the current low commodity-grade coffee prices may be tempting in the short run, but it would be an unwise business strategy considering the long-term implications. If farmers don't receive a decent price for their crops, they will cut production costs and compromise on quality. Or they may stop producing altogether. Either consequence could jeopardize Starbucks' supply. In the end, we recognize that farming, like any other business, must be economically feasible to ensure long-term sustainability.

Starbucks has taken some specific measures to address issues facing smallholder coffee farmers. In doing so, we've balanced Starbucks' business interests with our guiding principles, to arrive at some solutions that address the short-term problems while setting the course for the long term. These solutions include new pricing strategies and contract terms, loan programs, higher standards for suppliers, sustainable coffees, and quality improvement initiatives.

Prices are what concern farmers the most. In the past, Starbucks purchased its coffees at premiums over and above the prevailing price for commodity-grade coffee, determined by the New York "C." The premiums would vary, depending on several factors including the quality and flavor of a particular coffee. When prices recently fell to historic lows, this method became disastrous for farmers because these prices were not enough to cover their costs of production. Accordingly, Starbucks has moved away from this pricing strategy and started negotiating more of its coffee purchases based on outright prices, independent of the prevailing commodity price. This approach provides stability and predictability for both buyers and sellers and ensures that coffee farmers earn a living and continue to supply Starbucks with high-quality coffees. In fiscal 2002, Starbucks paid an average of $1.20 per pound, excluding freight, for high-quality green arabica coffee, which was nearly three times the average price of commodity-grade arabica and more than five times the price of robusta coffee beans.

The more direct the relationship with farmers, the better. Farmers see the value in reducing the role of middlemen and signing more contracts directly with buyers. These transactions still call for third-party services, but, nevertheless, farmers capture a larger share of the purchase price. Due to a radical change in coffee procurement, nearly one-third of Starbucks' coffee supply in fiscal 2002 was purchased through direct relationships.

Given the current economic climate, farmers want the security of knowing they have buyers for future harvests and are more agreeable to long-term contracts. To ensure the consistency of its supply, Starbucks has long favored long-term contracts with reliable farmers who are known for the quality of their crops. More than one-third of Starbucks' coffee supply in fiscal 2002 was procured through long-term contracts.

Offering better prices and terms to coffee farmers is only part of the solution. Starbucks recognizes that many farmers experience a shortage of cash with no promise of relief until the next harvest. Due to a chronic lack of working capital, farmers are often forced to sell their crops early, which reduces their chances of getting decent prices. In 2002, Starbucks helped make $500,000 available through Ecologic Enterprise Ventures and the Conservation International Foundation to provide affordable financing to smallholder farmers in Latin America. As a result, loans were made to nearly 900 farmers, helping them to bridge the cash flow gap during the growing season so they could earn more for their crops. Starbucks also directed $1 million through Calvert Community Investments to provide credit at favorable rates to coffee farmers.

In September 2001, Starbucks was one of the first in the coffee industry to introduce coffee sourcing guidelines intended to support and encourage the long-term sustainable production of high-quality coffee. The guidelines were developed with the support of Conservation International's Center for Environmental Leadership in Business and were being piloted during the 2002 and 2003 crop years. They use a flexible point system to reward farmers who meet strict quality, environmental, social, and economic criteria with financial incentives and preferred supplier status. Points can be accrued based on a supplier's ability to meet these sustainability guidelines. Suppliers who earn more points in the program will receive additional premiums— up to $0.10 per pound—and higher purchasing preference when Starbucks purchases green coffee. Since Starbucks introduced the guidelines, it has received more than fifty applications from producers interested in implementing the guidelines and gaining preferred status. Moreover, Starbucks' sourcing guidelines served as a model for the Costa Rican government when it created a state Sustainability Seal for local coffee producers who used sustainable methods.

During the current pilot stage, we are gaining critical feedback from coffee farmers on Starbucks' sourcing guidelines, which will help us make adjustments so they can be more easily adopted. We have no illusions that the Starbucks sourcing guidelines will be an overnight success. It takes time to make significant changes in origin countries and will require flexibility and patience.

Sustainable coffees build on the same themes of Starbucks' sourcing guidelines. The difference is the involvement of a third party to independently certify or verify that the coffee is produced under certain conditions. Starbucks markets several types of sustainable coffees including Serena Organic Blend™ and Organic Costa Rica™, Shade Grown Mexico™, and Fair Trade Certified℠.

Organic coffee is grown without the use of synthetic pesticides, herbicides, or chemical fertilizers. These growing practices help maintain a healthy environment and clean ground water. Farmers who pursue official certification submit to three years of soil testing and annual testing thereafter. Once harvested, the coffee beans must be processed in mills and roasting facilities meeting guideline standards to be sold as certified organic. The process is lengthy and costly, and many farmers opt not to go this route. Nevertheless, many of the farmers Starbucks buys coffee from actually employ organic farming methods, but are not certified as such.

Coffees that are grown under the canopy of shade trees are some of the finest in the world because of their flavor and quality. There are environmental and ecological benefits to shade-grown coffee as well. In recent years, rain forests have been cleared to make way for large coffee-growing *sun* plantations, resulting in losses of bird and wildlife habitat, declines in biodiversity, and increased dependency on chemicals and pesticides. By encouraging growers to adopt or improve their traditional "environmentally friendly" farming methods, which includes growing coffee in the shade, the harmful effects are avoided.

Starbucks formed an alliance with Conservation International (CI) in 1998 to promote the production of shade-grown coffee using ecologically sound growing practices that help protect biodiversity and provide economic opportunities for smallholder farmers. This partnership has been extremely successful so far because of the results it has produced. First, the area in which Shade Grown Mexico is grown—the El Triunfo Biosphere Reserve in Chiapas, Mexico—is a region CI considers as one of the world's most important biodiversity hot spots. The farming methods used to produce shade-grown coffee are helping to preserve the flora and fauna of this area. In addition, this partnership enables Starbucks to purchase Shade Grown Mexico coffee through CI's Conservation Coffee Program, which totaled 1.7 million pounds in fiscal 2002. And finally, farmers producing Shade Grown Mexico coffee received an 87 percent price premium over local prices for their coffee.

The consumer interest in Fair Trade Certified coffee has been growing because of what it symbolizes—that a fair price was paid to coffee farmers. In the Fair Trade certification system, smallholder farmers organize in democratically run cooperatives and register with the Fairtrade Labelling Organization International (FLO) to sell their beans directly to importers, roasters, and retailers for a guaranteed price. Buyers are required to pay a minimum of $1.26 per pound for nonorganic green coffee and $1.41 per pound for organic green coffee. Starbucks uses this system to purchase Fair Trade Certified coffee, and is licensed to sell it in the United States through TransFair USA. Other licensing agreements are being established with similar organizations that enable Starbucks to sell Fair Trade Certified coffee in other countries.

In fiscal 2002, Starbucks purchased more than 1 million pounds of Fair Trade Certified coffee, which is sold as Starbucks Fair Trade Blend. Promoters of Fair Trade want Starbucks to purchase more of this coffee and extend its marketing campaign of Fair Trade Certified coffee in its stores. This has been a difficult proposition for us to consider because this coffee does not always stand up to Starbucks' quality standards. Coffee quality is a critical component of the Starbucks brand and has helped us to connect strongly with our customers.

Offering them poor quality Fair Trade Certified coffee will compromise our brand and the consumer's willingness to pay a premium for Starbucks coffee, resulting in Starbucks' inability to pay higher prices to coffee farmers.

Rather than dismiss Fair Trade Certified coffee altogether, Starbucks is investing in programs that provide farmers the technical knowledge to improve the quality of their coffees. One example is an initiative among Starbucks, the Ford Foundation, and Oxfam America to collaborate with CEPCO, the largest Fair Trade cooperative of 16,000-member coffee farmers in Mexico. Oxfam's experience with smallholder coffee cooperatives and Fair Trade coffee has led it to conclude that the cup quality, and the perception of quality among coffee buyers, can limit the amount of coffee sold at Fair Trade prices. Oxfam America and CEPCO are working directly with farmers to help them improve their postharvest quality control techniques, which will strengthen the quality of their coffee and make it more marketable. Starbucks and the Ford Foundation are funding this initiative.

Taking a Leadership Role

AS THE WORLD's most prominent brand and retailer of specialty coffee, Starbucks' actions do not go unnoticed. We realize the opportunity Starbucks has to lead by example within the business community, the coffee industry, and among our own partners. This would be a daunting challenge if it were not for the well-defined principles we have in place that serve to guide the decisions and choices we make for the company.

Starbucks' prominence in the marketplace and its role as a leader will never be taken for granted. Starbucks will always be open to improvements that make it a stronger employer, a better neighbor in its communities, more environmentally responsible, and more responsive to the needs of its suppliers.

Above all, Starbucks will always strive to be relevant to its customers. When customers walk into a Starbucks, the experience they have must meet their high expectations for quality on all fronts. This is our uncompromising promise and enduring commitment.

Chapter Twenty-Four

Immigration and Education:
Two Great Resources

JOHN T. KERNAN
Chairman and Chief Executive Officer, Lightspan, Inc.

IT'S NO ACCIDENT that the United States continues to have the most resilient and robust economy in the world. We enjoy a high-energy culture of relentless innovation and a skilled workforce that is the envy of every other nation. This diverse, prodigious, and versatile workforce is possible because we continue to attract immigrants who come to the United States seeking a better life. Immigrants do indeed realize their dreams here, generation after generation, because we provide the underpinnings for success in the form of quality universal public education.

The future prosperity of America depends—as it always has—upon our ability to educate the newest immigrants and the poorest among us. The good news is that we have the political will, the technology, and the financial resources to do a better job of this. The fiscal 2002 federal Education Department budget was $48.9 billion, an increase of $6.7 billion over the previous year. More than ever, the federal government is committed to finding which students need the most help and delivering our best instructional resources to them. This funding priority, combined with demographic data and the convergence of digital technologies, points to education as a growth industry for years to come. For investors, companies involved in education present an attractive opportunity to both strengthen their portfolios and support the future growth of the U.S. economy.

Trends: Past Is Prologue

AMERICA IS AN epic success story comprised of millions of individual success stories, each built upon the bedrock tenet of our culture: Anyone can come to this country and, through hard work, make a life that's better than the one he or she left behind. And that egalitarian ideal still holds true today. If it didn't, immigration to these shores would have ended long ago. Instead it's on the upswing again. About 700,000 legal immigrants enter the United States every year. Another 300,000 enter the country illegally, or overstay their visas. They enjoy the freedoms that only America offers, and they work, pay taxes, spend their income on goods and services, and provide a substantial stimulus to the economy.

Today immigrants comprise about 13 percent of the U.S. work-force, the highest percentage since the 1930s. That's a good thing, because a growing economy requires a growing population. We are growing through the addition of largely unskilled workers from Mexico and Central and South America, as well as skilled technology workers from around the world. Today's Hispanic immigrants, like the waves of workers who preceded them from Europe, Asia, and Africa, will pull themselves up by their bootstraps, and in so doing provide an essential lift to the American economy. First they will work in the jobs that no one else wants, and then, because they are motivated and hard workers, they will climb the ladder to more challenging positions. Many will become entrepreneurs. Following a well-established pattern, they will assimilate themselves into American life so completely that within a few generations, they will be participating at the highest levels of business, government, and culture in this country.

Education is the cornerstone of this process. Quality public education is the great leveler, the fulcrum that allows individuals of every creed and color to find their own path to fulfillment of the American promise. And today this process works faster than ever. The children of new immigrants attend school, learn, and gain opportunities to quickly prosper and improve their lives—and our society.

A National Commitment to Improving Education

EIGHTEEN YEARS AFTER the alarm was sounded in the landmark report *A Nation at Risk*, the No Child Left Behind Act, signed in 2002 by President George W. Bush, signified an important new federal commitment to public education. More focused than the scattershot approach of the past, No Child Left Behind demands accountability and then provides more educational resources to the children most in need of them.

This kind of foresight is necessary and good in the global economy. In the past it was enough to train people to read and write and perform arithmetic. That was all the knowledge necessary to be productive on an assembly line or in another industrial job. Today we need to educate people to become computer programmers and health care professionals. We need people who will be able to work with technologies that are just now being invented, in industries that don't even exist yet. This means that we have to teach students to think critically. Success in tomorrow's workplace will require analytical and problem-solving skills, as well as the ability to continue to learn over the course of a career.

Teaching students to become competent problem solvers and life-long learners requires new ways of reaching them, because, let's face it, textbooks and chalkboard lectures can't compete with fast-action videogames and the glamour of music television. Educators know this better than anyone. If you're going to get inside kids' heads today, you need to speak to them in a language they recognize, and that is the language of multimedia. Once you have the child's attention, you must deliver an educational experience that is built upon solid pedagogy and that will further that child's understanding. We already know how to do this. We have built systems to do it over and over again, so that students are fully engaged in learning, can proceed at their own pace, and succeed at learning what they need to know.

How do teachers feel about this? Initially there was some computer phobia and a reluctance to accept technology in the classroom, but today there is really no turning back. Teachers, students, administrators, and families have all seen the value of well-designed instructional technology and the power that it has to change lives for the better. Educators are generally traditionalists who like to stick with what works, but today most teachers are comfortable with computers. The early adopters have proven that well-designed instructional technology can definitely help students learn faster. And the fear that technology would replace classroom teachers has been allayed. Just as it did twenty years ago for office workers, technology simply gives teachers new tools to be more efficient at what they do. It provides them with exciting ways to engage every student in the adventure of learning, to accurately assess what students know, and to challenge each student to perform at his or her best.

We are now at the point where instructional technology is beginning to permeate our schools and homes through broadband connections, video game consoles, handhelds, and the ongoing digital revolution. As it continues to prove its effectiveness, its acceptance will become more and more widespread until e-learning is virtually omnipresent. The economy has put a temporary crimp in state education budgets, but those funds will come back, and state education departments will begin pouring money into technology. Meanwhile, federal funding for K–12 education is here now, and schools are clamoring for solutions that will help them meet tough new performance standards. That's why companies involved in providing effective technology to schools will do very well.

It's About Assessing Performance

CALIFORNIA REDWOODS ARE the tallest trees on the planet. Why? Because they live in fog and crave sunshine. An overshadowed tree knows only that it must reach further toward the sunlight. It does this, and when it does, its neighbor responds by stretching even higher. Now the first tree must again grow further, and so on. In this way these trees pull each other along, inch by inch, foot by foot, until eventually the whole towering forest is magnificently scraping the sky.

The point is that competition is a law of nature, and it is good. Until recently our schools had little incentive to compete, but we have just reengineered our education system to fix that. The biggest effect of the No Child Left Behind Act will be to focus everyone's attention on test scores. After decades of well-intentioned but sometimes ill-executed school reform, federal education policy makers are determined to do more than just throw money at schools and hope that problems get solved. Accountability is the new mantra, and from now on, success is being measured by test scores.

Using objective measures to gauge performance encourages competition. Clear, attainable standards have been set for individuals and schools. Like the redwoods, students, teachers, school districts, and states will stretch to meet these standards, and pull each other up until our entire educational system is performing at a higher level. School districts with low test scores will get the federal funding they need to implement solutions that raise achievement, and if they don't succeed, students and parents will be given other educational options. For the first time, test scores from every school in the country will be disaggregated, so we'll be able to see who needs more help, and where to target resources. When we see that certain groups test low, we'll channel federal resources to those segments that need the most help. They will get the support they need to effectively compete, and the bottom will thereby be pulled up.

How to Invest Successfully in Education Companies

THIS IS GOING to be a great decade for anyone involved in education. Teaching young people is still difficult work. There are still many challenges that must be met. But now we truly have the bipartisan political support and the pedagogical and technological know-how to take a big evolutionary step forward in the way we teach our children.

As we've already noted, today's kids are born into a multimedia world. In the classroom of the future, the old instructional modes of print and lecture will still be used, but they will be part of a larger bag of tricks that every teacher will be able to access. The teacher will be a learning coach, empowered with a repertoire of proven instructional models and techniques, and a universe of quality content. These well-designed instructional solutions will support the important mission of educators and help them teach students faster and far more effectively.

Educating children is both a science and an art, and the best of these instructional solutions are being created by teams of educators, computer programmers, storytellers, and artists. These teams rely on the findings of researchers in cognitive science, psychology, and game theory to create engaging, interactive, self-paced content that really helps kids learn—better test scores prove it.

Companies that have a track record of creating instructional solutions proven to raise test scores—especially among low-income students—will be especially attractive to investors, because those companies are going to sell a lot of products to a market that is hungry for what they offer. Companies selling instructional solutions that are not proven to raise test scores will not do as well.

Case Study #1: Curriculum That's Proven to Work

Children of migrant workers have traditionally been one of the most difficult groups to educate. Because these families must follow work wherever it leads, there's little continuity of instruction. It's difficult for teachers to even assess what migrant students know, much less give them instruction that meets their specific learning needs.

Meet the Mata family. Natives of Mexico, Marta and Ezequiel Mata and their three children now live in a small roadside house in Kennett Square, Pennsylvania, a town that is known as the mushroom capital of the world. Located twenty-five miles southwest of Philadelphia, the small farming community produces tons of shiitake, portobella, enoki, and other mushrooms. Local farmers rely upon migrant laborers like the Matas to bring in the harvest, day and night.

Fortunately for fifteen-year-old Maria, eleven-year-old Yuliana, and nine-year-old Salvador, funding from a federal grant has allowed Kennett Square migrant students to use Lightspan Achieve Now, our interactive curriculum that is used both in the classroom and at home. The school district provides the Mata family with a PlayStation® PS one™ console to use at home. The children use it to learn reading, language arts, and mathematics with Lightspan Achieve Now, which aligns to the same state and national standards that teachers are addressing in the classroom. While the Matas may live in an unheated shack, their children are making the most of the day with a multimedia curriculum that compels them to keep learning.

A study tracked Kennett Square elementary school students who used Lightspan for between four weeks and four months and found that 50 percent posted gains on oral English-language proficiency exams. Another study conducted by the University of Delaware showed that in just one year, low-income students who used Lightspan gained 24 percentage points in reading and 16.1 points in math on standardized exams.

Today the Mata children have dreams that go far beyond their parents' ambitions: Yuliana would like to become a teacher, while Salvador wants to be a policeman. Maria is thinking of Penn State for college and would like to someday be an architect. Education is giving these kids a leg up, and opening up to them a viable path to the kind of success that enriches us all.

From the beginning, we designed Lightspan to increase the amount of time that students spend learning, and to help get families more involved in the education process. We made sure that our product was cost-effective enough that it could be used by virtually every child. And we designed the curriculum to engage students through the use of digital video and game-style production techniques that make Lightspan lessons fun and rewarding.

Case Study #2: On-Target Assessment Makes the Difference

With more than 57,000 students, the San Antonio School District (SASD) is the eighth-largest school district in Texas. Eighty-five percent of its students are Hispanic and 93 percent come from low-income families. Students from this demographic background have traditionally not been very successful in school. But these students are proving that they are great learners. That's because SASD teachers have an extremely accurate picture of what their students know, which enables them to give students precisely the instruction they need.

SASD teachers use Lightspan eduTest Assessment, an online solution that lets educators quickly identify the academic strengths and needs of their students. This program enables teachers to determine exactly how students are performing in relation to district, state, and national standards for reading, language arts, and mathematics. They use this information to guide instruction, giving each student the content they need—and to build greater family involvement by sharing it with parents.

Lightspan's eduTest makes it easy for teachers to create reports that document students' academic performance in great detail. The reports are easy to understand too, so teachers can print them out and share them with parents. And getting parents, especially immigrant parents, involved in their children's education is about the best thing you can make happen in education.

TWO HUNDRED AND TWENTY-SEVEN years ago, some people identified themselves as Americans, and demanded their freedom. They won it and bequeathed it to their children, who in turn preserved it for their children, and on down to you and me.

In the last century we exercised that freedom and dominated the world economy, using our formidable might to win wars, protect human rights, and send people to the moon. Compared to other nations we may have, at times, seemed the gawky adolescent, full of boundless energy and not certain what to do with all the power in our possession. But we were blessed with an abundance of natural resources and the entrepreneurial spirit of an immigrant nation. We created our own tradition as the trailblazers of new frontiers in science, technology, medicine, and industry.

Freedom facilitates the sharing of knowledge, and that is what has made us who we are. Americans do not hoard knowledge. As a matter of habit, we share it, nurture it, and grow it. We multiply its value by spreading it far and wide, and nobody does it as well as we do. We Americans have a great track record when it comes to casting light into dark corners, uncovering the unknown, and solving mysteries—just ask the last inhabitant of the Oval Office. Indeed, some of our obsessive information sharing can get messy, and much of it may have little consequence. But we also make important new discoveries faster than ever, and these beget even more new discoveries. And then we apply what we've learned to improve our lives in a continuous cycle of discovery and refinement.

The freedom-leads-to-knowledge formula works: The trajectory of American progress is so spectacular that it can't be ignored. We have made it obvious that more knowledge enables the growth of human capabilities, and today our capabilities continue to expand because our schools, companies, and other organizations are becoming ever more knowledge-centric.

This trend will continue to accelerate. If you don't think so, consider that in 2000, analysts estimated that the total amount spent on education in the United States, from preschool through college (and counting job training), was between $660 billion and $750 billion. E-learning is the killer app, and it is coming online faster than most people realize. We are a nation of learners, and we export our culture to the world. The opportunities are global, and the time to invest in instructional technology and e-learning is now.

Part Five

Geopolitical Implications for Today's Investor

Chapter Twenty-Five

Investing in Our Physical and Fiscal Security

JULES KROLL
Executive Chairman of the Board, Kroll Inc.

W E FACE TWO THREATS in America today, one physical, the other fiscal. The attacks of September 11, 2001, and other terrorist activities have permanently undermined our sense of physical security. No longer is the threat occurring somewhere else or "over there"—be it Israel, Indonesia, or Italy. At the same time, our fiscal house is under unprecedented siege. The questions raised on the reliability of financial statements come not from so-called new economy "bubble" stocks but from companies providing goods and services that are the cornerstone of our economy, like energy and telecommunications. In this new world, investors need to identify which areas to avoid and which companies and markets are attractive by virtue of their role in protecting us from these physical and fiscal threats.

The terrorist threat is not a new one. Civilization is in the midst of a thousand-year war. Muslim extremists are an extremely inflammatory, active, and effective force. Their goal is basic: to kill Christians and Jews and to destroy the modernity that interferes with their way of thinking. They are not alone, unfortunately. Other terrorist and criminal elements also hold similar, deep ideology, and their numbers are not tiny.

In contrast, the financial threat *is* new. For much of the twentieth century, the United States was the consummate safe haven and market of choice for the world's investors. Now, the reliability of America's financial infrastructure; the functioning of our capital markets; and the roles of corporate boards, bankers, and auditors are coming under unprecedented scrutiny for their failures. These failures have repercussions around the globe, because the investment platform has no political boundaries. Moreover, while America's financial system is under attack, the financial integrity of most other countries' systems is not much better—in fact, most systems are much worse.

The need now is to invest in the internal and external structures to protect us from these two threats.

Improvements to Our Physical Security

ON THE PHYSICAL THREAT FRONT, since September 11, we have slowly begun taking steps to improve our security. Most of the strides have been made by the United States military, in Afghanistan and elsewhere. But we have been sorely hampered in our foreign intelligence efforts, where we are lagging a decade or more behind where we should be given the threat. The Central Intelligence Agency must begin rebuilding our overseas intelligence capability, and shift from its overdependence on electronic intelligence to a new emphasis, or reemphasis, on human intelligence.

At home we should develop a domestic intelligence force, separate from the Federal Bureau of Investigation. The FBI is a police organization, and Kroll's experience shows that people who are good at police work are not necessarily good at intelligence—and vice versa. As a police organization, the FBI is charged with making arrests. In contrast, an intelligence operation collects and disseminates information. As a recent report by the Council on Foreign Relations noted, "With just 56 field offices around the nation, the burden of identifying and intercepting terrorists in our midst is a task well beyond the scope of the Federal Bureau of Investigation."

Nor can we rely on the estimated 750,000 local, county, and state law enforcement officers to bolster this intelligence effort. They lack basic information from national authorities—like updated terrorist watch lists and real-time intergovernmental communication links—as well as meaningful intelligence training.

Instead, state and local police, as well as firefighters and emergency medical personnel, should be given the proper tools and skills—now lacking—to handle their job in the war on terrorism as emergency "first responders." This includes basic equipment like protective gear, respirators, and oxygen; and more sophisticated hardware, like communication devices and portable and handheld equipment to detect explosive, chemical, biological, and radiological materials—in addition to the training to use the equipment. For example, the Center for Domestic Preparedness in Alabama is at the present time the only facility in the nation where first responders can train with chemical agents. But at peak capacity, it can train only 10,000 responders a year, according to some estimates.

Of course, federal agency response teams can help—but they will invariably arrive too late. However, there is still significant debate over even this issue. Federal authorities are extremely hesitant about turning over primary response capabilities to local authorities. The National Guard is currently looking to take on these responsibilities. It argues that its members are best suited to handle these situations. Unfortunately, this dialog interferes with ongoing efforts of providing first responders with much-needed resources. It focuses the debate on "Who will be the first responder?" instead of "Is the first responder equipped to respond?"

Domestically we have made strides to protect prime targets for attack—particularly our airports. For example, we've hired 55,000 federal screeners to check passengers and luggage, and most airports now have explosive detection equipment. This security system must move to the next level of sophistication. Instead of treating each passenger and piece of luggage as equal in risk, we must develop an intelligence-based system that uses risk-based criteria to prescreen and monitor passengers and luggage.

But far too much focus has been placed on yesterday's targets—the airports—instead of tomorrow's targets, which could cost human life or bring the global economy to its knees. The events of September 11 have drastically altered the landscape of potential terrorist targets. Historically, terrorist activity has been limited to "single point of attack" events, which, while lethal, were limited in their ability to drastically alter everyday life in the United States. Now, terrorists have demonstrated that they can conduct very complicated—and highly effective—mass-casualty events anywhere in the world. The terrorist threat will never be the same again.

For example, our seaports are highly vulnerable. A USS Cole-style incident, occurring not in far-off Yemen but at a domestic port, would have major repercussions for America's container traffic and energy imports. Seaport container traffic into the United States is highly concentrated. Over 40 percent of maritime containers arrive through the California ports of Los Angeles and Long Beach. This traffic is also highly valuable. Nearly half of the value of all U.S. imports arrives via sea containers, according to the U.S. Customs Service. The American Association of Port Authorities has a price tag for implementing adequate physical security at the nation's commercial seaports—but only 5 percent of this effort has been funded.

In addition, intermodal land/sea containers are very vulnerable, a low-cost way for delivering an explosive device, which could create a domino effect of global gridlock in world cargo shipments. As U.S. Customs Commissioner Robert Bonner declared last year, "Terrorist groups are not bent on killing Americans; they want to cripple our economy as well. One way for them to do this would be to use the principal means of international trade—sea containers—to deliver weapons of mass destruction, including a nuclear device, to the United States."

Steps are underway to counter this threat, but have yet to go far enough. For example, the Custom Services' Container Security Initiative prescreens containers before they are shipped to the U.S. and identifies high-risk containers based on advanced information risk targeting. But as of November 2002, only eleven of the world's top twenty seaports participate in the initiative. Also, under the Customs-Trade Partnership Against Terrorism (C-TPAT), importers voluntarily agree to increase security of their cargo from the foreign loading dock to the U.S. border, in return for reduced customs inspections and other compliance burdens. But more incentives are needed for the private sector—and more enforcement muscle for the Customs Service—to make the program effective. As of January 2003, just 300 companies are certified and eligible for swifter processing benefits under C-TPAT.

Similarly, our energy resources are susceptible to attack, and not just in distant locales like the Middle East and the North Sea. The northeast United States gets most of its refined oil from refineries located in Texas and Louisiana. "A coordinated attack on several key pumping stations—most of which are in remote areas, not staffed, and possess no intrusion detection devices—could cause mass disruption to these flows," the Council on Foreign Relations warned.

America's food and water supply is especially open to biological threats. Great Britain's recent experience with livestock disease illustrates the quick impact and lasting effects in this area. Our water supply is vulnerable, as water systems are locally owned and have limited laboratory capacity to test for contaminants. A biological attack is particularly difficult to counter because symptoms do not appear immediately and the window of opportunity to treat the agent can be very narrow: nine to eleven days for smallpox, and thirty-six to forty-eight hours to respond to anthrax. Most public health systems are sorely underfunded and understaffed, and few medical professionals have the training to identify and treat biological attacks. Most public health agencies do not have the resources for emergency hot lines, and it can take up to three weeks for a public health department to register a disease incident in the national database, according to some reports.

Making all the needed improvements will cost money, and some companies will benefit. For example, firms providing the equipment, training, and long-term maintenance contracts for first responder devices are investment opportunities in this new world. The Council on Foreign Relations has warned that "making a case for investing in security safeguards for low probability/high consequence events can be a hard sell to a tax-wary populace or CEOs under pressure to guard the bottom line."

But it also cited ancillary benefits to these outlays. The tools used to detect terrorists can also fight criminal acts of cargo theft; for example, the Customs-Trade Partnership Against Terrorism program is a successor to a similar effort in the mid-1990s by the U.S. Customs Service to fight drug smuggling. Also, emergency equipment used to save lives in a terrorist attack can be used in industrial accidents or natural disasters; public health investments help manage disease. "As a result, some of the costs may be offset by reduced losses and lower insurance rates. In short, sustaining support for actions to confront the new security environment may not be as difficult as it first appears because many of these measures can tangibly improve the quality of life for our society as well," the Council concluded.

Fiscal Improvements

ON THE FISCAL FRONT, improvements are also underway but have yet to go far enough to attack the systemic flaws in our financial system. Auditors, corporate board members, and security analysts must all do two things—shed their conflicts and increase their skepticism—to restore credibility for investors.

The Sarbanes-Oxley Act of 2002 has been hailed as the most significant change in U.S. securities laws since the 1934 Securities Exchange Act. It limits—but does not prohibit—auditors from engaging in nonaudit services for its accounting clients. The Securities and Exchange Commission is, at this writing, tweaking the law, considering rules that prohibit linking audit partners' compensation to the selling of nonaudit services. But the enforceability of such rules is questionable, and anyone who has read a proxy statement knows accountants make most of their revenue from nonaudit services. This conflict cannot be resolved until the accountants bite the bullet: Auditors should be paid to audit, and nothing else. The audit function is too vital to the integrity of the corporate books to be compromised by efforts to generate revenue or boost market share. Yes, shareholders will pay a higher price for audit services, which will no longer be used as a loss leader for more lucrative nonaudit consulting work. But it is necessary insurance.

In mid-2002, the New York Stock Exchange (NYSE), at the request of the Securities and Exchange Commission, reviewed its corporate governance standards. The NYSE mandated that independent directors make up the majority of the boards of listed companies and tightened the definition of "independent director." All well and good. But it also left a sizeable loophole: A director is independent as long as the board of directors determines he or she is independent.

So, for example, one NYSE board recently decided a retired accounting firm partner (still drawing a sizeable pension from his former firm) was independent enough to serve on the company's audit committee—and oversee the company's auditor, the director's former firm. At a Nasdaq company, a nonemployee nephew of the chairman is deemed to be independent, and heads the company's audit committee. At another NYSE company, one director also sits on the board of another public company, which is both a major competitor and a key supplier.

Unfortunately, there is no shortcut to the legwork required to establish director independence. It takes hard digging. For example, one leading corporate governance database—used by major executive/ director recruiting firms—labels a director at one Nasdaq company as "independent" despite his long-time role as an investing partner with the chairman and chief executive officer of the company.

Of course, director independence is no guarantee of a company's success. General Electric Company, widely regarded as one of America's best-run companies, had until recently a heavily "insider" board. Meanwhile, prior to its collapse, Enron Corporation had a relatively "independent" board, which did not stop it from evolving into public enemy number one. The NYSE realized it couldn't anticipate all circumstances that signaled potential conflicts of interest and in its corporate governance rules warned: "a 'conflict of interest' occurs when an individual's private interest interferes in any way—or even appears to interfere—with the interests of the corporation as a whole." But judgments of "independence" and "conflicts" remain in the eye of the beholder; investors must remain on constant alert.

As this was being written, Wall Street brokerage houses and federal and state regulators were hammering out a new structure for securities research, de-linking the compensation of stock analysts from the amount of investment banking fees they help generate. There has been considerable hand-wringing over how this new, independent research will be funded, but the general consensus is: There will be less research. Is this so bad? Investors rarely directly paid "hard dollars" for research, instead paying via "soft-dollar" brokerage commissions—maybe because the research was not worth real money. After all, do investors really need twenty-three securities analysts saying the same thing about General Motors?

To restore their credibility among investors, securities analysts, corporate directors, and auditors must go beyond just shedding their conflicts: They must dig deeper and exercise their obligation to dissent. It is no coincidence that the investors who should be most concerned about the failures of auditors, directors, and analysts—the institutions—have been virtually silent in the current debate. In a recent speech, New York State Attorney General Elliot Spitzer squarely placed the blame on them: "If there was a group at fault, it was the institutional investor, whose equity powers were not exercised."

Similarly, in a mid-2002 speech, Bevis Longstreth, a former SEC commissioner, noted that "institutional investors, as a class, have shown virtually no serious concern over these failures, despite numerous warning flags for more than a decade." Longstreth suggested there might be a good reason for this apathy: The best institutional investors "flourish in, and therefore prefer, a market made more imperfect by the failures ... Why take steps to improve the pricing for everyone?" After all, it's the institution, not the individual, that can afford to pay for the exclusive, independent research that goes beyond the biased, mass-distributed output of many big brokerage firms. For securities analysts, digging deeper means no longer just taking the word of the chief financial officer or chief executive officer. They must instead do their own legwork, like surveying suppliers, calling customers, sounding out labor unions, and independently verifying performance. Fewer analysts may be doing research. Fewer companies may be covered. But for individual and institutional investors, the securities research that does exist should become more accurate and valuable.

In corporate governance, some leading companies are already showing the way. General Electric recently began requiring that directors annually visit two GE businesses without corporate executives present, in order for board members to have more direct interaction with operating management. GE is also mandating that directors hold board meetings without management present and requiring they limit the number of additional board seats held, eliminating directors who spread themselves too thin. Another example: Coca-Cola recently announced it was expensing employee stock options, giving investors a truer picture of compensation costs; other companies have since followed Coke's lead.

In accounting, reform has led to an even broader healthy debate over replacing the complex, American rules–based system, as reflected in generally accepted accounting principles, with the principles-based standard used in Europe. There, the focus is on the spirit— rather than the letter—of the law, making it more difficult for corporations and accountants to outmaneuver the standards, according to proponents. Others counter that a European-style, principles-based accounting system gives companies too much freedom to interpret their own accounting.

Whatever system ultimately takes hold, a global accounting standard is long overdue. For decades consumers have been able to readily compare the features of a German Volkswagen, American Ford, Japanese Toyota, Korean Hyundai, Italian Fiat, and Swedish Volvo. Why can't the investor readily compare the German, American, Japanese, Korean, Italian, and Swedish income statements and balance sheets in valuing these automobile stocks? Some practices commonplace in one country are shunned in another. For example, Germany long permitted its leading corporations to establish "reserves," which companies dipped into during down years to smooth out earnings and post steadily rising net income. Yet "earnings management" is an anathema in the United States. It is time the accounting systems caught up with the global markets to end artificially skewing the allocation of capital.

The physical and fiscal threats facing America today will be not be solved by laws or regulations, but by commitment backed by investment. We have the tools to protect us from these threats; in some cases, initiatives are already underway. We have the money; we are among the richest nations on earth. Now we must decide: Do we have the will?

Chapter Twenty-Six

Waging a Different Kind of War

GENERAL WESLEY CLARK

I N SEPTEMBER 2001, after the terrorist attacks on the World Trade Center and the Pentagon, the United States found itself at war. As President George W. Bush explained, this was to be "a different kind of war." On October 8, a wave of air strikes against Taliban and Al Qaeda communications, headquarters, and other facilities in Afghanistan opened the operation.

At CNN headquarters in Atlanta, where I was providing military analysis and commentary, déjà vu hit me hard. Maybe I was almost alone in this feeling, but to me the attacks seemed so familiar and predictable, it was as though we were refighting the Kosovo operation on a different piece of ground. I could sense the timing, the target sets, the questions about target selection, the soon-to-follow criticisms of unintended casualties, and the strident critique from some quarters in Europe.

I had no uniform on, and no "U.S." insignia on the collar of my business suit, but as I described the strikes, I kept referring to the American forces as "we," rather than "they." Some of these men and women had served under my command not long before. We had discussed plans and tactics, and shared the challenges and frustrations of conflict in the Balkans. It had been just a little more than a year since I had retired from active service, taken the final parade at Fort Myer, and, regretfully, put away the uniform I'd been so proud of for thirty-four years. And for me this was anything but "a different kind of war."

For many in the American public, of course, this kind of war—no big buildup of forces, no clear-cut pronouncements of strategy and aim, the general air of uncertainty—was new and different. It wasn't like 1990, when Iraq invaded Kuwait. Then, the objective seemed clear-cut—the conventional aggression by Iraq against the independent nation of Kuwait was obvious, and so was the remedy.

And yet many of my colleagues in the news media used the Gulf War as a reference point, since this too was a distant war in an Islamic land little appreciated in the United States. Baghdad was compared with Kabul. The familiar figure of Colin Powell, now secretary of state, then chairman of the Joint Chiefs, as well as the two Bushes, anchored the comparisons.

I found myself self-consciously reminding many others about the Kosovo campaign, for it was here that the patterns had emerged. But I shouldn't have been surprised that so few had seen the connections. As General Powell himself counseled me, as I was preparing to write my book, "Wes, the American people never got involved in the Kosovo campaign; it wasn't their war." As in so many judgments, he was right.

Of course, aside from the difference in public support and interest, the wars in Kosovo and against terror appear dissimilar. The Kosovo campaign was against a state and its leader, while the war on terror is against a shadowy international conglomerate that knows no boundaries. The war in Kosovo was discretionary—we chose to wage it—while the war against terror was forced on us by a vicious attack on innocent people within the United States itself. The Kosovo campaign was limited in geography and intensity, while the war on terror appears to have no real boundaries. These are important distinctions—but there are also fundamental commonalities, and the Kosovo campaign offers critically important lessons as we move deeper into the war on terror.

The War Against Terrorism

SOON AFTER THE terrorist strikes against the United States on September 11, 2001, it became clear that the Taliban regime in Afghanistan would not surrender the prime suspect, Osama bin Laden, or any other members of his organization, Al Qaeda. The

Taliban thus made itself the initial target of the U.S. counter-terror campaign. Osama bin Laden and Al Qaeda would come later.

The initial air campaign struck at only a few targets—airfields, ammunition storage sites, a few communications sites, previously identified terrorist camps, and a handful of surface-to-air missile and radar sites. After a few days the inconclusiveness of these strikes was obvious to all observers.

From the outset there had been a good deal of handwringing from the public commentators about the difficulties of the campaign in Afghanistan. We heard about how the Soviet Union had failed in its decade-long effort to control Afghanistan, even after deploying more than 100,000 troops and suffering some 15,000 dead. The geography, climate, and topography of the country became talk-show staples. Now it seemed that the only weapons available quickly were aircraft and missiles—and were they enough?

Then, bit by bit, the campaign shifted to focus on the Taliban forces themselves. Tank and truck parks were struck. Slowly, and carefully, small teams of American and, eventually, British special forces were infiltrated to do reconnaissance and to direct the air strikes. Within days, encouraged by the devastating effects of the special forces-precision strike combination, the forces of the opposition Northern Alliance began to maneuver against the Taliban stronghold at Mazar-e-Sharif. The precision bombing directed by the Special Operations Forces forced the Taliban into a fatal dilemma: stay deployed in defensive positions outside the key cities and fall to American firepower, or retreat into the cities and face the certain hostility of a repressed populace. The Taliban died in the trenches, and broke and ran. They became encircled in populated areas, only to eventually surrender. They had no answers.

First was the fall of Mazar-e-Sharif on November 9, 2001, followed by the siege of Kunduz, the advance to Kabul, and within a few weeks the elimination of the Taliban regime in its home city of Kandahar. The victory was remarkably swift and surprising, accomplished by about 300 people on the ground, several hundred carrier-based aircraft, long-range bombers, and fewer than 3,000 U.S. soldiers and Marines in nearby countries guarding a few air bases, plus the already established infrastructure in the Persian Gulf.

By early December, the first major operation after the fall of the

Taliban had begun, a slow, cautious advance into the mountainous terrain of Tora Bora, reputed to be the hideout and redoubt of Osama bin Laden. Again, the local Afghan tribes, accompanied by special operations forces and supported by precision air strikes, drove the enemy away. But all the facts surrounding the operation have yet to be released, and it increasingly appears that this was a rearguard and deceptive operation by Al Qaeda, rather than a fight-to-the death last stand, and that the local Afghan tribes allowed significant numbers of the enemy to slip through their net and over the border into Pakistan.

President Bush declared on October 11, 2001, that the stabilization of Afghanistan was part of our mission, despite the strong preferences within the administration to avoid "nation-building." An interim government was drawn together from disparate Afghan groups. Soon afterward, a peacekeeping force was inserted into Kabul to help ensure the survival of the newly appointed Afghan leader, Hamid Karzai. Eventually building up to a total of roughly 4,500 multinational (but not American) troops under British leadership, the International Stabilization and Assistance Force had no mandate to operate outside the Afghan capital. Nor, despite Karzai's pleas and the requests of UN Secretary General Kofi Annan, was the force increased in size or made more capable.

In the meantime, while efforts to create an Afghan police force and to train a national army were commencing, the United States continued to pursue the remnants of Al Qaeda, then assembling in eastern Afghanistan and apparently preparing to resume offensive action against the coalition of Afghan tribes loyal to Karzai's interim government. The military action, which came to be known as Operation Anaconda, proved to be the largest American ground operation of the war, involving three battalions of the 101st Airborne Division as well as hundreds of Afghan tribesmen accompanied by U.S. and British special operations forces.

Operation Anaconda also reflected the new warfare. This was not to be like the bloody, month-long World War II Marine assault on Japanese caves at Iwo Jima, nor even like the massively supported Vietnam War assault by elements of the 101st Airborne up Hamburger Hill. Instead, the U.S. positions were planned on the high ground, so the troops could remain in position and call in precision strikes on any enemy forces who were attempting to flee their hideouts. American troops were to be the anvil. The Afghan tribes would probe and push and help develop the targets that the accompanying special operations forces would call in—they were to be the hammer. Unmanned aerial vehicles and other manned aircraft with real-time TV links would monitor the battle, and precise strikes would destroy the enemy, position by position, until he surrendered.

The battle didn't begin as planned. At least one of the advancing Afghan columns was ambushed before it could move into its initial position. There was some bad weather, and intelligence information was imperfect: There were more Al Qaeda and Taliban in the area than expected, and some were in or near the locations at which the American troops were set down by their helicopters. American soldiers were pinned under heavy fire—some forty were wounded during the first days of the battle. Apache attack helicopters and strike aircraft were brought into the fight. Two special forces transport helicopters were seriously hit, and eight special forces troops were killed. After the first day, however, the American intelligence, firepower, and communications dominance assured a predictable outcome, and from that point on actions appeared to unfold as planned. Twelve days later, it was over—the Al Qaeda and Taliban remnants were either dead or dispersed, and the only controversy was how many of the enemy had been killed.

A great public flurry erupted as American troops sustained their first casualties in battle since the tragic events in Somalia almost a decade earlier. "For this war, the Americans will take casualties if necessary," the commentators observed. But it wasn't planned that way—rather the opposite. It was, after all, modern war.

A New Style of Warfare

WHY DID THIS new style of warfare emerge, this aversion to casualties, the reluctance to put ground troops into the fight, the reliance on airpower, the continued tensions over unintended civilian casualties, and the frictions and constant scrutiny by the press? It's the story behind the story—the waging of modern war—driven by technology, international law, twenty-four-hour news coverage, and a resource-rich American military, that is the heir of all the military developments and tragedies of the twentieth century. And what does this portend about the future course of operations in the war against terror? The answers lie revealed in the Kosovo campaign of March–June 1999, where these patterns first appeared.

From the outset of warfare, a driving aim was to outreach the opponent. Longer spears and stronger bows gave way to rifled, long-range artillery, aircraft, and intercontinental-range missiles. Another trend was accuracy; from ball shot to rifles, then to matched sniper rifles, high-powered optics, and laser spotting devices for small arms. For the larger weapons, wire-guided, man-in-loop technology gave way to automated target recognition, laser-homing, and satellite-guided capabilities. After the Gulf War, "precision strike" became the materiel developers' watchword. By 1999 the capabilities were fully fielded to the U.S. Navy, and the first of the all-weather Global Positioning System bomb kits had been readied for use by the B–2 stealth bombers. Targeting went from spies and telescopes to radio-direction finding, stereoscopic range finders, then overhead satellite imagery, and finally unmanned aircraft with real-time, full-motion video transmitted to command centers thousands of miles away, such as the Predator Unmanned Aerial Vehicle. The Kosovo campaign saw widespread use of precision strike as well as advanced reconnaissance means. And it is here that the processes and procedures for their effective use on the battlefield began to be developed.

Advances in military technology and procedures have intensified the reluctance to commit ground forces in combat. The operation in Kosovo was marked by a prolonged struggle within military and political circles over the possible use of ground forces. Even the Army itself fought against its own commitment in a variety of ways. And despite the vastly different circumstances surrounding the war on terror, the fundamental political and institutional forces that appeared during the Kosovo campaign have already re-emerged in the Afghanistan campaign and are likely to persist in whatever next steps are contemplated.

Further, there is the problem of post-conflict operations, which today generally fall under the name of "peacekeeping" as part of a larger effort at "nation-building." While this is just beginning in Afghanistan, and will be important there and in any future operational theaters, the challenges and responses are not likely to be so different from operations in Bosnia and later in Kosovo. Here again, then, is relevant material worthy of consideration.

But it is not only technology, organizational capabilities, and circumstances that drive the patterns of military activities—it is also the military leaders themselves. They have tremendous impact on the decisions, the attitudes, and the willingness to dare, risk, and gamble of their political superiors. The actions in Afghanistan clearly reflected the thinking of the various branches of the U.S. armed forces: the Air Force's prescribed strikes against strategic targets like communications, airfields, air defense radars, and headquarters sites; the Army's prudent strategic and tactical planning. Big forces require large logistics bases and secure ports of entry. Above all, the U.S. military aimed to protect the welfare and safety of its most valuable "weapons system," our uniquely well-trained and highly motivated force of volunteers.

Surprisingly little analysis of the alternatives or explanation of the strategies has been made available, nor have we learned much of the people and processes driving them. The struggles between the theater commander and the chiefs of the Army and Air Force have been hidden away, as has the nature of the relationships among the theater commander, the chairman of the Joint Chiefs of Staff, and the Secretary of Defense. But the stresses, strains, criticisms, and pressures are there nevertheless. Thus far there is every indication that General Tommy Franks, the theater commander, though subjected to questioning and criticism, has received an appropriate degree of authority and enjoys the ability to communicate and work directly for his immediate superior, Secretary of Defense Donald Rumsfeld. This is certainly an improvement over what I experienced in the Kosovo campaign.

But relations in the military chain of command are functions not only of personality but also of position, responsibilities, and organizational expectations and doctrine. Understanding the inner workings is critical to appreciating and anticipating the course of the war. The best look at these inner workings is from the Kosovo campaign, where a divided executive branch and strongly parochial service chiefs combined with a partisan Congress and weakened presidency to drive inner workings of the command structure into the open.

The Bush administration has also managed to keep its famously rumored internal split between the Departments of State and Defense largely away from the public view. Secretary of State Powell's giant stature became both a blessing and a problem for the administration early on, and, inevitably, countervailing forces appeared in the form of Secretary of Defense Rumsfeld and the Pentagon. But, as in the military chain, individuals are only one element of the mix, because the two institutions, State and Defense, are positioned naturally for rivalry in every aspect of the planning and execution of foreign policy. Again, the experiences of the Kosovo campaign provide a remarkably good basis for understanding the respective institutional roles, responsibilities, and preoccupations that drive this competition. From my perspective as a participant both within the Pentagon and later as a theater commander, the competition was fundamental and to a large degree inevitable. It depended on the top leadership only for the artfulness with which it was managed.

Of course, the campaign in Afghanistan wasn't an all-American show. Even the greatest power in the world has to have, at least, access to the theater of operations—Afghanistan, in this case—as well as support from facilities in nearby countries and friends on the ground. Pakistan, other Central Asian and Persian Gulf states were critical. European powers seemed less relevant, although it was a good opportunity to build common cause with Russia. And the British rushed to proclaim wholehearted support for the mission.

Unlike the Kosovo campaign, where NATO provided a structured consultation and consensus-shaping process, allied support in the war on terrorism was to take the form of a "floating" or "flexible" coalition, with countries supporting the United States in the manner and to the extent they felt possible. The United States, for its part, would act in accordance with the principles of self-defense. It would be bound by no one. As one senior member of the administration told me, "We read your book—no one is going to tell us where we can or can't bomb."

Although European leaders sought to help, and NATO declared that the attack on the United States represented an attack on every member of NATO, the strategic direction of the campaign seemed to be purely American. The NATO decision-making structure wasn't used; instead, NATO was essentially bypassed.

This represented an unfortunate misreading of the lessons of the Kosovo campaign. Whereas in the popular view, the allies hindered the bombing, the actual truth is virtually the opposite: Allied target approvals made the overall impact of the strikes far greater than if the United States had acted unilaterally. The real lesson of Kosovo is this: To achieve strategic success at minimal cost, a structured alliance whose actions are guided by consensus and underwritten by international law is likely to be far more effective and efficient in the long term.

At this writing, some four years after the NATO campaign against Slobodan Milosevic's ethnic cleansing of Kosovo, Serbia has a new, democratically elected government. It is struggling with the problems of transforming itself from a fascist relic of the Cold War to a Western-oriented democracy. The Albanian Kosovars have returned to their province, and a democratic transformation is underway there, too. While hard feelings and bitterness remain, and some 40,000 foreign peacekeepers have helped assure stability, there is no fighting— just a struggle to overcome the legacies of the past and develop democracy and free-market economies. And Milosevic, the man who helped instigate and direct four Balkan wars in a decade, is undergoing a war crimes trial by a UN-mandated international tribunal at The Hague. All this was achieved at a remarkably slight cost, minimal destruction on the ground, no NATO casualties, and relatively few civilian deaths despite the use of some 23,000 bombs and missiles.

What caused this outcome was not just the weapons of war. In fact, one might say they were but a relatively small factor in the ultimate outcome. Rather, there were forces far more powerful than bombs and bullets at work. These were the wholehearted political commitment of European nations, the thrust of international law, and the binding structure of NATO.

An Alternative Approach to Winning the Struggle

IT IS HERE, most of all, that the study of the Kosovo campaign is so relevant. It suggests an alternative approach to winning the struggle against terrorism. What if, instead of relying on the nation's right of self-defense, we had gone to the United Nations and sought the creation of an International Criminal Tribunal on International Terrorism, taking advantage of the outpourings of shock, grief, and sympathy to forge a legal definition and obtain the indictment of Osama bin Laden and the Taliban as war criminals charged with crimes against humanity and genocide? Would we not have had greater legitimacy and won stronger support in the Islamic world?

Could we not have used the increased legitimacy to raise the pressures on Saudi Arabia and other Arab states to cut off fully the moral, religious, intellectual, and financial support to terrorism? Could we not have used such legitimacy to strengthen the international coalition against Saddam Hussein? Or to have encouraged our European allies and others to condemn more strongly Yassir Arafat's use of terror against Israel? Wouldn't reliance on a compelling UN indictment have given us the edge in legitimacy throughout much of the Islamic world that no amount of "strategic information" and spin control can provide? On a purely practical level, could we not have avoided the embarrassing quarreling during the encirclement of Kandahar in early December 2001 when the appointed Afghan leader wanted to offer the Taliban leader amnesty, asking what law he had broken, while the United States insisted on no amnesty? And could we not have avoided the continuing difficulties of maintaining hundreds of prisoners in a legal no-mans-land at Guantanamo Bay, Cuba, which has undercut U.S. legitimacy in the eyes of much of the world?

Some will argue that international law is hollow, lacking sovereign authority. Others will say that the United Nations is biased against the United States. But the simple truth is that the international law they demean is of our own making. We created much of it in our own image, along with the United Nations itself. In the twilight of World War II we recognized the need for allies, we understood the need to prevent conflict, not just fight it, and we recognized that we must banish from the world what President Harry Truman, addressing the founding of the United Nations, called "the fundamental philosophy of our enemies, namely that 'might makes right.'" As Truman went on to say, we must "prove by our acts that right makes might." What a tragedy it will be if we walk away from our own efforts, and from sixty years of post–World War II experience, to tackle the problem of terror without using fully the instruments of international law and persuasion that we ourselves created.

Moreover, using a structured alliance such as NATO to form a base for the coalition could have brought allies into the fight to a much greater extent than they are today. I knew during the Kosovo campaign that the allies were really committed when their governments came to warn me that NATO must not fail. Their own governments, they said, might fall were NATO to lose that campaign. They were being held accountable by their own voters for the strategy and tactics of the campaign. It wasn't pleasant for them—or for me—but holding leaders accountable is the essence of democracy, and the NATO mechanism insured such accountability during the Kosovo campaign, even if all the intelligence collection and dissemination and much of the operation was in American hands.

Sadly, because many of our friends and allies today are not accountable, that level of commitment appears missing among many of our friends and allies today, despite the ships, planes, and troops they have assigned to work alongside the U.S. forces. The consequences are profound, for as the president himself warned, the war on terror is going to require far more than simply military activities. Indeed, the most important aspect of the war may be in law enforcement and judicial activities. Much of the terrorist network draws support and resources from within countries friendly or allied with us. And here there are very real limitations to the use of American military force. What we really need are closer alignments of our police and judicial activities: greater cooperation in joint police investigations, sharing of evidence, harmonious evidentiary standards and procedures, as well as common definitions of crimes associated with terrorism. Through greater legal, judicial, and police harmonization, we need to make the international environment more seamless for us than it is for the international terrorists we seek.

For better or worse, however, the war against terror appears to be under exclusive American control. And every twinge of American decisionmaking that smacks others as U.S. unilateralism undercuts our friends abroad, the very people who must align their laws and procedures with our own if we are to win. Of course, what some label as U.S. unilateralism, others would call strong leadership.

What matters, however, is not the label but the results. It is obvious, even with the limited information publicly available, that the police and judicial measures taken to detect, identify, track, detain, interrogate, arrest, charge, convict, and punish terrorists and their accomplices within friendly countries has been less than fully successful. Achieving this success will be easier the more that American actions can be drawn from the legitimacy of the United Nations and American direction ratified by other states and multinational authorities. This is one of the prime lessons of the Kosovo campaign.

Meanwhile the fence-sitters and the ambivalent, shadowy sympathizers of the mid-September "floating coalition" have drifted away, Iran meddling in the political wilderness of Afghanistan and sponsoring Palestinian terrorism, Syria aiding other terrorists, and China watching anxiously from the sidelines, fearful of U.S. hegemonic aspirations in Central Asia and continuing its own robust military buildup. Could we not have achieved greater traction with these countries through reliance on a more formalized structure for consultation and even some decisionmaking?

Of course, consulting and working decisions closely with allies is difficult, time-consuming, and frustrating. Not surprisingly, they often have ideas different from our own. But those who abjure the effort may have underestimated the benefits, for allies will provide a crucial ingredient to long-term American success, especially in this campaign.

A final observation from among the lessons emerging from reflection on the Kosovo campaign is this: Just as the Kosovo war wasn't won by bombs and bullets alone, neither will we win the campaign on terror exclusively through the use of force. We have to deprive our adversaries of the incentives, the legitimacy, and the hope that they can ever succeed. As Napoleon himself reportedly said, "In war the moral is to the material as three is to one." And in our understandable concern to take prompt and effective action, we must not lose sight of the larger, broader, less concrete but ultimately more important struggle over human values and beliefs. We need a new and larger strategy.

President Bush has spoken correctly when he defines the struggle against terror as a battle for "civilization itself." But what the Kosovo campaign showed is the very power of our ideas, our belief in human rights and dignity, the importance of the rule of law, and the rights of people to govern themselves. No matter how angry we are, or how frightened, those are lessons that must be applied effectively to the campaign against terror if we are to win. And that is a task that remains to be done, and done soon, if it is not to be too late. NATO's campaign in Kosovo showed us that we don't have to fight alone; it showed us how to wage war based on values and law, rather than on narrower national interests. And it pointed the way to a new national strategy of engagement, combining all these ideas with America's unique position in the world to "make a difference when it can."

C h a p t e r **27** *T w e n t y - S e v e n*

Prospects for Containing
Future Terrorism

GRAHAM ALLISON

*Douglas Dillon Professor of Government and Director of
the Belfer Center for Science and International Affairs,
John F. Kennedy School of Government, Harvard University*

A<small>L QAEDA'S TERRORIST ASSAULT</small> on September 11, 2001, awakened the world to the stark reality of megaterrorism: terrorist acts that kill thousands of people at a single stroke. In the twinkling of an eye, possibilities earlier dismissed as analysts' (or Hollywood's) fantasies became brute fact. President George Bush rightly and resolutely declared war on Osama bin Laden, Al Qaeda, and all terrorist groups with global reach.

Yet as the U.S. government pursues a war for which it had not prepared, it must, in the idiom, "go with what we've got." Assembling an international coalition of very strange bedfellows, acquiring intelligence from sources and by methods it had mostly neglected, and jury-rigging defenses against the most obvious vulnerabilities, it gallops off in all directions. Even now, long after the fateful day in September 2001, a clear and coherent strategy for combating megaterrorism has yet to emerge.

In contrast, Mr. bin Laden and his Al Qaeda network have been thinking, planning, and training for this war for most of a decade. September 11 demonstrated a level of imagination, sophistication, and audacity previously thought impossible by the U.S., or any other, government. As the press has reported, less than a year before the September 11 attacks the FBI had assured the administration that it had a "handle" on all Al Qaeda operatives within the United States.

Some things have gone well for the United States and its allies in the first phase of the war on terror. Air strikes, coordination with the Northern Alliance, and Special Forces operations led to the Taliban's collapse more rapidly than most observers expected. More than 2,400 suspected terrorists have been arrested or detained by more than ninety governments around the globe. More than a dozen planned or attempted terrorist incidents have been disrupted. Most important, as of this writing no significant attacks against the United States have occurred since September 11, 2001.

On the other hand, Osama bin Laden was still missing, as of this writing. Few top Al Qaeda associates have been captured or confirmed dead. Efforts to improve homeland security have progressed at a predictably slow pace given the gargantuan practical, political, and bureaucratic challenges. The bombings in Bali and Tunisia and the attack on the French oil tanker off the coast of Yemen demonstrate that Al Qaeda may be reorganizing and rejuvenated, or just awakening from a brief hibernation. The United States—and most of the world—remains seriously vulnerable to terrorist attack.

Even in the midst of the continuing campaign, responsible leaders must acknowledge the possibility that much more catastrophic terrorist acts may be yet to come. Along the spectrum of megaterrorism, the worst case would be a nuclear explosion in a large city. Although biological and chemical weapons can cause huge devastation as well, "the massive, assured, instantaneous, and comprehensive destruction of life and property" of a nuclear weapon is unique, as delineated starkly by Matthew Bunn, John P. Holdren, and Anthony Wier, authors of the report "Securing Nuclear Weapons and Materials: Seven Steps for Immediate Action" (Nuclear Threat Initiative and Project on Managing the Atom, May 20, 2002; available online at http://www.nti.org/e_research/securing_nuclear_weapons_and_mate rials_May2002.pdf).

Consider this scenario: A crude nuclear weapon constructed from stolen materials explodes in New York City, at the site we now call Ground Zero. Not only what was the World Trade Center, but all of Wall Street and the financial district, and the lower tip of Manhattan up to Gramercy Park, would disappear. Hundreds of thousands of people would die suddenly. In Washington, D.C., an equivalent explosion near the White House would completely destroy that building, the Old Executive Office Building, and everything within a one-mile radius, including the Departments of State and Treasury and the Federal Reserve—and all of their occupants (as well as damaging the Potomac-facing side of the Pentagon).

Analysts have warned for over a decade that, in the absence of a determined program of action, we have every reason to anticipate acts of nuclear terrorism against America. The question is whether the horror of September 11, 2001, can now motivate the United States and other governments to act urgently not only against Al Qaeda, but also on the well-identified agenda for minimizing the risk of nuclear megaterrorism. Although the challenge is great, policies that would make a nuclear terrorist strike nearly impossible are clearly within our reach.

How Real Is the Threat?

AS THE BUSH ADMINISTRATION took office in January 2001, a bipartisan task force, chaired by the former Senate majority leader, Howard Baker (now U.S. ambassador to Japan), and Lloyd Cutler, a former counsel to the American president, presented a report card on U.S. nonproliferation programs with Russia. The principal finding of the task force was that "the most urgent unmet national security threat to the United States today is the danger that weapons of mass destruction or weapons-useable material in Russia could be stolen, sold to terrorists or hostile nation states, and used against American troops abroad or citizens at home."

No serious analyst has spent more than a day examining the evidence without concluding that "loose nukes" are a first-order threat. As Mr. Baker testified to the Senate Foreign Relations Committee in March 2001, "It really boggles my mind that there could be 40,000 nuclear weapons, or maybe 80,000, in the former Soviet Union, poorly controlled and poorly stored, and that the world isn't in a near state of hysteria about the danger."

The danger can be summarized in three propositions. First, attempts to steal nuclear weapons or weapons-usable material are not hypothetical, but a recurring fact. In 2001, for example, the chief of the directorate of the Russian Defense Ministry responsible for nuclear weapons reported two incidents in which terrorist groups attempted to perform reconnaissance at Russian nuclear storage sites, but were repulsed. The past decade has seen repeated incidents in which individuals and groups have successfully stolen weapons material from sites in Russia and sought to export them— but were caught trying to do so. In one highly publicized case, a group of insiders at a Russian nuclear weapons facility in Chelyabinsk plotted to steal 18.5 kg (40.7 lbs.) of highly enriched uranium, which would have been enough to construct a bomb, but were thwarted by Russian Federal Security Service agents.

In the mid-1990s, material sufficient to allow terrorists to build more than twenty nuclear weapons—more than 1,000 pounds of highly enriched uranium—sat unprotected in Kazakhstan. Iranian and possibly Al Qaeda operatives with nuclear ambitions were widely reported to be in Kazakhstan. Recognizing the danger, the U.S. government itself purchased the material and removed it to Oak Ridge, Tennessee. In February 2002, the U.S. National Intelligence Council reported to Congress that "undetected smuggling [of weapons-usable nuclear materials from Russia] has occurred, although we do not know the extent of such thefts." Such assertions invariably provoke blanket denials from Russian officials. Russian Atomic Energy Minister Aleksandr Rumyantsev has claimed categorically: "Fissile materials have not disappeared." President Putin has stated that he is "absolutely confident" that terrorists in Afghanistan do not have weapons of mass destruction of Soviet or Russian origin.

Nuclear materials have also been stolen from stockpiles housed at research reactors, which exist in dozens of countries. In 1999 Italian police seized a bar of enriched uranium from an organized crime group trying to sell it to an agent posing as a Middle Eastern businessman with presumed ties to terrorists. On investigation, the Italians found the uranium originated from a U.S.-supplied research reactor in the former Zaire, where it presumably had been stolen.

Until recently, enough highly enriched uranium for two nuclear weapons sat—as it had for more than a decade after the end of the Cold War—at a poorly guarded research reactor in Belgrade, Yugoslavia. Only after lengthy U.S.-Russian-Yugoslav negotiations and an infusion of private sector money (from Ted Turner's Nuclear Threat Initiative) was the highly enriched uranium extracted in a precision operation and shipped to Russia for blending down to a non-weapons useable form.

Second, if Al Qaeda or some similar group obtained thirty pounds of highly enriched uranium, or less than half that weight in plutonium, with material otherwise available off the shelf, it could produce a nuclear device in less than a year. The only high hurdle to creating a nuclear device is fissionable material—an ingredient that is fortunately difficult and expensive to manufacture. But as a former director of the Livermore Laboratories (a premier American nuclear weapons lab) wrote a quarter of a century ago, "If the essential nuclear materials like these are in hand, it is possible to make an atomic bomb using the information that is available in the open literature." An even easier alternative is a radioactivity-dispersal device, which wraps a conventional bomb with radioactive materials that disperse as fallout when the bomb explodes. This type of device—a so-called dirty bomb—does not begin to approach the destructiveness of a nuclear bomb, but it would likely cause mass hysteria and inflict large economic costs.

Third, terrorists would not find it difficult to deploy a nuclear device in a major city in the United States or elsewhere. It would not be hard to sneak a nuclear device or nuclear fissile material into the United States or most other states via shipping containers, trucks, ships, or aircraft. Recall that the nuclear material required is smaller than a football. Even an assembled device could be shipped in a container, in the hull of a ship, or in a trunk carried by an aircraft. Since the attacks of September 11, the number of containers that are X-rayed at the port of New York/New Jersey has increased to about 500 of the 5,000 containers currently arriving daily—approximately 10 percent. But as the chief executive of CSX Lines, one of the foremost container-shipping companies, put it: "If you can smuggle heroin in containers, you may be able to smuggle in a nuclear bomb."

Recent efforts to bolster U.S. border security are laudable, but just begin to scratch the surface. More than 500 million people, 11 million trucks, and 2 million rail cars cross into the United States each year, while 7,500 foreign-flag ships make 51,000 calls in U.S. ports. That's not counting the tens of thousands of people, hundreds of aircraft, and numerous boats that enter illegally and uncounted. Given this volume and the lengthy land and sea borders of the United

States, even a radically renovated and reorganized system cannot aspire to be airtight.

This threat has emerged because, after the Cold War, the Soviet Union's nuclear arsenal and stockpile were no longer held behind prison walls. Post-Soviet societies have experienced a remarkable transformation over the past decade, becoming simultaneously freer, more chaotic, and frequently more criminal. The same dynamic that liberated individuals also undermined systems that previously controlled some 30,000 nuclear weapons and 70,000 nuclear-weapon equivalents in highly enriched uranium and plutonium at more than 100 sites across Russia.

Thanks to extraordinary professionalism on the part of Russian military and security guards, many attempts to steal weapons have been thwarted. The security forces have been greatly helped by far-sighted cooperative threat-reduction programs, set up at the initiative of Senators Sam Nunn and Richard Lugar, which have contributed almost $1 billion a year to Russian efforts to secure weapons and material. The U.S. government knows of no case at present in which those who wish to make nuclear weapons have acquired either the weapon or sufficient nuclear materials to make one. What must worry us, however, is what we don't know.

If Al Qaeda and other terrorist groups have not so far succeeded in acquiring nuclear weapons, or materials from which to assemble them, we should give thanks for our great good fortune. If they have acquired them, most people will quickly conclude that, under existing conditions, this was bound to happen.

How Serious Is the Enemy?

THERE CAN BE NO DOUBT that Osama bin Laden and his associates have serious nuclear ambitions. For almost a decade they have been actively seeking nuclear weapons, and, as President Bush has noted, they would use such weapons against the United States or its allies "in a heartbeat." In 2000, the CIA reportedly intercepted a message in which a member of Al Qaeda boasted of plans for a "Hiroshima" against America. According to the Justice Department indictment for the 1998 bombings of American embassies in Kenya and Tanzania, "At various times from at least as early as 1993, Osama bin

Laden and others, known and unknown, made efforts to obtain the components of nuclear weapons." Additional evidence from a former Al Qaeda member describes attempts to buy uranium of South African origin, repeated travels to three Central Asian states to try to buy a complete warhead or weapons-useable material, and discussions with Chechen criminal groups in which money and drugs were offered for nuclear weapons.

Bin Laden himself has declared that acquiring nuclear weapons is a religious duty. "If I have indeed acquired [nuclear] weapons," he once said, "then I thank God for enabling me to do so." When forging an alliance of terrorist organizations in 1998, he issued a statement entitled "The Nuclear Bomb of Islam." Characterized by Bernard Lewis as "a magnificent piece of eloquent, at times even poetic Arabic prose," it states: "It is the duty of Muslims to prepare as much force as possible to terrorize the enemies of God."

If anything, the ongoing American-led war on global terrorism is heightening our adversary's incentive to obtain and use a nuclear weapon. Al Qaeda has discovered that it can no longer attack the United States with impunity. Faced with an assertive, determined opponent now doing everything it can to destroy this terrorist network, Al Qaeda has every incentive to take its best shot. Indeed, a spokesman for Al Qaeda, Sulaiman Abu Ghaith, has stated that Al Qaeda members have "the right to kill 4 million Americans, including 1 million children, displace double that figure, and injure and cripple hundreds of thousands."

Separatist militants (in Kashmir, the Balkans, and elsewhere) and messianic terrorists (like Aum Shinrikyo, whose cult members attacked a Tokyo subway with chemical weapons in 1995) could have similar motives to commit nuclear terrorism. As Palestinians look to uncertain prospects for independent statehood, Israel becomes an ever more attractive target for a nuclear terrorist attack. Since a nuclear detonation in any part of the world would likely be extremely destabilizing, it threatens American and Russian interests even if few or no Russians or Americans were killed. Policymakers would therefore be foolish to ignore any group with motive to use a nuclear weapon against any target.

What Must America Do?

THE GOOD NEWS about nuclear terrorism can be summarized in one line: no highly enriched uranium or plutonium, no nuclear explosion, no nuclear terrorism. Although the world's stockpiles of nuclear weapons and weapons-useable materials are vast, they are finite. The prerequisites for manufacturing fissile material are many and require the resources of a modern state. Technologies for locking up super-dangerous or valuable items—from gold in Fort Knox to treasures in the Kremlin Armory—are well developed and tested. While challenging, a specific program of actions to keep nuclear materials out of the hands of the most dangerous groups is not beyond reach, *if* leaders give this objective highest priority and hold subordinates accountable for achieving this result.

The starting points for such a program of specific actions are already in place. In his major foreign policy campaign address at the Ronald Reagan Library, then-presidential candidate George W. Bush called for "Congress to increase substantially our assistance to dismantle as many Russian weapons as possible, as quickly as possible." In his September 2000 address to the United Nations Millennium Summit, Russian President Putin proposed to "find ways to block the spread of nuclear weapons by excluding use of enriched uranium and plutonium in global atomic energy production." The Joint Declaration on the New Strategic Relationship between the United States and Russia signed by the two presidents in the May 2002 summit stated that the two partners would combat the "closely linked threats of international terrorism and the proliferation of weapons of mass destruction."

Another important result the summit yielded was the upgrading of the Armitage/Trubnikov-led U.S.-Russia Working Group on Afghanistan to the U.S.-Russia Working Group on Counter-terrorism, whose agenda is to address the threats posed by nuclear, biological, and chemical terrorism. And out of the June 2002 G-8 summit meeting came an agreement to raise $20 billion over the next decade—half from the United States and half from other G-8 nations—for cooperative projects, initially in Russia, to secure and promote nonproliferation of weapons of mass destruction.

Operationally, however, priority is measured not by words, but by

deeds. A decade of Nunn-Lugar Cooperative Threat Reduction Programs has accomplished much in safeguarding nuclear materials. Unfortunately, the job of upgrading security to minimum basic standards is mostly unfinished: By Department of Energy reports, two-thirds of the nuclear material in Russia remains to be adequately secured. Bureaucratic inertia, bolstered by mistrust and misperception on both sides, leaves these joint programs bogged down on timetables that extend to 2008. Unless implementation improves significantly, they will probably fail to meet even this unacceptably distant target. What both sides require is personal, presidential priority measured in commensurate energy, specific orders, funding, and accountability. This should be embodied in a new U.S.-Russian led "Alliance Against Nuclear Terrorism."

When it comes to the threat of nuclear terrorism, many Americans judge Russia to be part of the problem, not the solution. But if Russia is welcomed and supported as a fully responsible nonproliferation partner, the United States stands to accomplish far more toward minimizing the risk of nuclear terrorism than if it treats Russia as an unreconstructed pariah. As the first step in establishing this alliance, the two presidents should pledge to each other that his government will do everything technically possible to prevent criminals or terrorists from stealing nuclear weapons or weapons-useable material, and do so on the fastest possible timetable. Each should make clear that he will personally hold accountable the entire chain of command within his own government to assure this result. Understanding that each country bears responsibility for the security of its own nuclear materials, the United States should nonetheless offer any assistance required to make this happen. Each nation—and leader—should provide the other sufficient transparency to monitor performance.

To ensure that this is done on an expedited schedule, both governments should name specific individuals, directly answerable to their respective presidents, to co-chair a group tasked with developing a Russian-American strategy within one month. In developing a joint strategy and program of action, the nuclear superpowers would establish a new world-class "international security standard" based on President Putin's Millennium proposal for new technologies that allow production of electricity with low-enriched, non-weapons-usable nuclear fuel.

A second pillar of this Alliance would reach out to all other nuclear weapons states—beginning where the threat of theft is currently greatest: Pakistan. Each should be invited to join the Alliance and offered assistance, if necessary, in assuring that all weapons and weapons-useable material are secured to the new established international standard in a manner sufficiently transparent to reassure all others. Invitations should be diplomatic in tone but nonetheless clear that this is an offer that cannot be refused. China should become an early ally in this effort, one that could help Pakistan understand the advantages of willing compliance.

A third pillar of this Alliance calls for global outreach along the lines proposed by Senator Richard Lugar in what has been called the "Lugar doctrine." (See Lugar's May 27, 2002, speech at the Moscow Nuclear Threat Initiative Conference, available online at http://lugar.senate.gov/052702.html.) All states that possess weapons-usable nuclear materials—even those without nuclear weapons capabilities—must enlist in an international effort to guarantee the security of such materials from theft by terrorists or criminal groups. In effect, each would be required to meet the new international security standard and to do so in a transparent fashion. Pakistan is particularly important given its location and relationship with Al Qaeda, but beyond nuclear weapons states, several dozen additional countries hosting research reactors—such as Libya and Ghana—should be persuaded to surrender such material (almost all of it either American or Soviet in origin) or have the material secured to acceptable international standards. The recent removal of two nuclear bombs' worth of highly enriched uranium from the poorly guarded Vinca research reactor near Belgrade, Serbia, exemplified the kind of intensive Russian-American cooperation required on this front.

A fourth pillar of this effort should include American-Russian led cooperation in preventing further spread of nuclear weapons to additional states, focusing sharply on North Korea (which admitted in October 2002 it possessed a nuclear weapons program), Iraq, and Iran. The historical record demonstrates that where the United States and Russia have cooperated intensely, nuclear wannabes have been largely stymied. It was only during periods of competition or distraction, for example in the mid-1990s, that new nuclear weapons states realized their ambitions. India and Pakistan provide two vivid case studies. Recent Russian-American-Chinese cooperation in nudging India and Pakistan back from the nuclear brink suggests a good course of action. The new alliance should reinvent a robust nonproliferation regime of controls on the sale and export of weapons of mass destruction, nuclear material, and missile technologies, recognizing the threat to each of the major states that would be posed by a nuclear-armed Iran or North Korea. Recent revelations about North Korea's clandestine nuclear weapons program, which may have already succeeded in producing one or a few nuclear weapons, make intensive, cooperative nonproliferation all the more urgent. Persuading North Korea to abandon its pursuit of nuclear weapons will require not only American and Russian leadership, but also the active participation of other regional powers, most importantly China, Japan, and South Korea.

Finally, adapting lessons learned in U.S.-Russian cooperation in the campaign against bin Laden and the Taliban, this new Alliance should be heavy on intelligence sharing and affirmative counterproliferation, including disruption and preemption to prevent acquisition of materials and know-how by nuclear wannabes. Beyond joint intelligence sharing, joint training for preemptive actions against terrorists, criminal groups, or rogue states attempting to acquire weapons of mass destruction would provide a fitting enforcement mechanism for alliance commitments.

As former Senator Sam Nunn has noted: "At the dawn of a new century, we find ourselves in a new arms race. Terrorists are racing to get weapons of mass destruction; we ought to be racing to stop them" (see "Our New Security Framework," *Washington Post*, October 8, 2001). Preventing nuclear terrorism will require no less imagination, energy, and persistence than did avoiding nuclear war between the superpowers over four decades of the Cold War. But absent deep, sustained cooperation among the United States, Russia, and other nuclear states, such an effort is doomed to failure. In the context of the qualitatively new relationship Presidents Putin and Bush established in the aftermath of the September 11 terror attacks, success in such a bold effort is within the reach of determined Russian-American leadership. Succeed we must.

C h a p t e r T w e n t y - E i g h t

Shifting Sands in the Middle East

AMBASSADOR DENNIS ROSS
Director and Ziegler Distinguished Fellow,
Washington Institute for Near East Policy

AT THE TIME OF this writing, Americans had heard President George W. Bush tell the nation that Saddam Hussein had ignored United Nations Security Council Resolution 1441 requiring that Iraq disarm. The premise articulated by the Bush administration for war was that the Iraqi regime was hiding armaments of mass destruction that could provide Saddam a coercive means to further destabilize the political situation in the Middle East, or even worse, slip these weapons into the hands of terrorists bent on attacking the United States. Saddam Hussein has represented a threat because he seeks nuclear weapons to use as a shield behind which he can pursue his intentions for regional aggression.

The question to ask is not whether America and its allies should be going after Saddam, but when it has happened, how quickly these forces can succeed in removing him and then get out to leave the Iraqis to run their own affairs under a democratic and friendly regime, while still remaining a strong player in Middle East politics. Assuming the U.S. government and its allies are successful in extracting Saddam Hussein permanently from power, what are the consequences for Iraq, the Middle East, and the United States?

Iraqis Without Saddam

FIRST, IT SHOULD be expected that the Iraqi peoples feel stunned by the true purposes of the invasion. The average Iraqi knows little about the United States and its intentions, and certainly less about the democracy the United States and its allies have intended to install in their country. Clearly, a large portion of the population has been eager to celebrate Saddam's exit. After eleven years of economic sanctions, two wars in which 700,000 Iraqis were killed, day-to-day hardship for the average Iraqi in a country that uses its wealth to build military prowess and public monuments, and unspeakable brutality by the Iraqi regime, many Iraqis welcome change. Consider for a moment the Iraqi public's response when Saddam declared an amnesty for prisoners. People spontaneously, and literally, tore down the prison walls in an act of frustration and hostility.

Peace cannot, however, be immediate in Iraq. This country is not a homogeneous society. Large ethnic populations exist, among them the Shiites, Sunnis, and Kurds as well as numerous smaller groups, that are likely to try to position themselves for power in post-Saddam Iraq. A strong impulse toward score settling and blood feuding is likely among groups in the aftermath of Saddam. The United States and its allies are going to have to take responsibility that this doesn't happen. Thus, the immediate response to an American-led invasion could only bring shock, bewilderment, internal conflict, but also hope for a better way of life.

The Iraqi people themselves, once they know that it is safe to do so, will celebrate and rejoice at Saddam's departure. That response will be seen by the Arab world as a whole, and few in that world will long be critical of the allies having liberated the Iraqis. Yet America will find that it's not so simple to turn Iraq into a stable political entity. We will find that it's going to take much investment and much effort for us to create a broad-based, representative government within institutions that make pluralism possible over time. Creating such a combination acceptable as part of Iraq's political culture and democratization is an important goal to be achieved. The more quickly we succeed in bringing this about, the more likely we will find that it does create a moment in the Middle East for creating greater stability elsewhere.

The Middle East Without Saddam

WHAT IS THE EFFECT on the Middle East of America's invasion of Iraq? Even to the casual observer of politics in the Middle East, the region reflects a hotbed of conflict and instability. The most immediate signal from America's invasion of Iraq is that the United States is willing to do anything necessary, including going to war, to stabilize the region. Peaceful, successful democratization of Iraq sends a signal to the Iranians and Syrians that promoting terrorism will not be tolerated by the United States.

Among Palestinians, America's ousting of Saddam and serious commitment to peace in the Middle East provides renewed hope that a settlement with Israel can now become a more serious matter. With the departure of Saddam, who was providing $25,000 to the families of every terrorist suicide bomber attacking Israel, the number of such incidents is likely to diminish. This may well lead the way to a period of calm in which Israel can approach the Palestinians in a direct and resolute way. Furthermore, Palestinian reformers will see that if there can be a change in Iraq and if there is an effort to build much more pluralistic and tolerant institutions there, that they will have more of a chance to succeed with similar initiatives. It will create in Israel, in the Israeli public, a perception that if Saddam can go, then there may well be a moment of opportunity with the Palestinians. Whether that moment is capitalized upon depends much on whether the United States can launch initiatives for peace at the same time that it focuses on developing greater stability within Iraq.

It's a two-fold consequence. First, the Palestinian reformers must see that a serious effort is being made, by not just the United States but the international community as well, to build new institutions in Iraq—representative institutions, institutions that would create a basis for the rule of law, that would provide for an independent judiciary, and that would create the basis for political parties. In other words, if they see an international effort in Iraq to create a very different kind of governing system, one based on tolerance of the diversity that is there, a system electing broad-based representative government, then I believe it will provide additional inspiration to Palestinian reformers to believe that time is on their side. This could, in fact, become the moment for reform, certainly among the Palestinians and maybe more generally in the Middle East. So it's going to create for them both a sense of hope and a sense of opportunity.

The outlook for Arafat to continue as the leader of the Palestinian movement becomes less solid. The reform movement among Palestinians is leading public opinion toward Arafat becoming a ceremonial head of state. For this actually to happen, outside pressure from Arab states must help to transform the Palestinian movement from Arafat's leadership to new directions for peaceful settlement with Israel. Arafat is unlikely to step down unless coerced by his Arab colleagues. But clearly, the presence of the U.S. military in Iraq adds incentive to both sides to meet in serious talks. The United States must take time from its engagement in Iraq to ensure that the immediate political stability achieved in the Middle East by the ousting of Saddam is used to the greatest benefit by Israel and the Palestinians to forge a peaceful settlement of differences. Expectations in Israel and with the Palestinians can then be raised.

Saudi Arabia also is seriously affected by America's involvement in Iraqi politics. Saudi rulers are under increasing pressure to pluralize their nation. Significant segments of the population, including women, have been excluded from economic and political participation. In Saudi Arabia, per capita income has dropped from $20,000 per year to around $7,000 per year. The majority of the population is under the age of twenty-five and restless, and unemployment is increasing. The government is being forced to respond to these conditions, and the opening of the Iraqi political environment under U.S. occupation signals opportunity to portions of the Saudi public. The government of Saudi Arabia needs to show that it won't remain static and to find ways to create a sense that there can be participation among its citizenry in shaping the future of the country. Improvement in the lives of Iraqi people will fuel this yearning in Saudi Arabia.

Perhaps most important of all is the impact of a U.S. presence in Iraq on terrorist organizations, Al Qaeda being at the center. Two opposite responses are possible. First, Al Qaeda leadership, Osama bin Laden specifically, may be profoundly impressed with American power and resolve, and he may slacken his terrorist campaign on the United States. The second, more unfortunate, perhaps more realistic, outcome, is that bin Laden and the militant Muslim world see the invasion of Iraq as an attack requiring renewed response. America and any allies participating in the war on Iraq certainly become targets of terror by this well-organized and financed force. There is no other interpretation for bin Laden than to consider the invasion of Iraq an affront to Islam rallying a widespread jihad.

The absence of hope in the light of indignities many Muslims around the world have suffered fuels extremist ideology. Osama bin Laden preys upon despair and frustration. Only an international effort to alleviate this despair through huge expenditure of foreign aid and good will can extinguish the flame that brightens Al Qaeda and other international terrorist movements. It is the global social, political, and economic environment fomenting terrorism that must change. This is a huge, time consuming, and expensive challenge the allies must face.

The United States Without Saddam

WHAT ARE THE consequences of the invasion of Iraq for the United States and its allies? First, the Bush administration is intent on bringing democracy to the Iraqi people. Establishing an executive, legislative, and judicial system of government under a constitution can be no simple task. The first decision is whether the transition is overseen by the U.S. military, using the Japan model of World War II, or by the United Nations, which is, in a sense, apolitical with regard to the internal politics of member states. The most likely format is a U.S. military occupation. This has profound implications for the United States.

The occupation of Iraq and transformation of the country into a democracy necessarily becomes a long-term investment by the United States. The war alone costs taxpayers billions of dollars; a military occupation and foreign aid to build the infrastructure necessary to support democratic institutions can only cost many billions more. American public opinion and its effect on congressional budgeting of the effort in Iraq needs to be absolutely solid.

Second, if America has succeeded quickly and uncovered Saddam's arsenal of biological and chemical weapons before he can destroy the evidence, our invasion can be viewed by the world as legitimate and not imperialistic. This image of America can be enhanced as we and our allies participate in rebuilding Iraq's decimated society.

Third, the U.S. presence in Iraq and resolve to see the transition through can take no less than many years and considerable funding. We shall find that it is not so simple to turn Iraq into a stable political entity. Within Iraq lie many obstacles to democratization. There has been no freedom of speech in the twenty years that Saddam has ruled the country. There is no tradition of debate and compromise about the direction of politics in Iraq. The Kurds in northern Iraq must be pulled into the democratic effort along with the Sunnis, Shiites, and other Iraqi ethnic groups. No one knows if and how this can be done using a time-tested model of American-style democracy that is inclusive of minority views. No one knows if the Iraqi people understand and respond to the notion of American justice. A hierarchical court system for civil and criminal justice must be established in a country without a legal profession as we know it. Basic institutions, hospitals, and schools have to be expanded to meet the needs of the Iraqi people and must show America's commitment to their well-being.

Fourth, the Bush administration has to call on American business leaders to promote investment in Iraq. As Iraqi oil begins to flow more freely without economic sanctions, the revenues have to be directed to improving quality of life for the citizenry. American business principles, including capitalism, have to be integrated into the new democratic way of life in Iraq. While independent entrepreneurship already exists in Iraq, its scale and sophistication have to be enhanced to meet the expectations of the people under an open and free society.

Fifth, the invasion, occupation, and transformation of Iraq into a democracy based upon the American model cannot be other than a rough road. The message to other Arab states may come across that if the United States does not like what it sees in internal politics or foreign affairs, it may take extreme measures to intercede. The impact of this message, whether intended or not, may work to destabilize the Middle East even further. Islamic nations may well see the democratization of Iraq as a threat. Democracy means the separation of church and state, a notion that is an anathema to Islamic states, even to our allies in the Middle East.

Yet it is crucial that American public opinion and resolve to playing the central role in Middle East politics has got to be steadfast.

Today many Americans distance themselves from the Arab-Israeli conflict and are much more concerned over terrorism elsewhere and the economy. How can the Bush administration and succeeding administrations keep America's eye focused on a central position in the Middle East?

An unknown factor is Iraq's future foreign policy. During the postwar occupation must the United States institute policy, or can the occupying overseers allow the new Iraqi government to establish its own policies toward Iran, Syria, Turkey, Israel, Saudi Arabia, and other Middle East nations? It is reasonable that for many years Iraq's foreign policy be neutral, as dictated by the United States and its allies, thus allowing the country to concentrate all effort on internal development.

International public opinion against the United States and allies partially has focused on a perception of America's intention to control oil after the invasion of Iraq. In recent years, Iraq, because of United Nations economic sanctions, was limited to producing about 1 million barrels of oil a day. Iraq has the capacity easily to grow output to some 2.8 million barrels currently and to 5 million barrels in a few years. Therefore, a by-product of the opening of Iraq could be an increase in world availability of oil, rather than control of oil output, as critics would complain. It is in the best interest of the United States and its allies to allow Iraq to generate as much wealth as possible to participate in the rebuilding of the country.

If done correctly, America and its allies' occupation and transformation of Iraq into an open and thriving democratic republic can do much to improve stability in the Middle East. First, the United States must act quickly to improve quality of life in Iraq and make that known to the Islamic world. Second, the United States must finish its work as quickly as possible and get out of Iraq, but remain an influence in the stability of the Middle East. The message to Middle East nations must be that America sensed a clear danger in the Saddam regimen, reacted with resolve and compassion for the people, deposed a tyrant, established a participative government, and exited the country. America and its allies interceded in the best interest of peace and stability for all nations and peoples in the Middle East and not for national purposes.

The message continues that the United States and its allies will not tolerate any destabilizing influences in the Middle East or else-where in the world. But care must be taken to prove that America is not imperial, not intent on exporting its way of life to areas of the world where there is political strife. Substituting democracy for total-itarianism in Iraq is not done to broaden America's control over global politics but rather to serve the needs of the Iraqi people and to prevent the export of armaments of mass destruction to terrorists.

The United States and its allies have an opportunity to demon-strate that our approach is not only military but also political and economic; we can change an environment that creates human repres-sion and suffering and exports terrorism threatening basic freedom. This is the challenge in Iraq before America and its allies.

Foreign Investment in the Middle East Without Saddam

WHAT, THEN, ARE the implications for foreign investment in the Middle East going forward? People are not going to want to invest in the region unless they believe that stability can exist and be sustained. If there is ongoing conflict, the impulse is not going to be to invest. If it looks as though Iraq is finally stabilized, that the Middle East markets can be developed, and that there are legal protections for investors, then the setting changes.

Reform in the Middle East has to reflect commitment to creating rule of law, transparency, and accountability. The main thing partic-ipants in the business world can do is to continue to emphasize, especially to their putative Arab partners, that potential exists, from the outside, for foreign investment. Such a possibility is genuine, but only if a very clear climate can be spelled out. If there is an effort to build infrastructure either in Iraq or in the Palestinian territories in the aftermath of action against Saddam, together with some efforts to transform the situation between the Israelis and the Palestinians that creates a predictable environment, this is what business wants to see. Knowing that a business can repatriate profits, knowing that corruption isn't going to be the hallmark of rule in the Middle East, knowing that everybody has an equal chance without favoritism, this is the message the private sector needs to hear.

Chapter Twenty-Nine

Peace, Democracy, and Free Markets in the Twenty-First Century

MICHAEL MANDELBAUM

Christian A. Herter Professor of American Foreign Policy,
The Johns Hopkins University School of Advanced International Studies

O N THE MORNING of Tuesday, September 11, 2001, two hijacked commercial airliners flew directly into the twin towers of the World Trade Center, the tallest structures in New York City. The heat from the explosion of the two airplanes and the fires they set melted the steel supports of the 110-story buildings and they collapsed, killing more than 2,800 people. Almost simultaneously another hijacked airliner crashed into the headquarters of the American Department of Defense, the Pentagon, in Washington, D.C.

The events of September 11 qualify as the most spectacular, riveting, grim, costly, and searing acts of terrorism in history. The shock of the attacks reverberated across the United States and throughout the world. In their aftermath, September 11 was widely said to have been a historical watershed, a moment when the assumptions that had governed the way the world conducted its affairs were abruptly swept away.

In fact, the attacks did not usher in a new world. Instead, they illuminated the main features of the world that already existed, a world that had emerged in its full form a decade earlier but had been two centuries in the making. It is a world dominated by three major ideas:

peace as the preferred basis for relations among countries, democracy as the optimal way to organize political life within them, and the free market as the indispensable vehicle for producing wealth.

Supremacy of the Free Markets

SOCIETIES RAISE THEIR grandest monuments to what their cultures value most highly. As the tallest buildings in a city noted for tall buildings, the twin towers of the World Trade Center were certainly monumental. They were the equivalent for the twenty-first century United States of the great pyramid of Giza in ancient Egypt and the Cathedral of Chartres in medieval France. The institution that the World Trade Center symbolized, and to which it was dedicated, was the free market, the central activity of which is trade. The planet's dominant method for organizing economic activity, the market did in fact occupy an exalted place in American society.

It enjoyed a commanding position outside the United States as well, and the September 11 attack also symbolized its global status. Once, Manhattan's tallest structures had been the Empire State Building, named for New York itself, and the Chrysler Building, the headquarters of an American automobile manufacturer that by 2001 had become a subsidiary of a German corporation. The even taller buildings destroyed on September 11 were named not simply for trade but for world trade.

People from more than eighty different countries died in the fires and the collapse. Most of them worked for firms concerned with one aspect or another of finance. Concentrated in lower Manhattan, the financial industry is the most cosmopolitan in the world because its product, money, is more portable and more widely utilized than any other. This product is the key to the international reach of markets: While a purely local exchange can and does operate on the basis of barter, markets stretching beyond a particular time and place require money.

The money on which international commerce and industry depends is collected in lower Manhattan and from there distributed to every continent. The World Trade Center thus symbolized the network of commercial and financial exchanges that by the year 2001 had spread all over the planet. In choosing it as their target, the terrorists perversely dramatized the supremacy of the free market and of the political system intimately associated with it in the United States and elsewhere, democracy, as defining features of the world of the twenty-first century.

The attacks on Washington, D.C., and New York were acts of war, and the war they inaugurated, the American war against terrorism, became the first war of the new century. They recalled the surprise attack at Pearl Harbor sixty years earlier. Like that 1941 assault, the events of September 11 triggered a campaign against the attackers, with the American government mobilized for military action. The government dispatched forces to Afghanistan to root out the terrorists based there and to overthrow and replace the government that harbored them.

Yet the advent of the war against terrorism was unlike the conflict that began for the United States on December 7, 1941, or any of the other great wars of modern history—the European conflict touched off by the French Revolution at the end of the eighteenth century, the two World Wars of the twentieth century, and the four-decades-long political and military struggle known as the Cold War. The previous wars pitted mighty sovereign states against one another, all of them seeking the control of territory. They were waged by vast armies, which clashed in great battles—Waterloo, the Somme, Stalingrad—in which the fate of great nations and huge empires hung in the balance. In the Cuban missile crisis of 1962, when the United States and the Soviet Union confronted each other armed with nuclear weapons, the fate of the entire planet, of the human race itself, seemed to be at stake.

By these standards, the war against terrorism, as waged in Afghanistan, scarcely qualified as a war at all. The United States conducted a campaign of aerial bombardment and modest mopping-up operations on the ground in Afghanistan. To wage this war, the aim of which was to protect their citizens against terrorist attacks, the United States and other countries relied less on their armed forces than on their intelligence services, local law enforcement agencies, border guards, and customs and immigration officials, as well as on their public health systems. The Pentagon, one of the targets of the September 11 attacks, was not the only nerve center of the American campaign against terrorism.

The attacks thus illustrated another defining feature of the world of the twenty-first century: the transformation, or at least the dramatic devaluation, of war—the age-old practice that, for the first two centuries of the modern age, did more to shape international relations than any other.

There was no possibility that the September 11 attacks would touch off a conflict anything like the great wars of the modern era, and the reason for this pointed to yet another signal feature of the world of the twenty-first century. In the past, a blow to the international system's strongest power would have been welcomed by its rivals. In the wake of September 11, however, every significant government in the world declared its support for the United States.

For this there was an obvious reason: Every major government in the world supported the market-dominated order that had come under attack and of which the United States served as the linchpin. While not everyone subscribed to the political values symbolized by the other world-famous landmark at the tip of Manhattan island, the Statue of Liberty, all saw the free market as the path to what had become, in the twenty-first century, a supreme and undisputed national goal: the creation of wealth. Thus, there was virtually no country that neither received nor hoped to receive capital from the New York financial community.

The market-centered international order of the twenty-first century commanded almost universal allegiance not only because every country saw potential benefit in it but also because there was no viable alternative. In the past, those who had challenged the existing order of things had equipped themselves with alternative programs for the organization of political and economic life. The slogan of the French Revolution expressed its aim: liberty, equality, fraternity. The revolutionaries of the nineteenth century who drew their inspiration from that great upheaval pursued concrete goals: the end of monarchical rule, the promulgation of constitutions, the establishment of nation-states instead of multinational empires. The revolutionaries of the twentieth century also had a slogan, "Workers of the world, unite!"—and a program, the abolition of private property and the installation in power of Communist parties. The perpetrators of the September 11 attacks had neither. They proposed nothing in place of what they sought to destroy. They acted in the name of a fanatical strain of Islam that was far removed from the precepts and customs of the great Islamic civilizations of history and that, insofar as it offered a political program of any kind, was intended to apply only to Muslims, who comprised approximately 15 percent of the world's 6 billion inhabitants.

Ideas That Have Conquered the World

THE COMMANDING POSITIONS of free markets and, to a lesser extent, democracy, and the dramatic devaluation of war are the main features of the conduct of human affairs at the outset of the third millennium. Peace, democracy, and free markets are the ideas that have conquered the world.

The three are all liberal ideas in the original, nineteenth century meaning of the term: All involve the promotion of human liberty. All entail restraints on the exercise of power by governments. Democracies erect fences around certain spheres of social life into which the government is forbidden to intrude. Peace deprives government of its chief historical purpose: the waging of war. In a market economy, which one of the earliest and certainly the most influential of its chroniclers, Adam Smith, called "a system of natural liberty," private property is controlled by individual owners rather than by the government.

The three ideas are liberal as well in that in practice they establish explicitly, impersonal, universal rules to govern politics, economics, and foreign policy. They are liberal, finally, in that all favor the interests of the individual. Political liberalism protects the individual against the state and gives him or her the power, via the ballot, to select and remove those in authority. The supreme goal of the market economy is to satisfy the desires of the individual consumer. Because it is government that conducts wars, and war that enhances its power, peace tilts the balance of power within society back toward the individual, as well as preserving those individual lives that would be lost in war.

To be sure, these three great liberal ideas were not, at the outset of the twenty-first century, established everywhere. Peace was anything but universal. As for democracy, many countries had governments that looked like the British parliamentary model or the

American federal system but did not function as they do. In the eighteenth century Grigori Potemkin, a minister of the Russian empress Catherine the Great, lined a route on which she was traveling with impressive-appearing but flimsy, hastily erected structures in order to persuade her that large settlements had been built there. They are known to history as "Potemkin villages." In the same spirit, many twenty-first century governments qualified as "Potemkin democracies." The free market was more widely accepted and broadly practiced than the other two ideas; indeed, it may have been, at the outset of the new millennium, the most widely adopted institution in all of human history. But obstacles to the free flow of commerce continued to exist throughout the world.

At the outset of the twenty-first century these three great ideas were not, therefore, universal. They were, instead, hegemonic. The term "hegemony" comes originally from ancient Greece. There it referred to the preponderance in the exercise of leadership or predominant influence by one Greek city-state, usually within the context of a confederacy of several of them. The hegemon towered over the others. Similarly, the three great liberal ideas have been a towering presence in the world after the Cold War. They have provided the most widely adopted set of political and economic principles and institutions. They have been practiced and promoted by the most powerful members of the international system. They have been the world's orthodoxy and have had no serious, fully articulated rival as ways of organizing the world's military relations, politics, and economics. Not all sovereign states have accepted each of them or have been able to practice them. But there have been no plausible alternatives. Asked where in Paris he would most like to live, a French architect is said to have picked the Eiffel Tower on the grounds that this was the only place in the city from which he would not have to look at it. Peace, democracy, and free markets are the Eiffel Tower of the twenty-first century.

As with the Eiffel Tower, the three ideas have not pleased everybody. Their opponents have been noisy, determined, and sometimes violent. The opposition ranks have included the Middle Eastern terrorists who perpetrated the attacks of September 11, 2001. They have included, as well, the thousands of Westerners who gathered to protest the international economic policies of the wealthy countries at the meeting of the World Trade Organization in Seattle in December 1999 and the meeting of the Group of Eight—the wealthy industrial democracies plus Russia—at Genoa in July 2001.

While both groups disliked—detested is perhaps a more accurate word—the liberal practices and institutions that dominate the world of the twenty-first century, and both sought to destroy them, neither had any real hope of success and neither offered anything to put in place of what they were assaulting. In the wake of the September 11 attacks, a European marching to protest the military operations the United States undertook in response carried a placard that read "Civilization is genocide." The slogan captured the emptiness of the opposition to the three dominant liberal ideas: It was at once incoherent and idiotic.

The international system was therefore like a fixed-price menu from which a diner could accept or reject different items. He or she could choose to skip the hors d'oeuvre, or the main course, or the dessert—or to go hungry altogether. In the first post-Cold War decade Burma, Cuba, Iraq, and North Korea did reject all three liberal ideas, and their people did in fact go hungry. But there was no other menu, no other series of equally appetizing political and economic choices. The political and economic weather varied from country to country, but the global climate was unmistakably liberal.

The Potemkin democracies and faux-market economies with their rigged stock markets and government monopolies were, in fact, eloquent testimony to the hegemony of liberal ideas. They were hypocritical enterprises; but, as La Rochefoucauld observed, hypocrisy is the tribute that vice pays to virtue. At the dawn of the twenty-first century peace, democracy, and free markets were deemed the essence of virtue. And most countries have gone beyond simply paying symbolic tribute to them. Most have tried to adopt them, at least in part. Their efforts to do so are dominating the global agenda at the outset of the twenty-first century.

Index

Abu Ghaith, Sulaiman, 293
accelerating inflation, gold and, 124–125
advice, value of, 85–86
Advisor Insight, 187–188
Afghanistan, 276–279, 309
Against the Gods: The Remarkable Story of Risk (Bernstein), 53
AIG (American International Group), 163–164
Albanian Kosovars, 283
Alexander, Magnus, 216
Allison, Graham, 287–297
alpha stocks, 68, 71
Al Qaeda, 276–279, 287–289, 292–293, 302–303
American Association of Port Authorities, 268
American Century Ultra, 193
American Funds, 198
Amoco, 93
analysis
    contrarianism, 63–64
    fundamental, problems with, 52–55
    investor sentiment, 60–63
    probabilities, 65–66
    technical, 55–60
ANDEAN Pact, 158
Anderson, Jonathan, 170, 171
Annan, Kofi, 166, 278
AOL Time Warner, 56–60, 62

Arafat, Yassir, 302
Arctic gas development, 97
Art of Contrary Thinking, The (Neill), 63
Asea Brown Boveri (ABB), 165
ASEAN (Association of South East Asian Nations), 158, 171, 175–176
    Free Trade Area (AFTA), 175, 177–178
Asia
    changes in China, 172–175
    dynamics and regional interplay, 170–172
    effects of China's growth on other countries, 175–178
    growth in, 169
    investor's outlook, 178–179
    political risks/terrorism, 172
Aum Shinrikyo, 293
Awad, James D., 137–142

Baker, Howard, 289
Barra (BARZ), 142
Barron's, 21, 22, 36, 62
Battle for Investment Survival, The (Loeb), 52
Bernhard, Arnold, 201–204
Bernstein, Peter, 53
Biggs, John, 212
"Big Money in Boston," 3
bin Laden, Osama, 276–277, 287, 288, 292–293, 302–303

biotechnology
  defined, 143
  historical developments,
      143–144
  major areas of drug develop-
      ment, 147–149
biotechnology stocks
  factors affecting, 145–147
  seasonal trends, 152
  selecting, 149–152
  uncertainty/risk, 153–154
Bloomberg Personal Finance, 53
*Bloomsbury Guide to Human
    Thought*, 143
Bogle, John C., 3–18, 212
bond market
  impact on debt, 100–101
  impact on stock market,
      101–104
  influence of, 99
  politics and, 106–107
  yield curve, 104–106
Bonner, Robert, 268
BP Statistical Review of World
    Energy, 91
Brancato, Carolyn, 213
Brandywine Fund, 30, 35–36
Bretton Woods Agreement,
    135–136
Brimhall, Craig, 77–86
BSEC, 158
Buffett, Warren, 8, 80, 81, 84,
    213
Bunn, Matthew, 288
Bush, George, 107
Bush, George W., 107, 257, 275,
    278, 286, 289, 294, 299
BusinessWeek, 21, 23, 183, 245

"Deal of the Century," 62
"How Worried Should You
    Be?," 25
"Pessimism Dampens the
    Stock Market Outlook," 22
Buttner, Jean Bernhard, 201–210
buying companies,
    knowledge/personal experi-
    ence and, 37–39

Calvert Community Investments,
    251
Cambridge Energy Research
    Associates, 94
Canadian Imperial Bank of
    Commerce (CIBC), 165
CARICOM, 158
Carter, Jimmy, 106
cash levels, determining, 35–36
Cavanagh, Richard E., 217
Center for Domestic
    Preparedness, 267
Central Bank Gold Agreement,
    120
Central Intelligence Agency, 266,
    292
CEPCO, 254
CERA Advisory Services, 97
Charles Schwab, 187
China, 158, 162, 296
  changes in, 172–175
  growth of, 170–171
  importance of, 169
  investment opportunities in,
      173–174
Chubb Group of Insurance
    Companies, 213
CIS, 158

Cisco Systems, 33, 34
Citibank, 164
Clark, Wesley, 275–286
Clinton, Bill, 107
Coca-Cola, 272
coffee
  industry, 247–250
  Starbucks Coffee Co.,
    245–247, 250–254
Coincident Index, 215–216
Commission on Public Trust and
    Private Enterprise, 212–213
Commodity Research Bureau
    (CRB), 133
Conference Board, The, 211–217
ConocoPhillips, 97
Conservation International
    Foundation, 251, 253
Consumer Confidence Index,
    214
Consumer Internet Barometer,
    214
Consumer Price Index (CPI), 134
consumer spending, risks associ-
    ated with, 113
contrarianism, 63–64
Cooley, Scott, 195–196
Core Earnings, 190
Corinthian Colleges, 31
Corporate Profiles, 187
corporate responsibility, changes
    in, 8–9
corruption, foreign direct invest-
    ment and, 167–168
costs, soaring, 12–13
Council on Foreign Relations,
    266, 269
Crescenzi, Anthony, 99–108

Crick, Francis, 143
CSX Lines, 291
currency debasement, gold and,
    124–125
Cutler, Lloyd, 289
Customs-Trade Partnership
    Against Terrorism (C-
    TPAT), 268, 269
Czech Republic, 159, 165

debt
  interest rates and increase in
    household, 101
  a sign of financial imbalance,
    112–113
deflation, gold and, 122–123
Dell Computer Corp., 33, 34
democracy, 311–313
Directors' Institute, The, 213
Walt Disney Co., 166
diversification, 30–21, 80–81
  mutual funds and, 193–195
  problems with over-, 47–48
DOE/IEA 2000 Energy Review,
    94
dollar-cost averaging, 79–80
Dzurinda, Mikula, 159

earnings, future value and, 33
Eck, John C. van, 109–125
Ecologic Enterprise Ventures,
    251
economic indicators, Conference
    Board's leading, 215
Economist, 65
ECOWAS, 158
education
  accountability, 258–259

commitment to improve,
257–258
immigrants, role of, 255, 256
investing in, 259–262
Lightspan Achieve Now,
260–261
Lightspan eduTest Assessment,
261
No Child Left Behind Act
(2002), 257
Eiffel Tower, 312
emerging markets. *See* foreign
direct investment in emerging markets
Employment Cost Index (ECI),
133
*Enquiry into the Paper Credit of
Great Britain, An*
(Thornton), 131
Enron Corp., 14, 140, 200,
220–221, 271
entrepreneurs, creation of, 13–15
Ereky, Karl, 143
E°Trade, 187
European Union, 158
experience, learning from, 20–22
ExxonMobil, 96

Fairtrade Labelling Organization
International (FLO), 253
Fair Value Model, 186–187
FBI, 266, 287
Federal Open Market
Committee, 110
Federal Reserve, 102–104, 106
Federal Reserve Act (1913),
109–110
Fidelity, 187, 198

Growth & Income, 193
Magellan, 193
Fitch Ratings, 115
Food and Drug Administration
(FDA), 143
Fooled by Randomness (Taleb),
66
Ford Foundation, 254
foreign direct investment (FDI)
in emerging markets, 155
corruption and, 167–168
economic development and,
158–161
economic freedom and,
161–162
emerging markets defined, 161
global trends, 156–158
in Iraq without Hussein, 306
political risks, 162, 163–164
risk management, 163–166
social problems and, 166–167
terrorism and, 167
Fortune, 3, 8, 9, 12
"Why Greenspan Is Bullish,"
23–25
Fosler, Gail, 212
Franks, Tommy, 281
fraud
need for fiscal security,
270–273
Sarbanes-Oxley Act (2002)
and, 219–226
free markets, 308–311
Friess, Foster, 29–39
Friess Associates, 29–39
fundamental analysis, problems
with, 52–55

GARP (growth at a reasonable
     price) school, 53, 71, 185
genchi genbutsu, 234
General Electric (GE), 166, 271,
     272
General Motors (GM), 61–62,
     230
Ghana, 296
Gilbert, Peter M., 212
global emerging market (GEM)
     See also foreign direct invest-
     ment in emerging markets
     trends, 156–158
Global Industry Classification
     System (GICS), 189
gold
     bullish price scenarios,
          122–125
     demand, 120–122
     inflation and, 129–130
     as a monetary asset, 115–116
     real price of, 134–136
     reasons for investing in,
          116–118
     standard, 115–116, 127
     supply, 118–120
     wealth measured by, 130–134
Gold Fields Mineral Services
     Ltd., 118
goldgram price of oil, 127–129
Goldman Sachs Internet Index,
     34
Goldman Sachs Research
     Publication, 170
Graham, Benjamin, 52
Grant's Interest Rate Observer,
     65
Greenspan, Alan, 23–25, 104, 212

Griswold, Merrill, 8
Grove, Andy, 212, 213
growth, value investing and,
     43–44
GTL, 93

Hackett, James T., 89–98
Hedge Fund Index, 189
Heidrick & Struggles, 213
Help-Wanted Advertising Index,
     214–215
Heritage Foundation, 162
*History of the Railroads and the
     Canals of the United States*
     (Poor), 184
holdings, monitoring, 36–37
Holdren, John P., 288
Honda, 231
*Horizontal Drilling—What Have
     We Found?* (Swindell), 93
Hormats, Robert D., 169–179
"How Bad a Slump?," 22
"How Worried Should You Be?,"
     25
Hoye, Bob, 121
Humulin, 143
Hungary, 158, 166
Hussein, Saddam
     foreign investment in Middle
          East without, 306
     Iraqis without, 300
     Middle East without, 301–303
     reasons for removing, 299
     United States without,
          303–306

IBM, 14, 174
indexing, 32

Index of Economic Freedom, 162
India, 296–297
Industry Surveys, 187
inefficiencies
    fundamental, 71–75
    historical earnings growth,
       71–73
    multi-factor variables, 73, 76
    optimization model for scoring,
       73–74
    quantitative, 67–71
    reward/risk ratio, 68–71, 76
inflation, gold and, 129–130
ING Barings, 164
initial public offerings (IPOs),
    14–15
interest rates
    impact on debt, 100–101
    impact on stock market,
       101–104
    politics and, 106–107
International Coffee Agreement,
    248
International Finance Corp.
    (IFC), 161
International Monetary Fund,
    112
Investability Quotient (IQ), 186,
    187
Investment Advisers Act (1940),
    225
Investment Company Act (1940),
    225
"Investment Outlook," 21
Investment Survey, 205–210
investor
    behavior, 86
    psychology, 19–27

    sentiment, 60–63
Iraq, without Saddam Hussein,
    300
Ireland, 160
Israel, 301

Janus Mercury, 198
Japan, 96, 114–115, 169, 176
Jet Blue, 31
John Wiley (JW), 142
Joint Declaration on the New
    Strategic Relationship
    between the United States
    and Russia, 294
Jones Day, 213
Jorgensen, Dale, 212
JPMorgan Chase, 164

kaizen, 234
Karzai, Hamid, 278
Kernan, John T., 255–262
Keynes, John Maynard, 110
Killinger, Kerry, 237–244
Kosovo, 275–276, 280, 281–286
Kranenburg, Hendrik J., 183–190
Kroll, Jules, 265–273
Kvint, Vladimir L., 155–168

Lampf, Pleva, Lipkind, Prupis &
    Petigrow v. Gilbertson,
    220, 222
La Rochefoucauld, François, 313
Leahy, Patrick, 221, 224
Leahy Amendment, 221
Levitt, Arthur, 212, 220
Levy, Leon, 65
Lewis, Bernard, 293
Liberty Growth & Income, 193

Libya, 296
Lightspan Achieve Now, 260–261
Lightspan eduTest Assessment, 261
liquefied natural gas (LNG), 96–97
Livermore Laboratories, 291
Loeb, Gerald M., 52, 65
London International Financial Futures and Options Exchange (LIFFE), 248
Longstreth, Bevis, 272
Lowenfels, Lewis D., 219–226
Lugar, Richard, 292, 296
Lynch, Peter, 6

macroeconomic policies, problem with, 114–115
Malaysia, 171
management of mutual funds
    changes in, 6
    role of good, 32
    value investing and role of, 44–45
Mandelbaum, Michael, 307–313
marketing of funds, changes in, 10–12
Massachusetts Investors Trust (M.I.T.), 3, 7, 8, 12, 15
McDonald's Corp., 166
McGraw-Hill Companies, Inc., 184
McGuckin, Robert, 212
McKinsey & Co., 213
Mendel, Gregor, 143
Merck, 142
MERCOSUR, 158
Merrill Lynch, 187

Microsoft Corp., 14, 33, 34, 174
Middle East, without Saddam Hussein, 301–303
    foreign investment and, 306
Miller, Bill, 6
Milosevic, Slobodan, 160, 283
Monane, Mark, 143–154
monetary policy
    current economic and financial risks, 111–113
    history of, 109–111
    macroeconomic policies, problem with, 114–115
Money, 11, 36, 37
Moody's Investors Service, 115, 201
Morgan Stanley, 96
Morningstar, 48, 192–200
    Style Box, 193–194
    X-Ray, 194–195
Morningstar Mutual Funds, 195–196
MPT Review, 67
MSCI, 189
M3, 133
mutual funds
    costs, 195–196
    diversification, 193–195
    growth of, 191–192
    risks, 197–200
    selecting, 192
mutual funds, changes in
    consequences of, 15–18
    costs, soaring, 12–13
    corporate responsibility, 8–9
    entrepreneurs, creation of, 13–15
    management, 6

marketing of funds, 10–12
shareholder behavior, 9–10
size and variety of, 4–5
stock funds, 5–6
turnover in strategies, 7–8

NAFTA, 158
Nasdaq Composite, 34
Nasdaq 100, 34
National Guard, 267
Nation at Risk, A, 257
NATO, 282, 284–285
Navellier, Louis G., 67–76
Needham and Co., 143–144
Neff, John, 6
Neill, Humphrey B., 56, 63
Neural Fair Value Model,
    186–187
Newsweek, 22, 23
New York Stock Exchange
    (NYSE), 270–271
Nigeria, 94
Nikkei stock market, 115
9/11 attacks, 140, 167, 276, 287,
    307–311
Nissan, 230
Nixon, Richard M., 127, 134
No Child Left Behind Act
    (2002), 257
North Fork Bancorp (NFB), 142
North Korea, 297
nuclear terrorism, 289–297
Nunn, Sam, 292, 297
Nygren, William C., 41–50

Oakmark funds, 41–50
Odean, Terrance, 53
Ohno, Taiichi, 234

oil
    alternatives, 96–97
    consumption statistics, 89
    determining excess supply
        amounts, 90–92
    factors affecting ability to meet
        demand, 90
    goldgram price, 127–129
    horizontal drilling, 93
    size of oil fields and availabili-
        ty, 92–93
    technological advances versus
        demand, 93–95
    3-D seismic, 93
    time versus price squeezes,
        95–97
Oil and Gas Journal, 96
    Online Research Center, 91
One Group Growth & Income,
    193
Operation Anaconda, 278–279
Organization of Petroleum
    Exporting Countries
    (OPEC), 91, 95
Outlook, The, 188–189
overdiversification problems,
    47–48
Oxfam America, 254

Paine, Lynn Sharp, 212
Pakistan, 296–297
Palestinians, 301–302
peace, 311–313
J.C. Penney, 45
Pentagon, 307, 309
Persian Gulf War, 276
"Pessimism Dampens the Stock
    Market Outlook," 22

Peterson, Peter G., 212–213
PhRMA, 144, 145
Poe, Randall, 211–217
Poland, 158
Polaroid, 142
political risks, 162, 163–164, 172
politics
    interest rates and, 106–107
    small-cap stocks and, 140
Poor, Henry Varnum, 184
Poor's Publishing Co., 184
Poor's Railroad Manual Co., 184
portfolio
    rebalancing, 84
    turnover, 7–8
Portnoy, Brian, 191–200
Potemkin, Grigori, 313
Powell, Colin, 276, 281–282
price-to-earnings ratios, role of,
    34
Private Securities Litigation
    Reform Act (1995), 220,
    221–222
privatization, global, 156–157
probabilities, 65–66
Public Utility Holding Company
    Act (1935), 224
Putin, Vladimir V., 290, 294, 295

Quality Ranking System, 186
Questrom, Allen, 45

Reagan, Ronald, 106–107
rebalancing portfolio, 84
recessions, factors affecting,
    111–112
regression to a mean, 83
research tools

    Conference Board, The,
        211–217
    Morningstar, 48, 192–200
    Standard & Poor's, 184–190
    Value Line, 201–210
reward/risk ratio, 68–71, 76
Riley, Ned, 19–27
risks
    biotechnology stocks and,
        153–154
    current economic and finan-
        cial, 111–113
    foreign direct investment and,
        162, 163–166
    mutual funds and, 197–200
    political, 162, 163–164, 172
    terrorism, 167, 172, 265,
        266–269, 275–297
    understanding, 81–83
Roosevelt, Franklin D., 134
Ross, Dennis, 299–306
Rubin, Robert, 107
Rudman, Warren, 212
Rule 10b-5, 219
Rumsfeld, Donald, 281, 282
Rumyantsev, Aleksandr, 290
Russell, Frank, 32
Russell Index fund, 137
Russell 2000, 137
Russell 3000, 35
Russia, 95–96, 159
    nuclear terrorism and,
        289–290, 292, 294–297

Saddam Hussein. *See* Hussein,
    Saddam
Samuelson, Paul, 16
Sarbanes-Oxley Act (2002),

219–226, 270
Saudi Arabia, 91, 95, 302
Schabacker, Richard, 55, 56
Schaeffer, Bernie, 51–66
Schaeffer's Investment Research
    (SIR), 52, 57, 60, 61
SchaeffersResearch.com, 61
Schwab,Charles, 187
"Securing Nuclear Weapons and
    Materials: Seven Steps for
    Immediate Action" (Bunn,
    Holdren, and Wier), 288
Securities and Exchange
    Commission (SEC), 8–9, 14,
    15, 220
Securities Exchange Act (1933),
    222–224, 225–226
Securities Exchange Act (1934),
    219, 222–224
Securities Investor Protection Act
    (1970), 225
security issues
    fiscal, 270–273
    physical, 266–269
    terrorism, 167, 172, 265,
        266–269
selling, small-cap stocks, 138
September 11, 2001. *See* 9/11
    attacks
Serbia, 160, 283, 296
Shanghai Gold Exchange, 122
shareholder behavior, changes in,
    9–10
Silk, Leonard, 216
Simmons & Company
    International, 89, 92
Sinclair, Upton, 52
Singapore, 171

Slovakia, 159
small-cap stocks
    bullish versus bearish, 140–141
    diversification and time frame
        for, 139–140, 141–142
    politics and, 140
    recommendations, 142
    research, importance of,
        137–138
    selling, 138
    volatility and, 137
Smith, Adam, 311
Smith, Delos, 212
Smith, Orin C., 245–254
Snow, John, 212
social problems, foreign direct
    investment and, 166–167
South Korea, 171, 176, 177
Southwest Airlines, 31
speculation versus enterprise, 7–8
Spitzer, Elliot, 271–272
stagflation, gold and, 123–124
Standard & Poor's, 32
    Advisor Insight, 187–188
    Core Earnings, 190
    equity research, 184–187
    Fair Value Model, 186–187
    500 Index, 16
    formation of, 184
    Global Industry Classification
        System (GICS), 189
    Hedge Fund Index, 189
    Investability Quotient, 186,
        187
    mutual funds analysis, 188
    Neural Fair Value Model,
        186–187
    publications, 187–189

Quality Ranking System, 186
STARS (Stock Appreciation
    Ranking System), 185–186,
    187, 188, 189
Standard & Poor's Analytical
    Stock Reports, 187
Standard & Poor's MarketScope,
    188
standard deviation, 81–82
Starbucks Coffee Co., 245–254
STARS (Stock Appreciation
    Ranking System), 185–186,
    187, 188, 189
Statistics Co., 184
StockCharts.com, 55
stock funds, changes in, 5–6
stock market, impact of bonds on,
    101–104
Stovall, Sam, 183–190
strategies, sticking with selected,
    32–33
Sun Life, 15
Sun Microsystems, 94
Swindell, Gary S., 93

Taguchi, Toshiaki, 229–235
Taleb, Nassem, 66
Taliban, 276–279, 288
taxes
    managing, 85
    value investment and, 49–50
TD Waterhouse, 187
Tech Data, 142
technical analysis, 55–60
Templeton, John, 83
terrorism, 167, 172
    See also Hussein, Saddam
    alternative approach to win-

ning against, 283–286
how real is the threat, 289–292
how serious is the enemy,
    292–293
international law, 284
need to improve physical secu-
    rity, 265, 266–269
new style of warfare, 279–283
nuclear, 289–297
prospects for containing,
    287–297
role of Americans, 294–297
war against, 276–279
Thailand, 171
TheStreet.com, 36
Thomson First Call, 149
Thornton, Henry, 131, 132, 134
Time, 61–62
timing, market, 54
Tortorella, John D., 219–226
Toyota Motor Corp., 229–235
Truman, Harry, 284
Trust Indenture Act (1939), 224
Turk, James, 127–136
Turner, Ted, 290
Tyco, 140

United Nations, 284
United States, without Saddam
    Hussein, 303–306
U.S. Customs Service, 268
U.S. National Intelligence
    Council, 290
US News and World Report, 23
U.S. Treasury market, 100, 102

value investment
    estimating intrinsic, 41–43,

46–47
growth, 43–44
management, role of, 44–45
overdiversification problems,
    47–48
portfolio turnover, 49
selling, 48–49
taxes, 49–50
time horizon for, 46
Value Line
    Convertibles, 210
    formation of, 201–204
    Investment Survey, 205–210
    Mutual Fund Survey, 209
    Options Survey, 210
    Ratings of Normal Value,
        202–204
    Special Situations Service,
        209–210
    stock ranking system, 204–205
van Eck, John C., 109–125
Vanguard Group, Inc., 14, 198
volatility, understanding, 81–83
Volcker, Paul, 212
Volkswagen, 230

Wall Street Journal, 35, 162
Washington Mutual, 237–244
Washington National Building
        Loan and Investment
        Association, 238
Watson, James, 143
wealth, measured by gold,
        130–134
wealth, methods for increasing
    advice, value of, 85–86
    budgeting and managing cred-
        it, 78

diversification, 80
dollar-cost averaging, 79–80
don't chase returns, 83–84
patience, need for, 81
portfolio rebalancing, 84
saving aggressively, 87–79
taxes, managing, 85
volatility, understanding, 81–83
Welch, Jack, 166
"Why Greenspan Is Bullish,"
        23–25
Wier, Anthony, 288
Wilshire 5000 Index, 35–36
Wilson, Earl, 78
World Bank Group, 161
WorldCom, 53–54, 200
World Economic Forum, 166
World Gold Council, 116
World Trade Center, 307–311
World Trade Organization
        (WTO), 170, 313
Wyckoff, Richard, 60

yield curve, 104–106
Yukos, 96

Zacks.com, 54, 59
Zarnowitz, Victor, 212, 214
Zhu Rongi, 176
Zimbabwe, 162

About Bloomberg

Bloomberg L.P., founded in 1981, is a global information services, news, and media company. Headquartered in New York, the company has nine sales offices, two data centers, and 87 news bureaus worldwide.

Bloomberg, serving customers in 126 countries around the world, holds a unique position within the financial services industry by providing an unparalleled range of features in a single package known as the BLOOMBERG PROFESSIONAL™ service. By addressing the demand for investment performance and efficiency through an exceptional combination of information, analytic, electronic trading, and Straight Through Processing tools, Bloomberg has built a worldwide customer base of corporations, issuers, financial intermediaries, and institutional investors.

BLOOMBERG NEWS®, founded in 1990, provides stories and columns on business, general news, politics, and sports to leading newspapers and magazines throughout the world. BLOOMBERG TELEVISION®, a 24-hour business and financial news network, is produced and distributed globally in seven different languages. BLOOMBERG RADIO℠ is an international radio network anchored by flagship station BLOOMBERG® 1130 (WBBR-AM) in New York.

In addition to the BLOOMBERG PRESS® line of books, Bloomberg publishes *BLOOMBERG® MARKETS* and *BLOOMBERG® WEALTH MANAGER.* To learn more about Bloomberg, call a sales representative at:

Frankfurt:	49-69-92041-280	São Paulo:	5511-3048-4506
Hong Kong:	852-2977-6900	Singapore:	65-6212-1100
London:	44-20-7330-7500	Sydney:	612-9777-8686
New York:	1-212-318-2200	Tokyo:	813-3201-8910
San Francisco:	1-415-912-2970		

FOR IN-DEPTH MARKET INFORMATION and news, visit the Bloomberg website at **www.bloomberg.com**, which draws from the news and power of the BLOOMBERG PROFESSIONAL® service and Bloomberg's host of media products to provide high-quality news and information in multiple languages on stocks, bonds, currencies, and commodities.